A Small Bit of Bread and Butter

A Small Bit of Bread and Butter

Letters from the Dakota Territory

1832-1869

EDITED BY MAIDA LEONARD RIGGS

ASH GROVE PRESS

SOUTH DEERFIELD, MASSACHUSETTS

A Small Bit Of Bread And Butter: Letters from the Dakota Territory, 1832-1869 edited by Maida Leonard Riggs

Ash Grove Press,
19 Elm Street,
South Deerfield, Massachusetts 01373.

Library of Congress Cataloging-in-Publication Data
Riggs, Maida Leonard, ed.
A Small Bit Of Bread And Butter:
Letters From The Dakota Territory,
1832-1869.

ISBN: 1-886172-22-6

1. Riggs, Mary Ann Longley, 1813-1869 — Correspondence. 2. Women's Studies—History. 3. Minnesota—Dakota Indians. 4. Minnesota—Settlement. 5. Missionaries—Correspondence.

Includes Index

Library of Congress Card Number: 96-083698

Ash Grove Press books are available at special discounts for bulk purchases for sales promotions, premiums, fund-raising, or educational use.

Printed in the United States of America
Cover and text design by Lisa Carta

DEDICATION

To Longley/Riggs cousins
who made this book possible,
especially Rosemary, for Remembrance
and Pearl for her love and support.

Contents

ACKNOWLEDGMENTS

This project has been a long time from seed to fruit, and one of the unanticipated pleasures has been the number of people, especially archivists and cousins, who have helped me. They deserve my deepest gratitude for their patient support and encouragement. I am especially indebted to Patricia J. Albright and Elaine D. Trehub at Mount Holyoke College who made the early records of Mary Lyon's students in Buckland available. Melinda McIntosh and Virginia Garrand at the University of Massachusetts Library made it possible for me to copy directly from the letters on microfilm to a word processor.

From the historical societies I was able to purchase films of Mary Longley Riggs' letters. Mary Plummer of The Presbyterian Historical Society, Philadelphia, and Dallas Lindgren and Ruby Shields of The Minnesota Historical Society, St. Paul were most helpful.

Permission has been granted by the following repositories to repro-duce selected letters: Center for Western Studies, Augustana College, Sioux Falls, SD, the correspondence of Mary A. C. L. Riggs to Martha Arms Taylor Longley, Moses et al. 1836; Presbyterian Historical Society, Philadelphia, PA, the correspondence of Rev. and Mrs. Stephen R. Riggs in the American Indian Collection, Lac qui Parle Mission, 1837-1851; Minnesota Historical Society, St. Paul, Minnesota, the Alfred and Mary Ann Longley Riggs Papers, 1832-1869.

I am indebted to several of my Longley cousins who have been most helpful in my search for the story of our great-grandmother. Elizabeth Riggs Gutch, an amateur genealogist, knew of and had the letters in the Center for Western Studies, Augustana College, transcribed. John C. Williams supplied photographs. Rosemary Dybwad, family members, and I explored the towns of Hawley and Buckland.

Jack and Elvira Scott had pictures of and stories about the *yellow mansion*, Mary Ann's Hawley home in Longley possession until 1858, where Mrs. Scott was born.

John R. Grimes, Associate Curator of Ethnology, Peabody Museum, Salem, showed me some of the Indian artifacts Stephen Riggs gave to the Newton Theological Seminary and helped identify some of those brought east by Henry Riggs, my grandfather, in 1888.

[i]

My dear friend Pearl Veerhault has been challenged by the genealogy of the Longley and Taylor families which she traced from the early 15th century in Lincolnshire, England, to their settlement in Hawley. Her research details how many times the family was devastated by Indian raids in Groton and Deerfield, Massachusetts and how often families intermarried.

Finally, a University of Massachusetts Faculty Research Grant has made some of this project a little easier.

During the last several years I have traveled with my great grand-mother in spirit, and there is no way to measure my indebtedness to her for the story of five generations of family life that she left for all of us to share. Her letters, an important aspect of her way of life, were an attempt to keep her family together, and her story has drawn many of us closer. At times, Mary Ann was a most difficult traveling companion for she drove me to work early and late to read her beautiful, but often difficult, writing. She kept me awake nights with puzzling thoughts, or memories of too little food, too much cold, or no doctor to aid in birthing a child. But I count this particular trip the most demanding and the most rewarding of my life.

Maida Leonard Riggs
January 1996

Introduction

M ary Ann Clark Longley Riggs, an educated, pioneer missionary
woman of nineteenth century America, lived through a period of
great excitement and turmoil in the history of the United States.
The country was experiencing the spread of education's Second Great
Awakening, the opening of lands west of the Mississippi River, and the
exploitation and resettlement of Native Americans. Towards the middle
of the century the United States was engaged in an increasing debate
about the issues of slavery that eventually led to the Civil War.

In over two hundred and fifty letters written to her grandfather, parents, siblings, children, and family friends, Mary Ann furnishes us with
an intimate account of life on the frontier among Native Americans
between 1837 and 1862. These letters tell of her education, teaching
experiences, arranged marriage, motherhood, and life among the tribes
living in the Dakota territory that later became Minnesota.

Mary Ann's maternal and paternal ancestors were English Puritans
who arrived in the Massachusetts Bay Colony in the 1630's. As the
families moved west through southern New England, they settled in
Groton, Shirley, Northampton, Buckland and Deerfield, Massachusetts.
Her grandfather, Colonel Edmund Longley, was one of the founders of
Hawley, Massachusetts. Mary Ann's father, General Thomas Longley,
commanded a regiment of Massachusetts Minutemen during the War
of 1812.

Mary Ann was born November 10, 1813, in Hawley, Massachusetts,
the sixth of Thomas and Martha Longley's twelve children, five of whom
died before the age of fourteen leaving her with two older siblings, Alfred
and Lucretia, and four younger, Joseph, Moses, Thomas and Henrietta.

Mary Ann and her sister, Lucretia, attended Mary Lyon's Female
Seminary in Buckland during the ten week winter terms, 1818 to 1830.
Since it was customary for young ladies to board with a town family, it is
probable that they stayed with their Taylor grandparents. Records of
their attendance at the seminary, subjects taught, texts used, and three

of Mary Ann's essays still exist in the Mt. Holyoke College Archives. In the summer of 1829, at age 16, Mary Ann taught school in neighboring Williamstown.

That the Longley family believed in higher education for both its daughters and sons is attested to by the record of the seminaries and colleges they attended. Mary Ann and Lucretia attended Ipswich Female Seminary, and Henrietta, Mount Holyoke Seminary. Alfred graduated from the Seminary Department at Oberlin in 1841 and was ordained in 1845. Moses Maynard Longley studied at Ashfield Academy and spent 1835 to 1836 at Amherst College, graduating from Oberlin in 1842 and the seminary in 1845. Joseph attended Oberlin from 1842 to 1844 and graduated from the Theological Seminary at Auburn, New York.

HISTORICAL CONTEXT

Treaties enacted from Maine to Mississippi culminated in the displacement of entire Indian tribes as a result of the Bureau of Indian Affairs' policy of Indian removal.

The Native American way of life was an abomination to Christians and attempts to Christianize Indians began as early as the seventeenth century. Missionary organizations developed in the Northeast to convert the native peoples to Christianity. Two such groups were the American Board of Commissioners For Foreign Missions (ABCFM) in Salem, Massachusetts, and the American Board of Foreign Missions (ABFM) in New York. The religious revival of the early nineteenth century stimulated renewed civil and religious concerns for the perceived plight of Native Americans, leading to the establishment of many missions in Indian territories.

Native Americans who were hunters and gatherers relied heavily on the bounty of the land to supply their daily needs. They believed that the land existed for the good of all and should not be owned. Missionaries not only tried to convert the Native peoples to Christianity, but also colluded with the United States government by teaching them how to settle and farm small parcels of land.

The United States government signed treaties with the Dakota Sioux promising money, food, and land along the Minnesota River in exchange for vast acreage of the Dakota territory. However, the money rarely reached the Sioux. Traders claimed that the native people were in debt to them for supplies, so the government chose to give the money directly to the traders instead of the Indians. The government also stored the promised food in warehouses using it as blackmail, not relinquishing it until the Dakota converted to farming. A split developed in the native community between farmer Indians, who accepted a house and a few acres to farm, and blanket Indians, who wanted to hold onto their culture and the ways of their ancestors. Many of the Indians were starving because they were denied access to the warehoused food, and buffalo herds and game were being depleted due to the influx of settlers. Even the Dakota who had chosen to become farmer Indians suffered from a lack of farming skills and from severe Minnesota weather.

Stephen and Mary Ann Riggs, missionaries, went to the Dakota Sioux at an inauspicious time. Cholera, malaria and whooping cough were epidemic among the Sioux. In addition, the treaty of 1837 had allowed traders to establish saloons at the edges of reservations, resulting in increased consumption of alcohol.

Mary Ann's life among the Indians of Minnesota was interrupted by the Sioux Uprising of 1862. Her family was forced to flee to Wisconsin and abandon twenty years of work. During her seven years in Wisconsin she was frequently ill. She struggled to reestablish a home even though her husband was away and her children were leaving for college. On March 22, 1869, she died of a cold that swiftly turned into pneumonia.

Mary Ann Longley Riggs was my great-grandmother. As you read these letters, I hope you will experience the passion and pathos of the woman I knew from the stories told by my grandfather. I hope that all who read her letters will feel as Mary Ann felt after reading letters from home: "We feel some after reading them, as a very hungry child would after having devoured a small bit of good bread and butter."

Maida Leonard Riggs

Longley Riggs Letters
Selection of Letters & Editing Policy

The letters contained in *A Small Bit of Bread And Butter* are a subset of over 250 letters written by Mary Ann Longley Riggs to her family and friends between 1832 and 1869. The earliest letters were in fragments; some incomplete, others faded. In order to conserve paper she wrote around entire pages filling every available space. One had both horizontal and vertical messages.

In the original transcription I scrupulously preserved Mary Ann's spelling, underlinings, insertions and crossed out words. However, this does not make for easy reading, so fs were changed to ss, and most spelling was standardized. Mary Ann's crossed out words were omitted and her insertions were incorporated into the text.

Mary Ann had several simultaneous audiences. For example, she often wrote to her family in Hawley, Massachusetts, and her brother, Alfred, in Ohio, on the same day. She also wrote many journal style letters which extended over months. Duplicate information contained in the letters is not included in this book in order to eliminate confusion and present the most coherent story.

Letters were carefully selected and edited to preserve their original character and to display the pattern of Mary Ann's life as missionary, wife, and mother without destroying its fabric. Several letters are included in their entirety; in others, passages have been reduced in length or eliminated altogether in order to avoid tedious repetition. Missionary letters of the day usually included paragraphs at the beginning and the end describing God's goodness and grace. Most of these paragraphs have been omitted because of their repetitive nature. In almost every letter, Mary Ann comments on the lack of mail that she received. Most of these paragraphs have also been edited out to save space. Some of the information in the chapter introductions came from Stephen Riggs' book *Mary and I: Forty Years With The Sioux* because it provided background not contained in Mary Ann's letters.

I am fully aware that the selection of letters, originally numbering over 600 typed pages, and their treatment, is subject to the criticism of scholars. For this I take full responsibility.

PERMISSIONS

Center for Western Studies, Augustana College, Sioux Falls, South Dakota, to publish selected letters from the collection of: Mary A.C. L. Riggs to Martha Arms Taylor Longley, Moses et.al. 1836-1869.

Presbyterian Historical Society, Philadelphia, Pennsylvania, to reproduce correspondence of Rev. and Mrs. Stephen Riggs, American Indian Collection, Lac qui Parle Mission, 1837-1851.

Minnesota Historical Society, St. Paul, Minnesota to reproduce letters from the Alfred and Mary Ann Longley Riggs Papers, 1832-1869, Minnesota Historical Society, St. Paul, Minnesota.

Chronology of Mary Ann's Life

1813	Mary Ann Clark Longley born in Hawley, Massachusetts
1828-1830	Pupil at Mary Lyon's winter school in Buckland, Massachusetts
1829	Teacher during the summer in Williamstown, Massachusetts
1832	Pupil in Amherst, Massachusetts
1833	Attempted to start a school in Agawam, Massachusetts
1834-1835	Pupil at Zilpah Grant's Ipswich Female Seminary, Ipswich, Massachusetts
1835	Recruited to teach in Indiana
1835-1836	Teacher, Bethlehem, Indiana
	Meets Stephen Return Riggs
1837	Marries Stephen Return Riggs
	Travels from Hawley to Lac qui Parle Mission, Dakota
	Alfred Longley Riggs born
1840	Isabella Burgess Riggs born
1842	Martha Taylor Riggs born
1842-43	Trip east to Hawley, Massachusetts with Alfred, 5, and Martha, 6 months
1843	Stephen Riggs' school and hymn book printed in Boston Dakota translation of New Testament printed in Cincinnati
	Thomas Longley drowned
	Moved to Traverse Des Sioux Mission

1845	Anna Jane born
1847	Moved to Lac qui Parle Mission
	Thomas Lawrence born
	Thomas Longley Sr. dies in Hawley
1849	Henry Martyn born
1851-52	Second trip east with Isabella, 11; Henry, 2
	Alfred goes to school in Illinois
1854	Mission home in Lac qui Parle burns
	Stephen Riggs helps organize the Hazelwood Republic near Yellow Medicine
1854	Alfred goes to Knox College, Galesburg, Illinois
1855	Robert Baird born
1856	Isabella goes to Western Female Seminary, Oxford, Ohio
1858	Martha Longley dies in Hawley
1859	Cornelia Octavia born
	Alfred goes to Chicago Theological Seminary
1861	Isabella and Martha graduate from Western Female Seminary
1862	Civil War begins
	Dakota Uprising, Riggs family flees Hazelwood to St. Anthony
1863	Wisconsin home
1869	Mary Ann dies

CAST OF CHARACTERS

LONGLEY FAMILY
> Martha Arms Taylor, 1784 - 1858
> General Thomas, 1774 -1848

LONGLEY CHILDREN
> Lucretia (Cooley), 1811 - 1881
> Mary Ann Clark (Riggs), 1813 - 1869
> Henrietta, 1826 - 1850
> Alfred, 1809 - 1851
> Moses Maynard, 1815 - 1904
> Joseph, 1823 - 1871
> Thomas, 1821 - 1853

RIGGS FAMILY
> Riggs, Stephen Return, 1812 - 1883, of Ripley, Ohio, Mary Ann's
> husband. Missionary to the Dakotas, 1837-1877. Editor of the
> *Dakota Grammar & Dictionary*; translator, with Samuel Pond,
> of the Bible into the Sioux language

RIGGS CHILDREN
> Alfred Longley, Dec. 6, 1837 - April 15, 1916;
> > *Zitkadan washtay; Mazaska Nonpa*
> Isabella Burgess, Feb. 21, 1840 - Jan 26, 1897;   *Hapan*
> Martha Taylor, Jan 27, 1842 - Dec 4, 1910;   *Hapistanna*
> Anna Jane, Apr. 13, 1845 - Feb 18, 1926;   *Wauskay*
> Thomas Lawrence, June 3, 1847 - July 6, 1940;   *Hake*
> Henry Martyn, Sept. 25, 1849 - Dec 27, 1936;   *Ishakpa*
> Robert Baird, May 22, 1855 - April 1949;   *Tookanshena*
> Mary Cornelia Octavia, Feb. 17, 1859 - April 9, 1948;   *Hakakto*

Burgess, Rev. Dyer of West Union, Ohio, Stephen Rigg's sponsor

Drake, Lucy Spooner, missionary teacher at Lac qui Parle, 1852-1854

Gavin, Rev. Daniel, Swiss missionary who had settled at Red Wing

Huggins, Mr. and Mrs., missionaries to the Sioux

Little Crow, leader of the Indian resistance to United States Indian policy

Pond, Gideon, 1834-1878, Samuel Pond's brother, missionary to the Sioux

Pond, Samuel, pioneer missionary to the Sioux, 1834-1866, author of *The Dakota or Sioux in Minnesota As They Were In 1834.*

Renville, Joseph, trader, interpreter and guide translator for Pond and Riggs, part Dakota

Williamson, John P., 1867-1915, missionary to the Sioux, author of *A Brother To The Sioux*

Williamson, T.S. MD, from Ripley, Ohio, missionary to the Sioux in Minnesota, 1835-1879

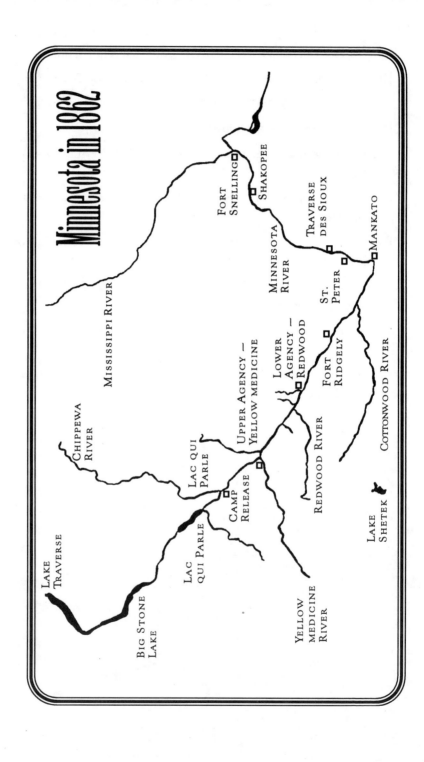

A Small Bit of Bread and Butter

Letters from the Dakota Territory

1832-1869

CHAPTER I

Amherst to Ipswich to Bethlehem

1832-1837

M ary Ann started writing letters home to her brother, Alfred, while
she was a student in Amherst in 1832. That year the upper
part of David Mack's store became a day school, the Amherst
Female Seminary. Hanna H. White of Ashfield, a friend of Mary Lyon,
and sister-in-law of Amherst College President Hitchcock, served as the
principal. There are no extant records of the Seminary to verify that
Mary Ann attended, but she wrote of the seminary ladies and of the
writing she did while in Amherst. In a letter from Agawam Mary Ann
shared her desire to become a teacher.

Mary Ann was one of the fortunate women of her generation to have
two role models: Mary Lyon in Buckland and Zilpah Grant, Headmis-
tress of Ipswich Female Seminary. Both women were avant-garde
mentors who believed that women were as capable of learning as men.

Ipswich Female Seminary was the first endowed seminary for women and the first to give diplomas, the forerunner for women's teacher training colleges in Massachusetts. While a student at Ipswich, Mary Ann wrote of her recruitment to teach in the mid-west.

She left Massachusetts to teach in Bethlehem, Indiana, where she found the culture quite different from that of her home town. Her escort west was the Reverend Dyer Burgess, a friend of Stephen Return Riggs. The Reverend Burgess knew that Riggs, an aspiring missionary, needed a wife and helped facilitate the arranged marriage between Stephen and Mary Ann. The couple traveled to Hawley, Massachusetts where they were married February 16, 1837.

Amherst, July 23, 1832
Dearest Brother A,

I received your letter on the 20th. Was somewhat surprised by its contents as in substance I [imitated] your example when I was at Williamstown. Allowing me to judge my remarks were less sarcastic and scornful than yours a year since about the same class of individuals. But let this pass for I am heartily sorry for everything wrong that I have done and will endeavor to do so no more. If I have not, I will unlearn contempt. . . .Thus far I have passed the summer pleasantly. There is rather more variety here than in our mountain hamlets. . . . The seminary ladies have had an opportunity of attending the exhibitions and the services on the 4th of July at the chapel [Amherst College]. On the last mentioned occasion Dr. Humphrey delivered an allegory on Temperance. We likewise had a ride to Mount Holyoke and Northampton on the 20th of June. The party consisted of 19 young ladies from the seminary, one teacher attended by two gentlemen from the village & two coachmen. The day was perfect—a contrast with the time when you, sister Lucretia & myself ascended its highest summit.

Mardi matin

I wish much to see you. Can you not ride over to Amherst and call on your sister M.? Your old friend W. W. whom we style Papin le Beouf, called on me soon after his return from Greenfield. I regretted that he did not see you. He boards at a temperance table which some of the students in derision and sport term "the starvation club." Brother, what think you of the cholera? It seems approaching & truly death standeth before the door. . . . Prof. Worcester delivered a discourse last Thursday afternoon adapted to the occasion. Stated its commencement, progress and ravages. Remarked that in about 15 years 50,000,000 had been its victims in the eastern continent. Also that the intemperate were among the first to feel its power.

On this account I feel particularly sorry that you have not starved your appetite for sweetmeats. But above all do make that preparation of heart which is necessary to meet the awful pestilence. The thought that this may be my last letter to you has passed across my mind. I do not cherish such gloomy forebodings. I have thought that I do not feel enough when such a terrible scourge has caused and is causing the nations of the earth to tremble beneath its terrors. Still there is secret hope or feeling in the human breast even when thousands are falling around us by some fatal epidemic, that they may escape. I entreat you not to let the secret hope that you may be passed by to tempt you to neglect that preparation which is needful to meet the king of terrors arrayed in his most terrible garb. . . .

Agawam, Mass., April 22, 1833
Dear Brother,

. . . . I have spent nearly a week in this place, but how much longer I shall remain & whither I shall go, God only knows. I have neither time nor inclination to enter into details respecting my situation here, there-fore suffice it to say that I came here a week today, expecting to open my school on Wednesday last, but was informed that I should probably not have more than 6 or 7 pupils. The members of the Baptist Society, al-though they had pledged their word to patronize the school some time since, declined promoting an object sanctioned & moved by "stiff necked" "blue skins" Presbyterians. Since Wed. some efforts have been made in behalf of the said school, but as yet with little success. I have been and am in a state of mortifying suspense. Miss Barnes, my room-mate at Amherst, teaches in the district school in the same bldg. where I may possibly teach the ensuing 3 months. Can you find me a school at the close of that time?

Ipswich, Thanksgiving eve
Dear Brother,

. . . . Last evening I spent an hour at Miss Grant's house, given for the young ladies, to cultivate their social affections & improve the manners I suppose. Some very beautiful specimens of [Carolinian] & Indian work, plants, & minerals, with a variety of shells & engravings which were tastefully arranged for our amusement. Unexpected music from another apartment, gave us a happy surprise & threw for a moment an air of enchantment around us.

Ipswich, Nov. 24, 1834

Miss Grant equals my highest anticipations. Affection, dignity, &
wisdom are harmoniously & equally blended in her well balanced
character. You will not censure me for forming my judgment this early,
when you recollect it is based upon the united testimony of better judges
than myself. I think she possesses just those traits you would admire in
the principal of such an institution as this. If one of a like spirit presided
in each seminary for ladies in our land, what a change would there be in
their education & character. Me thinks even the asperities of political
warfare would be softened, through the benign influence of those who
are now considered merely as a pleasing toy, a plaything by means of
which to while away an idle hour. . . .

There are many bright examples of intellectual worth, of talents of a
superior order, devoted to a high & noble purpose. Would that there
were more, that the happy era might soon come when New England
daughters & sons too, should prove themselves worthy of their pilgrim
fathers. . . .

Did I possess the means, I would give you a description of my
location. But it is quite out of my power as I have taken few walks
during my short residence here. You, however, can just fancy yourself in
a town upon the sea coast that has been settled a century, & you will
have a more correct idea of Ipswich than I could give you by description. My heart's desire regarding my situation for the winter is, in part,
realized. Whether it eventually proves a blessing remains to be determined, although I am aware much depends upon my own efforts. You
mentioned something in your letter we received before I left home,
regarding the West as a desirable field for teaching. I feel that it is, yet
me-thinks those who go thither, should be actuated by other & nobler
motives than of acquiring property. At least those who go to the far
west, cannot expect to amass wealth by teaching for years to come.
Having had the destitute & ignorant state of females in Illinois presented
by Miss Grant, I cannot but feel we desire to do something to rescue
them from ignorance so degrading. It was stated as a fact, that the
females married young & totally ignorant of the duties of a wife. One
case was mentioned as not a solitary one, where a family in Illinois

containing several who had arrived to maturity of years, & not one who could read, who had even heard of a bible, or of a God. Miss Lyman of Amherst boards in the same family with myself, which is an unexpected pleasure.

Ipswich, March 5, 1835
Dear Brother,

A letter from Mary so soon may perhaps somewhat surprise you, but probably not more than the fact, that in a few weeks I may be engaged as a teacher in Indiana. If so New Washington will be my home if my life is spared for two or three years. I now design returning home next week, where I shall remain a few days, perhaps two or three weeks & then go "west" accompanied by a lady from this Seminary, and under the protection of Rev. Mr. Ellis. The reward will not be great unless I include the consciousness of endeavoring to do good. This I do know however, that the proposed school is to commence on the 1st May, if nothing prevents, and the teacher is requested to be there several days prior to the commencement of school.

The decision is made. The Rubicon is passed. In a few weeks I shall locate in a rural spot not far from the Ohio. I shall then doubtless realize more than I now can, western life. Now the fact that I have pledged my word to go, that seems more like a dream than a reality. The proposed situation will not be such a one as I had pictured. There will be none of the romance and much of the reality of life. I do not anticipate such marvelous trials, such severe self denying labors as some describe. True, I may not enjoy all of the comforts of home. . . .

Bethlehem, Ind. July 10, 1835
[To Brother Alfred]

It is I think quite a different thing to experience the want of comforts to which you may have been accustomed . . . for I am not as comfortable as at home and must be guided by the voice of Providence rather than that of pleasure. I must economize, so may not be able to spend my vacation with the Dickinson's of Amherst . . . it is the duty of one in my circumstances to labor where I can be the most liberally rewarded, provided all other circumstances are equal. I do not say this, because I think the compensation here is insufficient, far from it, for I think it generous. . . .

Bethlehem, Sat. eve, Dec. 5, 1835
My dear Brother,

. . . . I am alone this evening, & it is one of my comforts that I can sometimes be thus for, with little or big society with whom I should esteem it a privilege to do so. But I fear it would not only require remolding but new materials. I sometimes fear I am doing little good in this respect, & that instead of raising others I am sinking & that I shall be impelled downward when I would guide others "onward & upward."

Monday morn

Yesterday was the fourth Sabbath in succession that I have been unable to attend church as there has been no service within five miles & when thus near, the weather has been such that I could not go comfortably on horseback. Thus you see I am experiencing a little of western deprivations. Since I last wrote I have taken a jaunt on horseback of about 40 miles to Salem in Washington. By the way I passed through Philadelphia which has no resemblance but in name to the city of "brotherly love." On the first day of the excursion we rode 32 miles without stopping to rest or refresh. You will believe I was not a little fatigued. On the next morning however, I arose quite vigorous. It was the week of Synod at Salem which Mr. Dickey desired to attend consequently I passed it among the hospitable people there. I found too, such society as I had not before enjoyed since my arrival.

Bethlehem, Ind., Dec. 17, 1835
My own Brother,

Your letter reached me while in school this afternoon. I read until I could not command myself sufficiently to do so before witnesses then laid it aside but could not let it remain though I was repeatedly obliged to screen my face & stop to gain self possession. . . . Uncle Joshua wrote that God was visiting in mercy the church & people in Hawley & this afforded me great comfort when I thought of Moses return thither. I pray that his life may be spared & his health restored, yet though it would rend my soul with anguish to part with those whose existence is so interwoven with my own, yet could I hope they had exchanged this world for the one "where the wicked cease from troubling and the weary find rest," I should feel that these blessings & my loss was their gain, but were there no such hope to cheer, oh the agony. God forbid that it shall ever be indured—But may we all "lay up treasures in heaven where neither moth or rust can corrupt or thieves break through & steal, where none shall thirst or hunger more." Dear brother let us repose our trust in one who cannot change, let our affections centre where no blight or mildew can blast or treachery or cruelty can crush. Let us forget the past only so far as shall stimulate us to renew diligent watchfulness for the future. It would afford me a high degree of pleasure could I forward you some botanical specimens but I have none. Not having a botany prepared for this section of the country my researches were not as successful as they otherwise could have been, & the few rare plants I did find I severed & conned & destroyed. When spring opens I hope to renew my excursions, but until then I am debarred from such pleasures.

. . . . Thank you for the remembrance of our birthday. I thought of thee, of home & of all whose presence was wont to gladden our hearts, & I confess the contrast did sadden mine. No kind wish, no fond look— no birthday greeting, or affectionate kin, naught but the sad remembrance that friends were far away & the thought that my brief life was one day shorter & I can scarcely credit my memory when I think I am 22. I too still feel like a child & wish a mother, father, sister or a brother near to whom to go, or rather that we were all of our dear family at our own loved home. Had we in childhood's happy days but dreamed of the future ills we should have prized those joys more highly & should have grieved that they so soon must end. But thus it is with life. Yet my loved brother, there is a world where friendship is perfected, refined & partings are unknown.

Did you notice the splendid "Northern lights" in November? It seems some of the New Yorkers thought their city on fire, but some of the Hoosiers had still more enlarged ideas of the conflagration, thinking the day of judgment was at hand. This is a specimen of the intelligence of the people here. They are I believe kind & this atones in part for the lack of many other qualities. . . .

Jan. 9, Sat. morn

I attended a debate last evening & was greatly amused. It exceeded anything I have ever heard. Such a combination of sense and nonsense, such high flown speeches & such blunt ones, such murdering of the king's English as I never before heard in one evening. Their proceedings I doubt not were intended to be quite parliamentary, for on rising they invariably addressed the chair in due form & then alluded to their honorable competitors or opponents, but one of the speakers scarcely uttered a grammatical sentence. Notwithstanding all this, there were some very good things said . . . .

Bethlehem, Ind., Jan 31, 1836
[to Alfred]

You imagine me more sad than is the reality. Usually I am quite happy. I have never regretted coming here and think were I now at home I should pursue the same course regarding the west.

Feb. 2, 1836

I received a letter from my protector, Mr. Burgess stating that a friend of his, a man of promising talents now a member of the Western Theological Seminary preparing for a mission to China, desired him to ascertain whether I was under any particular engagement and provided I was not, Mr. B. added, his friend would visit Indiana in April. In conclusion he says "Pray excuse him. Persons intending to go far hence to serve Gentiles have to adopt some extra methods in obtaining the companions of their future labors." Of course I shall decide nothing regarding the individual alluded to at present, but I ought soon to decide regarding my own duty — my fitness for a missionary.

Bethlehem, April 26, 1836
My dear Brother,

If you were me, how gladly would I open my heart, & try your wisdom in exploring its recesses, including its apparent contrarieties, & reading its whisperings. With such assistance I think I should know myself better, for never have I felt so ignorant & unable to decide regarding its convictions of duty—its feelings, as I now do. You probably recollect remarking in your last letter that after having decided some queries regarding my own duty, the only questions then be, "Is the gentleman fitted for the lofty enterprise? Has he a mind & a soul equal to the undertaking?" Perhaps could I unhesitatingly decide these points affirmatively, I should "scarcely doubt his capability of being a fellow pilgrim." I think him, viz. Mr. Riggs, intelligent, well informed and deeply interested in the cause of missions, but as yet I do not feel that regard which I am sure I ought to feel for a lone fellow pilgrim. You know I despise the affectation of romance and desire to bring my views down to sober reality, yet I cannot think of forming such a sacred and unalterable connection without good evidence of an interchange of affection, a congeniality of soul. As it regards this point I will acknowledge there seems to me a mystery which my ken cannot pierce or my foresight explain. Though Mr. R. seemed familiar yet there was not that frankness, that open heartedness, which I had hoped for. It might have been occasioned by my own demeanor, for notwithstanding all resolutions I had formed of forgetting my old aversion to introductions, & thinking only of the great & blessed work in contemplation, it would occasionally force itself upon me. Besides this I felt so sad that I probably seemed unhappy. Perhaps this lack might have resulted from diffidence, if so, ought he not in his letters, which I shall receive previous to forming any decision, to be frank & explicit?

It is not as yet decided regarding the field where Mr. Riggs may labor. Perhaps among the Sioux Indians, perhaps in India or China. I know not that the field ... should be regarded, even though one might have a preference or feel a peculiar interest in one more than in another, & I thought it an evidence of Mr. R.'s love for the cause of missions that he seemed quite so willing to go to the poor Sioux or Dakota. When you think of Mr. R. you must not fancy him so talented as Mr. Burgess' letter might imply (though I know not but he really is), but recollect that is the description of a warm, a very ardent friend. Neither must you think of him as being peculiarly interesting to a stranger, but as one smaller than middle stature, plainer than the mediocrity, even very homely if you please, & appearing to better advantage in conversation than in the desk [pulpit]. True, I cannot judge what he may be in the desk as he is not yet "licensed" & doubtless spoke under embarrassing circumstances last Sabbath. Still I do not wish you to flatter yourself that he is great, & indeed I do not think you would decipher that so essentially a requisite as goodness. I do wish my dear Alfred, to commune with my own heart, listen to the "still small voice" & obey its dictates. And when my heart seems so dark, it is a consolation to think there is one . . . who will lead us in the right way if we seek his guidance. Do write without delay as your letters are ever a solace. "Tis sweet to believe of the absent we love if we miss them below, we shall find them above."

Bethlehem, May 17, 1836
My own Mother,
  Perhaps you may be surprised so soon to receive a communication so different from the one I last forwarded. After it was dispatched I endeavored candidly to examine circumstances, hoping to read aright the inclinations of Providence, & follow their guidance. When I simply looked at Mr. R's situation, & remembered he too must have had feelings perhaps as various and acute as my own, I confess his apparent want of open heartedness seemed less ingratiating, & his conduct more natural. . . . With such feelings I determined to wait the reception of Mr. R's letter. Contrary to my expectations it reached me last week, & was all that I could wish & more than I expected. And as it will give you a more correct idea of him than any description of mine, I subjoin a part of his letter.
  "I should think from your conversation that you would have very little difficulty in deciding that it is your duty to become a missionary—but this will scarce touch the question whether you are willing to go with

me. If you can come to a decision when you write please give me the result. You need not be in the least afraid of committing yourself—for although I shall consider my offer, if accepted & any engagements bind-ing on myself—yet I shall not hold your acceptance in that way unless it still continues your pleasure.

"I believe I told you my expectations concerning yourself were fully realized. I now say they were more than realized but I wish you to make your decisions uninfluenced by my feelings. There are some consider-ations which seem to make it desirable that you should decide this matter as soon as convenient. For besides the unhappiness created by a state of suspense, a delayed decision might prevent me from entering into the "field" which is "white already to harvest" as soon as necessary. But I know you love the poor, the perishing heathen too much to cause any unnecessary delay. If however you cannot decide immediately from circumstances, just mention it & I will be the last to press a decision in such a case. And may the Lord guide you into the path of duty, & make his face to shine upon you, & enable you to make such a decision as will advance your own happiness & glorify him on earth. I will make no comment, though I shall wish your opinion regarding it. I know if I trust in God I cannot be disappointed in a companion unless the All Wise sees best, & I would entirely trust His goodness to provide me with such a one & enable me also to be such a one as will promote happiness & advance His cause."

. . . . I shall leave it optional with you, my mother, whether to disclose at present my future expectations—perhaps it might not be best as I have not replied to the part alluded to in Mr. R's communication, hoping first to receive a reply to my last letter home. Do not imagine Mr. Riggs to be remarkably talented but recollect Mr. Burgess's descrip-tion was from a woman friend. I shall content myself if he has good common sense, is kind & a devoted Christian. Neither fancy his address as particularly pleasing, but remember his time has been devoted to fitting himself for the work of a missionary. If it should seem my duty to accompany him, I could wish (though I am conscious such a blessing would be undeserved) the warm approval of all my dear & near kin-dred. As it will probably be necessary for me to procure a bonnet this

Summer, please send me word if you can ascertain what are worn.

Bethlehem, June 7, 1836
My dear Brother,

Many thanks for your good letter. Though like yourself I feel the inadequacy of the pen, still it seemed to me that our spirits had communed. And could you have read my thoughts as I read yours and pondered on your suggestions you would have felt how much happiness it was in your power to impart by such kind messages, and perhaps they may be our only medium of intercourse "for other twelve moons" though there is a possibility of my returning home next fall. Listen for a moment while I tell you the circumstances in which I am placed & then advise. If Mr. Riggs should labor among the Indians he will probably leave for the mission in the Spring. Were this to be the case I should most certainly feel that I ought to pass the winter at home, and as they would wish here to procure a teacher from Ipswich, it may be necessary for me to decide whether I will remain another term, before Mr. R. can determine regarding his future location. Would it not then be my duty to relinquish the idea of remaining here as long as I intended & endeavor to obtain some situation at the east where I could devote a part of my time to study?

Had I the means I should choose devoting the time entirely to such pursuits as seemed best calculated to fit me for my future labor, & I know of no place so eminently calculated for this purpose as Ipswich. But if I should do so I should expend even more than "the last farthing" of the avails of my labor here. Though I doubt not that the appropriations of my Board for the outfit of missionaries are sufficient to supply them with what is deemed requisite. Still it seems to me I should choose something that I could feel I was at liberty to dispose of as I pleased. Am I wrong? I doubt not pa'a's willingness to give me an equivalent to Lucretia's portion, but I should prefer that would be reserved for Henrietta's education that she may be fitted for usefulness, though I believe it is our duty as a family to give more than we do to the cause of missions. . . .

In reference to health. Permit me to say while you are in the west you

had better change much. Let the deep ravines and the sunny mounds &
the tall trees & the little flowerets know you. Let your inside be like an
old acquaintance perfectly familiar. It is all important that those who
expect to be missionaries should be prepared to endure hardships. . . .
What say you to this, dear Alfred? I know it is even so, but I am conscious that I am not well fitted to endure hardships, though I think my
residence in these wilds may perhaps inure me to some things I should
once have deemed hardships. I know it is not always the most hardy
that are enabled to endure most, or that are most successful, but I trust
as my sphere of labor may require.

Bethlehem, June 7, 1836
Such a multitude of thoughts come rushing upon me. . . when I think
of leaving all the tried friends & loved ones, with one of whom I can
know comparatively little; of entering upon untried scenes, now in a
strange land, my spirit would be ready to faint within me, did I not feel
that I had endeavored to seek heavenly wisdom to direct. But there is
one thought which, though it may seem of minor consequence, will
thrust itself before me and give me pain, viz. the possibility that my dear
kindred may not affectionately regard Mr. Riggs. I am conscious that
his habit & manner may differ somewhat from ours, still as far as merit
or worth is concerned I do not doubt that he is not only worthy, but
more than worthy of your mercy. . . . But I trust Alfred will regard whoever is regarded by his Mary & I am sure she will love any one worthy of
his affection.

Bethlehem, Oct. 3, 1836
My dear, dear brother,
Your late message of affection found me on Thursday last. . . . The
probability is that I shall not reach Pittsburgh until the first week in
November. There is a possibility, if not a probability, that Mr. Riggs may
accompany me on my return, but this would rather enhance than diminish the happiness your company would afford.
Mr. Riggs is now with us & on Wednesday we shall probably leave
for Ohio. The sitting of Presbytery is on the 17th & Synod on the

Thursday following. They will probably occupy nearly two weeks, so that my return to West Union will be delayed until the last of this month. Then I hope to set my face eastward. During Presbytery Mr. Riggs will probably be licensed & soon after make a formal application to the American Board. He now thinks everything in reference to our future destination is undetermined.

La Belle Riviere, Wednesday eve

Once more I am upon these waters & once more my home bound heart gladdens as I set my face towards home. But my thoughts are turned from their wonted channel by the rude songs & the cheer of the boatmen below & the rattling silver of the gamesters in the gentlemen's cabin. We shall probably reach Cincinnati in the morning and happy indeed should I be could I there hear a brother's voice & catch a brother's eye. Not that I am not well attended, but you know so much of a woman's heart as to realize or, at least from some faint conjecture, my feelings. . . .

If Mr. Riggs should return with me, I suppose he will be able to leave for the east very soon after Synod. Passed Madison one of the most flourishing villages in the state a little before sunset. I hope your health will be much improved by a visit to the home of our childhood. Are you quite sure you do right to have no plans, or to relinquish your hopes in reference to college even though you have seen 27 winters, and your health is frail & miserable?

> *But I can hardly think the frost*
> *Of seven & twenty winters mark*
> *My brother's brow. Oh are they lost*
> *Forever? Would that all our dank*
> *And deep ingratitude might hence*
> *Be blotted out from that book of*
> *God's Remembrance.*

And are we then so old? In truth I had almost forgotten I had numbered so many years until the reception of your letter apprised me of your own. Let the rapid flight of time admonish us to be up & doing. . . .

With much love, I am your
Mary

Thomas Longley
1774-1848

married
December 20, 1804

Martha Arms Taylor
1784-1858

Henrietta Arms Longley
July 12, 1826-1850

CHAPTER 2

Journey to the Northwest Territory

1837

Eighteen thirty-seven was not an auspicious time for the newly married couple to begin their missionary work. The month in which they were married witnessed the first indication of the financial panic of 1837. This situation, which was to last for the next seven years, resulted in rising unemployment and bank closings in major cities like Boston.

As the number of immigrants increased daily, land hungry settlers pushed on the edges of the western frontier. Impending war between the states loomed as debate heated up over the admission of slave and free states. In 1830 President Jackson signed the Indian Removal Act, and the Department of Indian Affairs was established to administer Indian territory west of the Mississippi. Indian affairs were, at best, turbulent. Fort Snelling, on a strategic river route for the Sioux, became the site of the Indian Agency and military post.

Government permission was required to settle in Indian territory, but Stephen and Mary Ann started their journey west without it. The trip from Hawley by stage through Hartford, New Haven, New York, Philadelphia, and Pittsburgh lasted more than a month as they visited with family, friends, and former missionaries along the way. During this part of the trip, Stephen was ordained and learned that a mission had been established at Lac qui Parle. The last part of the journey, across the prairie in an ox-cart, saw Mary Ann pregnant with her first child.

Mary and Stephen reached Lake Harriet June 1, 1837, and there made a home while awaiting assignment to the Lac qui Parle mission.

At the time of their arrival, most of the Native peoples of the area were starving and losing their lands to the government of the United States and the westward expansion of European settlers. This continual disintegration of the Indian lands and culture contributed to the growing resentment toward white settlers.

City of Penn, March 3, 1837

Again my dear Parents I have seated myself to talk with my pen with those who think of us and of whom we think often, very often. . . . I know that friends widely separated often lose the deep interest once felt in each other, and it is this thought that makes separation to me more painful. But I will not allow this thought a place in my heart. . . .

We were met here this afternoon and intended calling upon cousin Sylvia but Mr. R. has been busily engaged in making or trying to make arrangements about our baggage. . . . Even with this detention we have had a prosperous and pleasant journey. Surely I may be very grateful when I contrast my comfortable situation tonight with that of a poor English woman coming on board the boat from New York today. As she told us the story, her husband and herself recently arrived with their little ones from the mother country and were on their way to Illinois where her husband was to act as a gardener. This morning he came on board with her and two little twins scarcely able to stand alone, and stepped on shore for "the luggage" and the boat was off and the poor woman's husband left on shore.

Sat. morn, and a beautiful one it is. We now expect to pass the Sabbath here. We shall improve today by making a few calls &c though I feel far more like secluding myself entirely than by seeing the city. . . . We shall expect to receive letters at West Union. We shall probably be there the last of March or the first of April.

Anti Slavery Palace, [West Union] Wednesday morn, April 5, 1837
My own dear Parents,

. . . . My dear husband left me at Portsmouth & made a short tour in this Presbytery. I remained there several days, & then accompanied by brother Joseph Riggs & sister Elizabeth, I went to Ripley. At both places the kindness of friends led me to feel that I was not among strangers, though you will easily conceive they could not supply the place of husband, father, mother, brother & sister. Brother J. Riggs gave $30.00 to the board besides making us several presents. His kindness supplied my lack of a good English Merino, and sister Riggs had prepared her donation & took it by, as the apostle directs, 1 pr. warm blankets, also sheets & pillow cases. . . .

We find Mrs. Burgess not behind & perhaps before most of our friends in her plans & gifts. Besides a stove, she has provided sheets, pillow cases, towels, dried peaches, a fine blanket & comforter &c. Perhaps you will fear that with so many kind friends we shall be furnished with too many comforts. Pray then that we may be kept very humble, & receive these blessings thankfully from the giver of "every good & perfect gift." Mr. & Mrs. Burgess' hospitality is evinced by their open doors, & welcome board during Presbytery which commenced yesterday. This evening Mr. Riggs preached his trial sermon. It is the one I read from Daniel, "They that be wise shall shine as the brightness of the firmament, & they that turn many to righteousness as the stars forever & ever." Tomorrow will probably be his ordination. Now we expect to return to Ripley the last of this week, pass the next there & the succeeding in Cincinnati. There we go far hence to the Gentiles not knowing the things which may befall us there. Give our best love & respects to grandpa'a & all the dear friends. . . . so willing to assist our preparation for departure & residence among the poor Indians. Since my arrival here I have ascertained that a church has been formed at Lac qui Parle. Mr. Renville's Indian wife is a member. I wish a letter from this, our dear church at home, to the one at Lac qui Parle. . . . We have both had pretty good health since we left Massachusetts & I hope it may continue. . . . I should be glad to write on but I can only say may God bless you all.

West Union, April 6, 1937
Dear Mother,

. . . . I wish you would secure for me two yards of gingham like my dress and send it the same way {in a small box or packet to the American Board of Foreign Missions, Boston.} Please send it the first time pa'a goes to Greenfield. I procured it at Hall's. Do you suppose the good people of Hawley would feel like filling out a small box for the Dakota mission sometime? If not you can send me anything for, as I mentioned before, I have not procured any bed quilts yet & perhaps I may be glad of that calico quilt.

Cincinnati, Apr. 26, 1837
Dear brother Alfred,

Once more we are visiting the Queen of the West. Once more we have left behind us dear friends and set our faces to the far wilderness. Still my thoughts go further back than to those most recently left, to my tried and precious kindred away upon the hills of New England. I cannot thank you sufficiently that your letter was so cheering, even more so than you often write. It consoled rather than saddened and did not bring with it that sudden overpowering rush of tenderness and anguish which your letters sometimes bring. . . .

I know not whether I shall gladden or sadden your heart most by telling you we could find no miniature painter, who would send you my phiz for less than £5.00. I hesitated some time whether to sit for it and even after I had decided my heart almost failed me when I thought how many vitals or testaments might be procured with the amount. The only way I have consoled myself for such an expenditure on my homely face is, by hoping. . . that it will stimulate the possessor to more devotedness, more benevolence, more love to him and his cause in whose service we trust, we are engaged. And I thought too, before I decided you would be sadly disappointed if I should fail to get it taken.

My dear husband is out making purchases with Mr. Weed, the assistant sec. of this branch of the board, at whose house we now make our home. . . . Mr. & Mrs. Weed labored as missionaries among the Indians several years, and retain plain habits & kind hearts, & are as little citified & less even than most good people. Mrs. W. was a Lathrop of Pittsfield and a niece of Dea. Lathrop of Hawley. She recollects calling at our house a long time ago when on a visit to her uncle's.

Today a procession passed through the principal streets in the city, which led me to believe masonry was not dead or sleeping. I think if pa'a had witnessed the awful mockeries he would have felt his zeal for antimasonry rekindled, if he had beheld the trappings & the fooleries of these masons incognito known as "The Odd Fellows" of Cincinnati and Louisville. First in order came two (royal arch I suppose) on horseback, then the musicians, some with drums some with clarinets, bugles, etc. Then followed others on foot with aprons and bands of satin or velvet variously trimmed and ornamented. Some blue, some red, & some white richly wrought. These are marched with their little fingers locked together, some of them carrying spears & some swords. At certain distances three walked together supporting flags on which were inscribed "Benevolence" "Many are called but few are chosen" and the like. The one in the centre of some of the trios carried open bibles on which was laid an Ivory mallet, & those at the sides held spears, meeting over the bible. Again you would see one bearing a large gold key & another the rod that budded and two others the ark. It seems to me profanity extreme.

Wednesday eve

I did not feel like writing this evening but Mr. Weed's little sons have kindly placed a table for my use & I cannot refrain from using it. . . . We left Ripley accompanied by one of Mr. R.'s brothers and sisters last Monday and hope now to leave for St. Louis next Monday. We may be detained there or at Alton a week or two and at the fort a long time. We shall therefore confidently expect letters at the Fort Snelling. If you have not written don't delay a moment. Tell us all about your plans, & all about the dear ones at home. We have not as yet purchased any drawing books, which we had intended to do with the gift from brothers & sister, & shall not unless we can find less expensive books. Perhaps you can find some elementary drawing book, containing very simple lessons such as straight lines & curved, benches, logs & foliage from the little shrubs or tuft of leaves to the tall tree, with some lessons in perspective. If you can find such a one & will send it in the first packet ma'a sends, I shall be happy to receive and use it.

Sat. noon

Again dear brother, with heart & hand & pen I'll talk with thee. You wished me to write you what escritoire we purchased &c. The only good one to be found in the city was one which was altogether too ornamental of mahogany with brass corners and flat handles smaller than yours, but containing a drawer in the largest side. We took it however rather than have none, & shall furnish it with inkstand sandbox paper quills &c. &c. so that we can have writing apparatus convenient. . . .

La Belle Riviere, May 1, Monday eve
We are again on our way to "the far west" comfortably situated on the fine steamer Isabella bound for St. Louis. We shall be unable to stop at Bethlehem but I hope to see Jane D. at Jeffersonville where she is teaching, as the boat will of course stop sometime at Louisville & ferry boats are constantly plying between the two places. Though I am going rapidly from you, nature wears a very cheerful aspect. The green trees and occasionally an orchard in full bloom give the banks a beautiful appearance. The motion of the boat is such that I fear you will find my craglypias quite unintelligible, as you may have done when I have written from a jarring steamboat, but I wish to finish this to leave at Louisville in the morning. I was writing at our new escritoire placed on a berth for a table & our trunks &c. Around us with little of the practical or romantic about, though perhaps as much as graced the garrets of some of our famous poets with the exception of the loaded tables in lieu of oatmeal and gruel. If this however had been all the difference I should not have been under necessity of sending these lines with my poor miniature which Mr. R. and our brother Joseph R. say is pretty correct. I am of course no judge.

> *Depart faint image of affection deep*
> *To home's loved ones, but cause them not to weep*
> *By waking fond remembrances of the past.*
> *If gone by, joys too sweet, too dear to last.*
> *But speak to them of one who'll ne'er forget*
> *The friends, youth, but who does not regret*
> *The chosen path, the path that Jesus trod*
> *Though it should lead from every friend but God.*

Tues.
This morning we reached Louisville in safety, having passed Bethlehem during the night. The falls are in sight. They are not as beautiful if I had a good view of them as those in Shelburne. Give much love to all and allow me to repeat the injunction, write immediately

directing to Fort Snelling, Upper Mississippi. Please mention to mother that the newspaper with patterns never reached me. I hope another will be sent directed as above.... I know not but Uncle Sam will charge this letter by the ounce, but I hope he will carry it safely and speedily.

Steamer Isabella, May 3, 1837
My dear Mother,
 .... Mr. R. accompanied me to Jeffersonville, where I found Miss Jane Dickey surrounded with a promising school of misses, many of whom are members of the "Juvenile Missionary Society".... The thought that my pupils were actively engaged in so good a work was truly cheering, though my residence in Indiana seemed on many accounts to be "a day of sad things." I hope I was enabled to do some good which may long be felt.

Thursday, May 4
 We have been highly favored thus far on our way down the Ohio. We took a last look at Indiana about noon, & saw the waters of the separating Wabash join those of the Ohio, & yet flow on without comingling for 10 or 12 miles marking their course by their bluer tint & purer shade. The junction of this & the Cumberland have enlarged the Ohio to a broad river indeed. Fine islands stud it at various intervals, clothed in most delicate hues.

 The banks are much lower here than nearer the source, sometimes gently slipping to the water's edge, & bearing such marks of inundation as trunks & roots of trees half imbedded in the sand or cast higher upon the shore. At intervals we pass some beautiful bluffs, not very high but very verdant & more precipitous. Both have craggy rocks with evergreen tufted tops, & a few dwarf stragglers on their sides. One of them contains a cave, apparently dark enough for deeds of darkest hue, & very probably it may have witnessed many perpetrated by wandering bandits that prowled about these cliffs during the early settlement of Illinois.

Fri. eve, On the Mississippi
 This morning when we awoke we found ourselves on the muddy

waters of the broad Mississippi. They are quite as muddy as those of a shallow pond after a severe shower. We drink it however & find the taste not quite as unpleasant as one might suppose from its color, though quite warm. The river is very wide here & beautifully spotted with large islands. Their sandy points, the muddy waters, & abounding snags, render navigation more dangerous than on the Ohio. We have met with no accident yet & I am unconscious of fear. I desire to trust in him who rules the water as well as the land. We have studied French & written a little today. I have also found some time for sewing. . . .

Sat. May 8

We hope to reach St. Louis this evening, having been nearly six days on our way from Cincinnatti, a very long passage owing in part to strong winds, some failure in the draft of the steamer, stopping for freight &c. The cabin has been decorated & perfumed with flowers this afternoon, procured from the shores of Missouri. If I succeed in securing specimens, I will enclose some of them. Even the upper deck received a bouquet. We have just descended to our tiny stateroom after having enjoyed a most lovely sunset, where our eyes could scan several miles of the river with its wooded shores & islands. Tomorrow is the Sabbath and we hope to rest from our travels. . . .

St. Louis, May 10

Had you been with us this morning you would have sympathized with us when we heard that the Fur Company boat left for Fort Snelling last week. You can imagine our feelings, our doubts, our hopes, our fears, rushing to our hearts, but soon quieted with the conviction that the Lord would guide us in his own time to the field where he would have us labor. We feel that we have done all within our power to hasten on our journey & to give information in reference to the time for leaving this city. . . . We now have some ground for hope that another boat will ascend the river in a week or two, & if so, we shall avail ourselves of the opportunity. . . . Yesterday we endeavored to keep the Sabbath in this Sabbath breaking place—this depot of iniquity. It being almost impossible to obtain accommodations for ladies in this city & disliking a removal of our effects on the Sabbath, we made our home on the boat Isabella until we left for the boat on which we now are. Today for the first time, if memory has not proved treacherous, I have seen some of the dark sons of the forest, from the Seneca nation, a peaked, oppressed tribe. Most of them were dressed in coats &c, but one still wrapped his blanket round, & decked his straight black hair tufted with feathers, & his ears weighted down with gew gaws. Will my soul burn with love unquenchable for these tawny tribes while life remains? I trust it will.

Alton, Ill., May 12

. . . . Since the warm days of spring, those harbingers of summer have imparted their debilitating influence, and particularly since our arrival here, lassitude & weariness have hampered my capacities for writing, & taken possession of the "frail house I live in," and yesterday & today Mr. Riggs has suffered perhaps more than myself from the same or similar visitors. We think the water exerts some influence & hope in a few days to feel new vigor and increased strength of body & mind. We are now spending our time in a lovely family—a family that have led us to feel at home in a strange land, & cheered our hearts, drooping as they were at the sight of such manifestations of selfish tyrannical depressed human nature, as St. Louis afforded. . . .

We shall not soon forget the name of Gilman, or the hospitality that will be associated with it. Mr. G. invited us to his home the morning of our arrival, & we have found it a home though not our dear mountain home. We still live in hope of reaching Lac qui Parle this season though we have heard nothing definite of a boat for the St. Peters. In reference to this, "patience must be our motto."

Steamboat Olive Branch, May 12

. . . . We are now on our way to Galena, where we shall probably take a boat for St. Peters. We pursue this course though it subjects us to the inconvenience of changing boats, that we may be able to avoid traveling on the Sabbath if possible. One Sabbath at least will be reserved in this way, as the Pavilion, the only boat for St. Peters at present, leaves St. Louis on Sunday! This we felt would not be right for us, consequently we left Alton today, trusting that the Lord would speed us on our journey of 3000 miles, & enable us to keep his Sabbaths holy. Of the scenery we have just passed this afternoon, I can give you no just conception. It beggars description & yet I wish you could imagine the Illinois shore lined with high semicircular rocks half embosomed [sic] by trees of most delicate green & crowned with a grassy mound of the same tint. Or being more perpendicular & towering more loftily in solid columns, defying art to form, or demolish nature's works so—impregnable, and at the same time so grand & beautiful. But you must see them to feel their loveliness & their sublimity [sic]. I have just been gazing at these vistas of rocks mellowed by the soft twilight. A bend in the river, & an island makes them apparently meet the opposite shore. The illusion of a splendid city, built of granite & marble & shaded by luxuriant groves, are reflected in the quiet water. This river bears little resemblance to itself (as geographers name it) after its junction with the Missouri. To me it seems a misnomer to name a river from a branch to which it is so dissimilar. The waters here are comparatively pure & the current mild. Below, they are turbid and impetuous, rolling on in their power, & sweeping all in their pathway onward at the rate of five or six miles an hour.

Galena, Ill. May 25, 1837
My dear Parents,

.... A kind Providence has so ordered our affairs that we are detained here still, & I hope our stay may promote the best interests of the mission. It seems desirable that Christians to these villages on the Upper Mississippi should become interested in the missionaries & the missions among the northern Indians, that their prejudices may be overcome, & their hearts made to feel the claims those dark tribes have upon their sympathies, their charities, & prayers. You are doubtless aware we are in the great lead region of Illinois & Wisconsin. Yesterday Mr. T. procured a skiff & accompanied us to a lead furnace. This furnace is almost the only one in this vicinity that stops upon the Sabbath. We could not remain to see "a run out" as it is termed, but we saw the "fiery furnace," the molten lead, the long shovels, pokers & ladles, & the kettle that receives the burning metal. Then it is skimmed & dipped into forms

from 18 to 24 inches long. When cold these "pigs" are taken out &
usually weigh from 65 to 75 pounds. Though a bar of not more than
four or five inches thick, & apparently might easily be raised with one
hand, both of mine were inadequate though I might have succeeded by
repeated efforts. We obtained some specimens of the ore which I shall
be happy to forward at the earliest opportunity.

Lower rapids, upper Mississippi, 4 o'clock p. m.

We are now above the mouth of the Des Moines, toiling & puffing
in order to ascend against the strong & rapid current which extends for
2 miles. The firemen have already consumed a barrel of rosin in order to
increase the intensity of the heat. A few hours since we passed a little
group of Indians. They were Sacks and Foxes I suppose as those tribes
reside, or rather roam, in the vicinity that is in Wisconsin. Perhaps
Thomas and Henrietta are as ignorant as I was in reference to this
territory, & if they are, they may impute to their atlases unless I am
mistaken. If I have not forgotten Wisconsin is represented the same as
the Northwest on maps used in schools. It, however, is a part of the
Missouri Territory. But to return to the poor Indians. They had spread
their tents next to the shore with their horses grazing around them.
Some of the young ones were amusing themselves sailing in a little
pirogue (a canoe dug from a tree). Four of the tents were like a pointed
roof of a house with their ends open, & the others conical, & I should
judge were made of coarse cloth. If it were in my power, I would sketch
this group. I hope Henrietta will be able to when she comes out to teach
the red children. Soon after gazing at these sons of the forest we passed
a sinking boat, a poor crazy bark, & the very one on which we came
from St. Louis to Alton last week. . . .

Steamer Pavilion, Upper Mississippi, May 31
My Dear Parents,

We are this evening more than 100 miles above Prairie du Chien on
our way to St. Peters, which we hope to reach before the close of the
week that we may be able to keep the Sabbath on the shore & also
receive letters from home. While lingering at the Prairie we saw quite a

number of Indians. Their indolence and filthiness are enough to make the heart sick, but their ignorance & degradation enough to make it bleed. Some of them had little about them but a blanket, while others wore red pantalets tied with bead bands, & deerskin moccasins, & a very few loose hunting skins. Most of them wore a part of the hair at least braided the rest hung over the forehead & neck. The faces of the majority were disfigured with a coarse paint, the color of cochineal. They were variously painted, some with red cheeks & foreheads, others with a red circle round their eyes, & most with a stripe of the same where the hair parted in the middle of the head. I am told the paint used is Chinese courtesan, the very same used by many other ladies. Large coarse beads of tin ornaments larger than a dollar adorned the neck of several, & a majority wore plated tin ear rings hung around the ear in such a manner that a slight motion of the head would be communicated to the ornaments, quite similar in form to those of the fashionables in our more refined land. They have failed to carry out the fashion here by not boring the ear from top to bottom, & the paint generally used by the pale faces is not quite so "shiny" as that most in vogue with their more tawny sisters. Two Indian men I noticed with bells fastened a little below the knee & their step was more proud & firm than most of their brethren.

Usually though I could not tell the men from the women unless they carried packs. Then I knew they must be squaws for they not only carried their papooses slung behind, but all that must be borne.

During the day, many of them lingered near the groceries or lay on the sandy bank, baking in the sun. Some few strolled along the sandy shore, searching carnelians among the sand which they wished to sell that they might procure with their proceeds whiskey very probably. . . .

A neighbor Mrs. L. brought in a rolling pin & half pound of cinnamon & a pound of black tea, for us the morning of our departure from Galena. Such kindness has been very cheering. I think I did not mention Mrs. B. I. Gilman's liberality. Just before I left she slipped a ten dollar bill into my hand, & Mrs. W. G. supplied my cloak pocket with lemons for lemonade on the way. . . .

Your own,
Mary

Joseph Grout Longley
May 26, 1823-May 6, 1871

In the uniform of a Lieutenant in
the 1st Massachusetts Black Regiment
of the Civil War.

Lucretia Salome Longley Cooley
Wife of Sedwick Cooley
1811-1881

Moses Maynard Longley
July 14, 1815-April 12, 1904

Lac qui Parle Mission

1837 - 1842

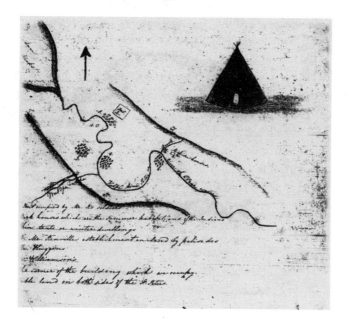

J oseph Renville operated the trading post, Lac qui Parle, located two hundred miles up the Minnesota River from Fort Snelling. Renville, part Dakota and part French, was instrumental in inviting missionaries to the territory. The Pond brothers, Gideon and Samuel, arrived at Fort Snelling in 1834, establishing a mission at Lake Calhoun where they were diligent in learning the Dakota language. Later they played an important role in the work Stephen Riggs undertook in translating Dakota into a written language.

Dr. T. S. Williamson arrived in 1835. Finding the Ponds' work well established, he took the advice of the Indian agent, Major Taliaferro, and moved up the river to Lac qui Parle where he and his wife founded a school. The number of students varied depending on the activities of the Indians. During this period there was growing resentment against the missionaries who were trying to introduce white, Christian work habits into the Indian culture.

For the first five years of their marriage, Mary Ann and Stephen lived in a room ten feet by twelve feet in the upper story of the school house, where the first three children, Alfred, Isabella and Martha were born. Besides growing family responsibilities, Mary Ann taught English and math to the Indian students at the school. Since Stephen was often away from home for extended periods of time, Mary Ann was left alone to cope with the Indians who were growing increasingly restless. The government agents refused to release promised food until the Indians agreed to settle on small farms and give up their vast territory. Traders continued to establish saloons on the edge of the reservations, and many Indians resorted to stealing and disorderly behavior which Mary Ann interpreted as a lack of respect for her privacy and possessions.

Fort Snelling June 2, 1837
My own dear Brother, [Alfred]

Last night was our first at the garrison, & though we are at Lieut. Ogden's quarters, & surrounded by walls strong & high guarded by trusty sentinels, I felt no more secure than in some lonely cabin, through whose open walls I could see "the moonbeams sweetly smile." I know if we will trust implicitly in an almighty protector he will never leave nor forsake us.

As we passed up the Mississippi & gazed upon the sublime handi-work of "nature's God," we wished you were with us to gaze, to admire & to adore. The prominent bluffs rearing their proud heads above & looking down on their more lonely compeers, enveloped almost with clouds & sky resting as it were upon the craggy tops, seemed to say, "How impotent is man." The bases of most were covered with verdure & forest trees, often reaching several hundred feet up the sides of the bluffs which stood rather like single mountains than a continuous bluff. Above all stood the rocky summit in some perfectly bare, in others spot-ted with trees of green. The scenery on the upper Mississippi surpassed all that I have witnessed, to say the least. I could give you no idea of its grandeur were I to fill this sheet with descriptions. When you come to us you can see for yourself.

I cannot tell you much in reference to our future situation as we have seen none of the missionaries yet, but expect to see them today. Mr. Pond & Mr. Renville have arrived from Lac qui Parle, & I suppose will return in about a week. The prospects of that station are favorable, & we have had thus far much cause for encouragement, though we have met many who think labors among the Indians are useless & will prove unavailing. Some too who seemed to think of our plans as though they were a matter of speculation or the result of singular taste. I know that if our motives are such as they should be, the world cannot understand or appreciate them. So I am not astonished when such remarks as are often made in reference to these poor & awfully degraded tribes come from those who professedly live for this world alone.

We found a Mrs. Denton here, formerly Miss Skinner of the Mackinaw mission, now the wife of a Swiss missionary among the

Sioux nearly 100 miles below on the river. She says they have very little furniture from choice—nothing I should judge, but cooking & eating utensils. I am not fully persuaded that it is the best way, though perhaps I shall be, before we have traveled several hundred miles by land. Early in the spring Mrs. D. was two days journey (by canoe) from her husband, who she learned was sick. As soon as the ice was broken up, she procured a canoe & two squaws & commenced her journey up the river. The first night she slept in the canoe with the little boy she had taken with her. The next as the boy was afraid in consequence of the squaws going considerable distance up the bank, she slept on the ground, & took no cold though there were two or three inches of snow upon the ground. I know not how soon I shall have as large a bed, as broad a canopy as Mrs. D's.

Lake Harriet, Monday eve, June 20
Dear Joseph,
   . . . . When you are prepared to teach these poor Dakotas the way to heaven . . . perhaps we may enjoy the pleasure of seeing you at our western home. But you have much to do to prepare to do good anywhere, you must begin now & form habits of doing good, you must endeavor every day to govern yourself, so that you will never again be angry or fretful. The Indians know when Christians get angry, & what do you suppose they think this Christian religion is? Do they think it is better than theirs? They know it is not good to get angry, & think it is very bad when they see it in others. We have some strawberries here & I think they will be abuntative [sic] in a few days & gooseberries also. These I think are almost all the summer & cranberries the fall fruit. So we shall need to learn to do without apples & a great many other good things, but we shall have more left than we deserve. I think Joseph would be willing to spare us some of his apples & this thought will give us much pleasure.

Lake Harriet, June 20, 1837
Dear Brother Thomas,
   Yesterday Mr. R. & myself commemorated a dying Savior's love for the first time on missionary ground. The reason was one of peculiar

interest, sitting down at Jesus' table with a little band of brothers &
sisters, one of whom was a late Chippewa convert who accompanied
Mr. Ayer from Pokagama, a prominent Pokagen coming to this place for
supplies. One of the Methodist missionaries, Mr. King & a colored man,
& members of this church from the Fort & mission completed our band
of 15. Several Sioux were present & gazed at the strange scene before
them. *Ho wax te* or Ho wash ta, as we should write in English, a medicine man, was present, & his head decked with a stuffed bird of brilliant
plumage, & the tails of another of dark brown. This name means "Good
voice" & he is building himself a log house not far from the mission house.
A humble & devoted follower of Jesus, he might be instrumental of
great good to this people. He might indeed be a "good voice" bringing
glad tidings. . . .

. . . . Last evening we had a family prayer meeting. It was a pleasant
session, & though we mourned that no Sioux would meet & pray &
praise with this happy Chippewa, we rejoiced that any sons of the forest
were brought from darkness into light. And notwithstanding we sang
& prayed in an unknown tongue to most of us, we could unite in spirit.
There was something very fervent & devotional in the tone of his
service, & some sounds struck my ear as being similar to Greek. . . .

Lake Harriet, June 22, 1837
My dear Grandfather,

We are now on missionary ground, & are surrounded by those dark
tribes, of whom we often talked at your fireside last winter. I doubt not
you will still think & talk about them & pray for them also. And surely
your grandchildren will not be forgotten. We reached this station two
weeks since, after enjoying Lieut. Ogden's hospitality a few days, & were
kindly welcomed by Mr. Steven's family, with whom we remain until a
house now occupied for a school can be so prepared that we can occupy
a part. Then we shall feel still more at home, though I hope our rude
habitation will remind us that we are pilgrims on their way to "a house
not made with hands, eternal in the heavens." The situation of the mission house is very beautiful, on a little eminence just upon the shore of a
lovely lake skirted with trees. Beyond, towards the fort, commences a

finely undulating prairie which reaches to the rivers. About a mile north of us is Lake Calhoun, on the margin of which is an Indian village of about 20 lodges. Most of these are bark houses, some of which are 20 feet square, & others are tents of cloth or skins. Several days since I walked up to the village & called at the house of one of the chiefs. He was not at home, but his daughters smiled very good-naturedly upon us. We seated ourselves upon all the bed, sofa, & chairs they had, which was a frame extending on three sides of the house & covered with skins. This family, from the old chief down to the third generation includes about 16 individuals, but many of their lodges contain 20 or more. Since our visit at the village two old chiefs have called upon us. And said this was a very bad country, we had left a good country, & had come to live in his bad country, & he was glad. The other called on Sabbath evening when Mr. Riggs was at the Fort where he preaches occasionally. He inquired very politely how I liked the country, & said it was bad. What could a courtier have said more?

The Indians come here at very odd hours of the day without ceremony, sometimes dressed & painted very fantastically, & again with scarcely any clothing. One came in yesterday dressed in a coat, calico shirt & cloth leggings, the only one I have seen with a coat, excepting two boys who were in the family when we came. The most singular ornament I have seen, was a large striped snake fastened among the painted hair, feathers, ribands of an Indian head dress, in such a manner that it could coil round in front and dart out its snaky head, or creep down upon the back at pleasure. During all this the Indian sat perfectly at ease, apparently much pleased at the astonishment & fear manifested by some of the family. We wish very much to talk with them when we see them, but we can do so only through our interpreter, though we can ask them the names of a thing, where they are going, & a few other questions in Sioux. It will take a long time to acquire the language. Messrs. Pond, who have been here the longest, are unable to converse very much on religious subjects in Dakota, though they can usually understand & are understood on common topics. Almost all that has been acquired by this language has been by living among the Indians without the aid of interpreters. If a good interpreter could be obtained it would be of great assistance to the mission. . . . We have decided to remain until September at least, when a missionary meeting is expected, & the probability is that we shall stay a year, as Mr. Stevens is very desirous of assistance & can accommodate us with a part of a house with a trifling expense, so that we can, while Mr. Pond is with us, enjoy perhaps as good an opportunity for acquiring the language as at "Lac qui Parle."

On our arrival here we found more fellow laborers in this wide field than we had anticipated. The Methodists have missionaries among the Sioux some few miles below this, & farther down are two Swiss missionaries sustained by a society in Switzerland.

Saturday eve, June 24

This afternoon the members of our mission family have witnessed a most interesting ceremony, the marriage of a white trader with an Indian woman with whom he had lived 15 years. The service was partly English & partly Dakota, & was performed by Mr. Samuel Pond, Mr. Stevens making the first, & Mr. Riggs the concluding prayer. Two of the children of the married couple were present, one a very interesting little girl of 10 or 12 years, who is a member of the mission family & school. It was apparent that she & her mother felt a little unpleasantly, though they conducted themselves with propriety on the occasion. The mother was dressed in moccasins, blue broadcloth pantalets & skirt with a fine calico short gown, ornamented with 5 bright patches of tan, three or four inches in diameter on the waist in front. Several dozen strings of dark cut glass beads hung upon her neck & her ears were loaded with ear drops. A blue broadcloth blanket thrown over her shoulders, completed her wedding dress, save two brass finger rings which I had forgotten. The ceremony was very interesting to me, not only in itself, but because it reminded me of one [Lucretia's] extremely dissimilar which I shall long remember. Besides this, it was the first marriage at this station, & the husband hopes to come forward on the morrow & unite with the little church here. This church is very small including the older members of the mission, Lieut. & Mrs. Ogden & two soldiers at the Fort, & two or three others.

Lake Harriet, June 27, 1837
Dear Sister Henrietta,

You will perceive I have spoiled your page through mistakes, & when it is once soiled, nothing can restore its beauty. Thus you will find it through life. If the day which dawns brightly & purely upon you is darkened by some bad action, one wrong word, it cannot be made spotless again. You may feel truly sorry but that will not wash away a single dark spot. Then how necessary it is that we are careful, very watchful over our words, thoughts, & actions, that we may not have cause for bitter regret. I suppose you feel desirous to know how I employ my time, & what I am doing for the Dakota (pronounced Dah koe tahs). At present when I rise in the morning & put my room in order, I read some in the testament. I have commenced Barnes on the Romans. After breakfast I often write some Sioux words, if not I sew. We have now copied one vocabulary & commenced another. When we commence house keeping, which we hope to do as soon as next week, I shall have additional duties, but now my time (that is business hours) is spent in writing, & studying Sioux, writing letters, sewing, listening to the Dakota, which I cannot understand, & in charge of the girls' sewing. This occupies an hour and a half. One little girl has made a dress of my fitting—it answers very well. We have commenced another, & have several more to make, as they make all their own clothes, with some assistance & care, & sew some for the family. There are about three of them, & the oldest I think is 11 or 12 years old. I think you would like to sew with them.

Home, July 8, 1837
My dear Mother,

This first letter from our present home should surely contain a message to mother. Would that you could look in upon us, but as you cannot I will try to give you some idea of our home. The building fronts the lake but our part opens upon the woodland back of its western shore. The lower room has a small stove given us by Mrs. Burgess, a few chairs & a small table, a box & a barrel containing dishes & flour, corn meal, beans, & store furniture. Our chamber is low, & nearly filled by a bed, a small bureau & stand, a table for writing made of a box, & the rest of our 1/2 doz. chairs, & one rocking chair cushioned by my mother's kind forethought. These articles, with our trunks &c. leaves but little space unoccupied when daily arranged in order. The rough loose boards in the chamber are covered with a coarse and cheap hair & ton carpeting to save labor. The one below will require some cleaning, but I shall not try to make it or keep it white. It would be useless, & almost, if not impossible. I have succeeded, so far very well according to my judgment, in household affairs with Mr. R's assistance. That is, very well for me. I brought the cake, put in my cloak pocket when I left to this place, & think it will be pretty good when steamed. I have forgotten what I wrote about the bed quilt. I do not need it now though it may be convenient hereafter. I have two good dark comfortables, four black kits, one furni-ture spread & enough for another, & one bed quilt, not new. I do not think you had better make it while you have no one to help you, but if you should conclude to make it for me, I should choose a colored lining & not very thick with cotton.

Some Indian women came in yesterday with strawberries which I purchased with beans. Poor creatures, they have very little food of any kind at this season of the year & we feel it difficult to know how much it is our duty to give them. If we make a practice of giving there will be no stopping place. I think it will at least be right to buy what they bring to sell, & pay them abundantly, & thus encourage industry & supply them with some food.

We are reminded of our Mass. home very often. Our writing table which serves as a chest is covered with a part of the green flannel you gave me. My box, my pincushion, watch & braided chair cover, speak of you. Other things also are mementos of your & others' care & kindness. We are not troubled with all the insects which used to annoy me in Ind., but the mosquitoes are far more abundant. At dark, swarms fill our room, deafen our ears, & irritate our skin. For the last two evenings we have filled our room with smoke almost to suffocation to disperse these over officious insects. It would be in vain for me to wish for a quiet night of sleep with a mosquito bar which we have recently ob-tained. . . . Write soon. I am glad Henrietta is able to write so well, &

that she has worked her cape so soon. I hope she will be very careful to have fun & grow better every day.

Lake Harriet, July 13, 1837
Dear Brother Alfred,

It afforded us pleasure that my miniature gives you such happiness. I do not wish any more remuneration than we have received—apply all that you have to some good purpose & that will be enough. Perhaps I shall think of some small articles which I may wish from home, if so I presume if you are there you will willingly send. We commenced housekeeping on Thursday the 8th inst. just two years from the time the first blow was struck by Mr. Stevens at this station. Prior to this, the Messrs. Pond had created a dwelling at Lake Calhoun about a mile distant, & made some progress in the language & greatly conciliated the favor of the Indians. Mr. S. Pond who was licensed & ordained in Connecticut last spring, breakfasts with us & joins Mr. Riggs in reading the Greek Testament at worship, while I read from the plain English Bible. We occupy, as I mentioned in a previous letter that we intended to do, a part of the building created for a school house. Two small rooms, one of which is a chamber, afford us very comfortable accommodations, much more so than we had allowed ourselves to anticipate.

Lake Harriet, July 31, 1837
My own dear Mother,

Having finished the ordinary duties which Monday brings, my thoughts fly to her who may yet be toiling on & on, spending & being spent again & again for the comfort of her family. And may they for whom so much has been endured "rise up & call her blessed" who has forgotten self in her care for them. When you are languid & wearied even to exhaustion, will it not comfort & cheer you to think your children are gratefully seeking to imitate your example of benevolent self-denial? May this too be your consolation, & may all that you have rocked in infancy & watched over with a mother's love till now, requite that love by their efforts to benefit their fellow creatures & Glorify God. The school connected with this mission is almost the only thing which can be seen of the efforts now making for these Indians, & this most of us feel little confidence in, as it regards the mass of Indians. Being a boarding school its influence must be very limited for many reasons. One obvious is that none except they that have white fathers can meet even the small sum required yearly, & few of these take much pains to educate their half Indian children when perhaps they have white wives & children whom they must care more for. Until my location here I was not aware that it was so exceedingly common for officers in the army to have two wives or more, but one of course, legally so. For instance at the Fort before the removal of the last troops there were but two officers who were not known to have an Indian woman, if not half Indian children. You remember I used to cherish some partiality for the military but I must confess the last vestige of it has departed. I am not now thinking of it in connection with the peace question, but with that of moral reform. Once in my childish simplicity I regarded the army & its discipline as a school for gentlemanly manners, but now it seems a sink of iniquity, a school of vice. And oh how lamentable is the influence which we wish to exert. And yet we are all from the same Christian country.

I believe however that the Indians are so discriminating that they will perceive the different motives which actuate us in our labors if we daily live as disciples of Jesus, reflect his image, & walk in his steps.

But to return to missionary labors for these poor Dakotas. We hope Mr. Pond will soon be able to preach to them of Christ in their own tongue, & perhaps a Sioux school will be opened when they return from their next hunt. Mr. Riggs is indefatigably engaged in acquiring the language, though he feels that he makes very little progress. It will be a long time before we shall be able to speak & write in Dakota as we now do in English. I know that I am doing very little towards acquiring it, but the warm weather & the domestic duties to which I have been so little accustomed, seemed to unfit me for study. I hope, however, I shall be able to accomplish more in future, as I feel less fatigued today than I have before on Monday since we reached here. This quite encourages me. I scarcely need say that Mr. R. does all to aid me which a kind husband would do, even to the milking, & much more. As regards various household affairs such as making good bread, butter, coffee &c &c, I succeed better than I feared, & I hope I shall soon be able to do all that devolves upon me in as little time as possible.

Wednesday morn, Aug 2

We are enjoying a fine cool breeze which is peculiarly refreshing after the heat of yesterday. The thermometer stood at 92 in our room during the afternoon, two or three degrees higher than it has been at any time this summer, excepting on the 22nd of July when it was the same. After such long & warm days, the nights are oppressive unless the earth is cooled by a shower. This is frequent, & accompanied by such peals of thunder rolling long & loud, & such vivid lightening as I have seldom or never seen.

Aug 4

Secluded as we usually are from the world, & just commencing our missionary labors, I can have little news to write. I do not wish for more intercourse with "the world" for this or for any reason, for Mr. R. & myself feel it rather desirable to avoid, rather than to seek, the intimate acquaintance of men at the garrison. You can perhaps imagine how much of our time consecrated to the Indians might be required & squandered were we greatly to encourage visits from the fort, & to return them when made. Situated but a pleasant drive from Ft. Snelling, which is isolated from it most seasons, those who have little or nothing to do but to kill time, & with few of the amusements of fashionable town life to aid them, would quite frequently enjoy an excursion to "the lake"....

We wish, however, to treat all with Christian kindness, & to encourage such an acquaintance as will promote the best interests of the mission. I said situated as we are &c, perhaps I should not have used an expression that would imply so much, as you will perceive by what I have written that we might have more intercourse with the gay & fashionable, than in most of the mountain towns in Mass. Besides this, we see friends from the states occasionally as we have had very frequent arrivals this season. You will not deem us shut out from the world entirely, while six or seven steam boats are in this port in about the same number of weeks. Perhaps during the winter months we may feel our-selves further away from the states & from those quiet little nooks among the hills of New England, where lie so many quiet plain hearted, consci-entious & church going sons of the Pilgrims. Would that there were more, & that their influence was felt far & wide, then the wife of the commanding officer would not on the Sabbath accompany a party of pleasure to the falls, & be applauded for it by a professing Christian. Then the garrison shanty would not be open on that holy day.... We expect Dr. Williamson here in Sept. & then we shall perhaps come to some more definite determination about our situation. . . . Mr. Boutwell from Leech Lake was here at the time of the treaty. He has been tried in many respects, & I think manifests a meek & Christian spirit. He married a part Chippewa from the Mackinaw school of whom he spoke with such affection. He remarked that it would have been impossible for him to have continued at his station if his wife had been a lady from the states unacquainted with Indian character & the Chippewa language.

Dear Henrietta,

.... It is now nearly sunset, & time for our Wednesday evening prayer meeting. . . . The Indians have nearly all left the village at Lake Calhoun, & will probably not return until the corn is large enough to eat. They left because their half starved children would ruin the corn had they remained by cutting the corn stalks to obtain the juice. Their parents therefore are obliged to choose the one of two evils & leave their ground to the merciless blackbirds. You will think this is a poor specimen of family government & it is probably not poorer than others. Mr. Riggs has been cutting hay for the cow, which we have today. They commenced hay making the first of this month, thus you will see the seasons are very late here. I do not remember whether I mentioned that the choice pota-toes which brother Thomas took so much pains with, were spoiled. The frost nipped all but the ones so carefully wrapped, & that was decayed before our arrival here. Perhaps Thomas will send us some seed, though we have very good potatoes here.

On the broad prairie of the far west, Sat. eve, Sept. 9, 1837
My own dear Mother,

Just at twilight I seat myself upon the ground by our fire, with the wide heavens above for a canopy, to commune with her whose caring heart follows her children wherever they roam. This is the second day we have traveled on this prairie, having left Traverse des Sioux Thursday afternoon. Before leaving that place, a little half Indian girl, daughter of the trader where we stopped, brought me nearly a dozen of eggs, the first I had seen since leaving the states, which afforded us a choice morsel for the next day....

Lac qui Parle, Sept. 18

The date will show you of our arrival at this station where we have found a home. We reached this place on Wednesday last, having been 13 days from Fort Snelling, a shorter time than is usually required for such a journey, the Lord's hand being over us to guide & prosper us on our way. Two Sabbaths we rested from our travels, & the last of these was peculiarly refreshing to body & spirit. Having risen & put our tent in order, we engaged in family worship & afterward partook of our frugal meal. Then all was still in the wide wilderness, save when at intervals, some bird of passage told us of her flight, & bade our wintry clime farewell. Thus an opportunity was afforded for reading, meditation, & prayer....

The day passed peacefully away, & night's refreshing slumbers succeeded. In the morning we were on our way before the sun had begun his race, & having rode 15 or 16 miles, according to our best calculations, we stopped for breakfast & dinner at a lake where wood & water could both be obtained, two essentials which frequently are not found together for 10 or 20 miles. A fire was soon built, the worship of God enjoyed, after which breakfast was prepared, a duck having been killed on our way. Such a dish as this was peculiarly grateful to us hungry travelers, & soon we were again on our way, not stopping often like pleasure hunters or flower gatherers, but pressing onward like those who have a goal in view, while it was day. I have given you this minute account that you may better imagine us with our two one-ox carts taking the lead, & followed by Dr. Williamson's wagon so fully loaded as to leave me a little corner. Mr. Riggs walked beside the horses, & the Dr. sometimes before, & then behind, pursuing our way over hill & plain, between lakes, & through marshes & streams of mud, day after day, until our journey was accomplished. I can give you but a faint idea of this wide prairie stretching itself between the two great rivers of the west. Sometimes we traveled several miles on a broad plain with no hill or woodland to break the perfect circle of the horizon, again our way would be over a succession of gentle hills with lakes or marshes between, & here & there an island of wood, which seemed large at a distance, but grew smaller as we approached, so deceptive is the appearance on a prairie. Often did we see woodland in the distant horizon before us but, mirage like, it disappointed our hope, proving to be a few scattered trees, or some small shrubs. Most of the wood upon the prairie is on islands, inconvenient if not inaccessible for travelers. These islands of wood are not injured by the fires which Indians kindle in the fields, which are gradually consuming the small wooded spots on the prairie that are not guarded by such a fire proof barrier as water.

The quantity of water we crossed during our journey was very small, though several muddy, sluggish brooks bear the name of rivers. I think the water which gushes from Hawley hills would equal the rivers that we passed on our way here. They at least appear very small in comparison with the wide world they prairie [SIC]. The quantity of water in the lakes & marshes is far greater, and were it not for these, this prairie would probably become a desert.

The evening after we arrived, we were shown the "little chamber" where we spread our bed & took up our abode. On Friday Mr. R. made a bedstead by boring holes & driving slabs into the logs, across which boards are laid. This answers the purpose very well, though rather uneven, & corresponds with our present table, which is a box that we brought from Ohio. Yesterday was the Sabbath & such a Sabbath as I never before enjoyed. Although the day was cold & stormy, & much like November, 25 Indians & part Indian assembled at eleven AM in our school room for public worship. Excepting prayer, all of the exercises were in Dakota & French, & most of them in the former. Could you have seen these Indians kneel with stillness & order during the prayer, & rise & engage in singing hymns in their own tongue, led by one of their own tribe, your heart would have been touched. The hymns were composed by Mr. Renville, the trader who is probably 3/4 Sioux, & his son took the lead in singing twice during the service, & Mr. Huggins once. In the afternoon we had, as we usually shall have, services in English, during which no Indians were present.

Wed. eve

.... If you can procure from any friend's library Long's Expedition to the Source of St. Peter's River & you will find a very interesting account of the Dakotas in the first volume, & one as nearly correct as any to be obtained. The Renville alluded to is the trader at this post. He & several of his children, are members of the church at this station....

Sept. 25, Monday eve

I would gladly add a few lines daily until my paper is filled. I wish you could join us now & pass a few days or weeks. After climbing a ladder you would descry our little aerie under the eaves, on the south east side of the house, with the sides well "daubed" with mud & lime, & the roof well shingled over.

Sept. 27

I have just been down in the school room trying to teach some Dakotas who are learning English, the figures & multiplication table. They succeed as well in learning our names as I do in learning theirs, & I suppose one, two, three, four is no easier than Wajita (Wah-Zhe-Tah) Nompa (Nompah), Yamni (Zah-me-ny) Tjopa (To-pah). I feel rather fearful that they will soon tire of what they can understand so little, for I cannot explain anything to them, as I should in English.

Mde-i-ye-dan, Lac qui Parle, or the lake of echoes,
Sept. 27, 1837
My own dear Alfred,
.... The date of this will tell of our removal from Lake Harriet &

explain the tardiness of our letters. Having determined for various reasons which I have mentioned in a letter to mother that it was best to come here this fall, we made our preparations speedily, & embarked on a Mackinaw to Traverse des Sioux, a trading post & crossing place of the St. Peters. On arriving there a distance of 60 miles by land, & 120 by the river, we were out a week including one Sabbath while we rested from our journey pitching our tent on the river's bank. At Traverse des Sioux we commenced our tour across the prairie. . . . By rising early, & traveling diligently, we accomplished this part of the distance of about 140 miles in six days, including one day of rest as before. . . .

I know not that I can tell you much about the state of this station. Dr. Williamson, I should judge, is a man who seldom speaks about it. As an instance of what I should think his humility, I'll mention one fact. Last summer Dr. W. accompanied the Indians in their hunt. The first day he divided his own supplies, which would probably have been sufficient for him during the hunt, wishing them to feel he was willing to fare as they did. The hunt proved insufficient, the best hunters being unable to kill as many deer & fowl as they probably would have eaten, if they had been alone. The whole company consisting of three fourths women & children, had to supply the deficiency with roots which they call "tapesin." They grow spontaneously in some parts of the prairie & resemble turnips or potatoes. The women dig them with a sharp pointed stick & their hands. Potatoes they also dig with the latter, using their heavy hoes, which form a part of their pack for a hunt only as a means of defense whenever alarmed, speedily digging a hole in the ground where they can hide from the enemy. . . . Dr. Williamson subsisted for two weeks mostly on roots.

Thurs., Sept. 28

I have just been preparing a wild duck for dinner & I presume you would find wild fowl abundant here & perhaps you might succeed in bringing venison for a repast. We have had some once which the Indians gave us, & I thought it not inferior to beef. Other wild meat, which we have had a specimen of, we have found very good, such as geese, grouse or prairie hen, ducks, plover & pigeons. We do not often have a fresh morsel, for Mr. Riggs has neither the time nor the skill re-quired. . . .

Lake of echoes, Oct. 8, 1837
My Mother,

Though it is scarcely a week since I finished my last letter home, & the probability is that no conveyance will for a long time occur, it is a pleasure to have a sheet on hand, on which I can talk with my dear mother. Today, which is the last of the week, has been with me a busy day though I can see little I have accomplished. In the morning I accom-panied Miss Poage to Mr. Renville's & to the Indian village on this side of the St. Peters. One object in going today, was to show Mr. Renville's daughter how to prepare some yeast for bread. After this we walked over to several of the lodges, or bark houses near, & found quite a num-ber of the women beating out corn. You are aware that they dry their corn by exposing it on scaffolds to the sun, after braiding it by the husks in long strings. When dry, it is taken to enclosures of skin, perhaps a tent hung round, & skins laid upon the ground, where the women beat it from the cob with sticks three or four feet long, completing the opera-tion, if imperfect, by shelling with the hand. We found the two wives of the chief thus busily engaged together. One of them asked if we had beaten our corn, & on telling them we had not, one replied that four of us could do it very soon. When we told them we did not know how, she said we might watch them & learn.

This afternoon *Wanatonas*, a Yankton chief & his wife came in to get some cinnamon Dr. W. had promised him. He is quite celebrated & the one of whose self torture Long gives such an interesting account in his Expedition to the Source of the St. Peters &c. This chief, having been on a journey during which he feared much from the Chippawas, made a vow to the sun that if he returned in safety he would fast four days & nights successively & distribute all of his property. Returning safely he performed the dance to the sun, cutting a hole in his arms & breast for the ropes to pass through, which were secured to a tall vertical pole, around which he danced & swung himself, until two of the slits gave away &, on the fourth day, when he swooned, his uncle cut the third. Afterward he performed the rest of his vow by distributing his horses, lodges, dogs, &c.

I cannot avoid telling you of this evening's disappointment. At dark, the man who had been to Traverse des Sioux, returned, bringing all our effects that were left there, but the very barrel packed expressly to bring up this fall, even though all the other articles were left. It contained most of our stove furniture, such as tea kettle, boilers, &c, & our tin ware, & many other things that we thought we could not well dispense with. I did not feel reconciled, & perhaps I do not feel quite right, though I wish what is best for us & I am sure God knows & will do what really is so, & will bring good out of the inconvenience occasioned by a want of proper cooking utensils, &c.

Thursday eve, Oct. 12

This day, which is just now departing, has been kept by the mission families as a fast, with particular reference to a violation of the Sabbath by native church members. One member at least, having engaged in playing ball after the morning service, & his father been an eye witness, not knowing, as he says, that playing was forbidden on the Sabbath, though he knew it was wrong to work. We hope it was ignorance alone, & that being enlightened by the truth, they will heartily repent & give their testimony & example to the sacredness of the Sabbath. All of the mission feel this trial & Dr. W., in some measure their spiritual father, feels it very deeply....

Sat. eve Oct. 21, 1837

Another week has fled my dear mother. With us, it has brought no change save that which departing time ever brings. We are one week nearer the eternal world, & have one week less to labor among these heathens. I sometimes feel that I am doing nothing & can do but little for their benefit. The various little domestic duties, which seem to claim attention, take up more time than I anticipated, or at least than I hoped would be the case. And when I think of the additional duties & cares which may be mine, I feel insufficient for these things. Perhaps like Martha, I am "cumbered" about by many things, if not "much serving," when I should cast all my cares on one able & willing to bear all our burdens. I hope I shall be enabled to judge correctly in reference to the importance of the claims upon my time, & cheerfully meet those that are most so, even though I must neglect many that seem pleasant & in some accounts desirable. Could I see & tell you what I wish, I know that a mother's kind counsel would afford me pleasure, but I cannot be sufficiently grateful for the kind friend God has given me in this land, even though my mother is not here. And I am persuaded that though distant, she still has the sympathies, the affections, of a mother. But there sometimes seems to be an obstacle in the way of enjoying that full degree of these, that I might, could I, face to face, talk over what I hesitate to write. Perhaps I am wrong in thus depriving myself of the precious privilege of opening my heart as fully & freely in reference to feelings & circumstances of which I have forborne to write, as I have been wont to do in days that are past. For this reason I often find the thought rising involuntarily "Oh, could I see mother." Still I trust I am willing to be separated from you all, if I can thus do most either directly or indirectly to advance the cause of Jesus. I say indirectly, because, when I feel as though the prospect of my being able to do much for these Indians is the darkest, it affords me pleasure to think that perhaps I may enable my dear husband to do more than he could do alone. This thought is very cheering, & should, I think, assist me to perform the many little duties that devolve upon a wife, with patience & delight.

Monday eve, Oct. 30

We are now enjoying the mild smoky weather of "Indian Summer." The prairie around is on fire, as we can distinctly perceive at night, though not sufficiently near for the blaze to be seen during the day. The hazy atmosphere & warm air, however, are as infallible proofs by day as the distant fires by night. I can imagine something of the awful grandeur of the scene upon the broad prairie when fire & smoke are commingled in various directions around. The Indians set fires for various reasons, such as rendering assistance in hunting, serving as a beacon to their friends or rendering the water less impure the ensuing summer, though often they may be unintentional, resulting from carelessness. They are frequently dangerous & render traveling unpleasant, if not unsafe, a little later in the season. If the fires are near or approaching the only safeguard is speedily building a fire & burning a space on which you can take refuge when flight would be in vain.

When I tell you that I have been occupied this afternoon somewhat similar (though on a far smaller & plainer scale) to those made previous to Lucretia's wedding, you will not be surprised to know that one of our missionary sisters, Miss Poage, is to be married on Wednesday, if nothing unforeseen prevents. Had you been present, the dissimilarity doubtless would have struck you more forcibly than the similarity, for all that could be seen would bear a strong contrast to the preparations then made. And in this case, I suppose the principal reasons for preparing for any guests were these or similar ones. It seems rather desirable that the Indians should witness a Christian marriage, that they should see that we regard & respect the ordinance, & at the same time perceive a difference between this & a meeting on the Sabbath, & feel that we intend to treat them in a friendly manner. How such wishes will best be accomplished I know not, but will give you a faithful account of the services &c when they are past.

Nov 2, Thurs.

Yesterday the marriage to which I referred was solemnized. Could I paint the assembly, you would agree with me that it was deeply & singularly interesting. Fancy for a moment the audience who were witnesses of the scene. The rest of our missionary band sat near those of our number who were about to enter into the new & sacred relationship, while most of the room was filled with our dark faced guests, wrapped in a blanket, or a buffalo robe, their chief "wedding garment," and coarse & tawdry beads, broaches, paint, & feathers, their wedding ornaments. Here & there sat a Frenchman, or half breed, whose garb bespoke their different origin. No turkey or eagle feather adorned their hair, or party colored paint their faces, though even their appearance & attire reminded us of our location in this wilderness. Mr. Riggs performed the marriage ceremony for the first time & Dr. W. made the concluding prayer, & through Mr. Renville's interpreting, explained the ordinance & its institution to the Dakotas.

After the ceremony Mr. Renville & family partook with us of our frugal morsel, leaving the Indians to enjoy their feast of potatoes, turnips, & bacon, to which the poor, the lame, & the blind had been invited. As they were not aware of the supper that was provided, they did not bring their dishes, as is the custom, so that they were scantily supplied with milk pans &c. This deficiency they supplied very readily by emptying the first course, which was potatoes, into their blankets, & passing their dishes for a supply of turnips & bacon.

I know not when I have seen a group so novel & interesting as I found on repairing to the room where these poor creatures were promiscuously seated. On my left sat an old man nearly blind; before me the woman who dipped out the potatoes from a five part boiler, sat on the floor, & near her was an old man dividing the bacon, clenching it firmly in his hand, & looking up occasionally to see how many there were requiring a share. In the corner sat a lame man eagerly devouring potatoes, & around were scattered women & children, the young men having left immediately after the exercises were closed, as the invitation to the supper was designed to be in accordance with scripture. After the last ladle was filled from the three-parted large pot of turnips, one after another hastily departed, borrowing dishes to carry home the supper to divide with the children that had been left at home in charge of the tent....

I received a letter from Miss Crosby a few days since, which affords me both pleasure & pain. Pleasure to learn that the young ladies in her school possess so much of a missionary spirit as the fact that they have made two bedquilts & one comfortable for this mission, & wish also to know how much would be required to support a scholar in our school, if we have one. You see we shall not lack bed clothes, as those are to be forwarded in a box the ladies in Hanover [Massachusetts] have been preparing through Miss Crosby's Christian mentality, I suppose. Accept love for yourselves, & all the dear ones at home, from your children.

Lac qui Parle Mission, Nov. 9, 1837
My dear brothers Thomas and Joseph,
    The letter, promised so long, shall at last be commenced for I never

feel more like writing than when a packet has just been dispatched thither. And by having an unfilled sheet on hand bearing the name of some loved distant one, I find time to add a few lines when I otherwise should not. And perhaps, if you would try this plan, you might find it equally efficacious, & I should more frequently receive a *tanka* (tawnkah) sheet, whose lines were neither few, nor far between. Will you not at least make the experiment & suffer no week to pass by without some record of what you have read or anything else that you may have accomplished? Then I shall know more about you, & shall think of you more frequently & more correctly. The evidence of your progress, the mark of increasing manliness, thus manifested, will help me to realize that Thomas & Joseph are not the "little boys" I left at home a few years since, but men. Men who will soon I hope be active & useful members of society! Whether in New England, or in some far distant & benighted corner of the earth.

Friday eve, Nov. 10

Has this day been remembered at home as the natal day of one too far distant to participate personally in the pleasures enjoyed in a father's house? I flatter myself that it has been thus remembered, & that neither Alfred or Mary Ann have been forgotten in the morning & evening devotions. Today I am *wikeemna nompa sampa topa weekehameany nomepah sahmpah to pah* that is, two ten & four more. The figures show the order of the Dakota as 2 1 4 3 ten, two, more four. I have just been looking at my last birthday present from mother. Such tokens of affection call up the forms of many far away, & revive the recollection of numberless favors received that cluster round their memories, & will, I trust stimulate me to greater activity, devotedness, & patience in the work before me. . . .

Last Sabbath was communion season when Mr. Riggs & myself, for the first time united with this little church in the wilderness in commemorating the Savior's dying love. About seven years before, I first sat down at the Lord's table with the church in Hawley. I was reminded of this during the interesting services of the day. Instead of a large band of brothers & sisters, a few were gathered together, & of this little number, seven were Dakota, or part Dakota. . . .

I make very slow progress in learning Dakota & could you hear the odd combinations of it with English, in which we allow ourselves, you would doubtless be somewhat amazed, if not puzzled to guess our meaning, though our speech would betray us, for the little Dakota we can use, we cannot speak like the Indians. The peculiar tone & ease are wanting, & several sounds I have been entirely unable to make, so that, in my case at least, these would be "Shibboleths" not a few. And these cause the Dakota pupils to laugh very frequently, while I am trying to explain, or lead them to understand, some of the most simple things about arithmetic. Perhaps you will think them impolite, & so should I, if they had been educated in a civilized land, but now I am willing to bear with them, if I can teach them anything during the hour that is allotted me for this purpose. As yet I have not devoted my time to any except those who are attempting to learn English, & my class will probably consist of five girls, & two or three boys. Two of the boys, whom we hope will learn English, are full Dakota, & if their hearts were renewed, might be very useful as preachers of the gospel to their own degraded heathen. Is this too much to hope, too much to pray for?

Friday, Nov. 24, 1837

One year since early this week I reached my Massachusetts home after an absence of a year & a half, & found all of our dear family in safety, sickness & death having made no ravages among our little band. Were I now there should I find it had still been thus? I have just returned from the schoolroom to our "little chamber in the wall," & you would not be surprised if I acknowledge that I sometimes fear my labor will be in vain, for I can seldom make myself understood. Still I feel that some have made considerable progress of which, I send you the transcript of a letter prepared by a Dakota man for a brother of Mr. Huggins in Ohio. The writer, *Wamadiokia* (Wah-mah-de-o-ke-a), received very little instruction besides learning the alphabet, & a few words, being obliged to hunt during the winter to furnish his family food, they having no corn. He, however, improved what opportunities he had, devouring the lessons that were prepared for the other Dakotas

& making himself master of them. Thus by his indefatigable & persevering industry, he is able to read & write, acquirements that would place him among the "self taught men" & link his name with a Flint, Franklin & Sherman were there such in the Dakota nation.

The translation of course has not all the simplicity & force of the original, though it will give you a pretty correct idea of it.

> The Dakota commenced learning to read, but now they some have left off. Tavaloe continue now a little, & they will perhaps continue to know. Those who have left their books do not now hear the word of the Great Spirit. They think his book is not sacred & not honorable & therefore do not want it.
>
> It is so with these, but as for me, I wish to know well the instruction of the sacred book. The medicine man, (Dr. Williamson) Mr. Huggins & the Grizzly bear (Mr. Pond) have taught me some things; therefore I hold them very strong in my mind. And I think if I know that any Dakota who is about to kill one of their cattle, spirit dogs (horses) hogs or tame deer (sheep) I should very much forbid it.
>
> We make a field, but the summer is so short we make but little corn. Huggins has taught me to plant, but I cannot farm yet, for I am a Dakota still & cannot work as white men do.
>
> If you write a book I shall see it.
>
> — *Wamadiokiya*

Friday eve, Nov. 31

The month now closing has been more serene & lovely than we had anticipated. The weather here is far less variable than in New England, & though it doubtless will be colder & more windy, I think we shall find our new home very comfortable, even though the falling snow melted by our warm fire, should occasionally greet us through our roof in rain, as it does tonight. It is the day after Thanksgiving eve at home,

& were you all gathered round the Thanksgiving table yesterday, save Stephen & Mary?

We had a frugal meal here in the wilderness & had perhaps great or greater cause for thankfulness as any of those who sat at richer feasts, for we partook of the fruit of this untamed soil prepared in a mill that has recently been created & scarcely in operation yet. Several times previously we had enjoyed a good dish of mush, or hominy, ground in our coffee mill, but if this mill succeeds, it will supply us with better bread & with far less labor than when prepared in a hand mill of any kind. The stones, ropes & plan for the mill were sent from Ohio when we came out, the mission families having hitherto been accommodated with the use of a hand mill of Mr. Renville's. And now my dear brothers, accept the best wishes of your distant brother & sister, a warmhearted good night in addition.

Lac qui Parle, Wednesday morn, Dec. 15
Dear Parents,

My first use of the pen after the peculiar manifestation of God's loving kindness we have so recently experienced, shall be for you my dear parents, you who know so well a parent's joy, a parent's solicitude, & a parent's responsibility.

That you will with us bless the Lord as did the psalmist in one of my favorite psalms, the 103rd, we do not doubt for I am sure you will regard my being able so soon to write as a proof of God's tender mercy. I have been very comfortable most of the time during the past week, though the last few days I have suffered with sore breasts in consequence of taking cold I suppose. One is now very much better, being affected only externally, the other is still much swollen & most painful especially when drawn. I hope however that Dr. W's kind care & the Dakota woman's skill in drawing the breast, will be instrumental in making them well & whole both internally & externally.

Ma'a I am sure will think the Dakota woman conferred a great favor & that they deserve much credit for the ability & willingness to perform so difficult a part of nursing. That it is quite universal with them will not seem singular, as they are kept at the breast usually until four years old & sometimes a year or two beyond.

As our little one cries and I am his chief nurse now, I must lay aside pen & paper to attend to his wants, for Mr. Riggs is absent procuring with Dr. W. & Mr. P. the translation of Mark from Mr. Renville. Again the nameless little one has fallen asleep & I may resume my pen. I said nameless, perhaps I should not have regarded him thus for Mr. P. gave him a Dakota name yesterday which he says is considered as very good among the Indians, viz Wamdiyapiduta, Scarlet eagle tail, so that now our family consists of Tamakoci (Tak-mah-ko-che) This country, Payuha (Pay-yoo-hah) Curley head & Wamadiyupidute (Wah-mah-da-yoo-pa-doo-tak) Scarlet eagle tail. I suppose you will be interested to know how we succeed without nurse or assistants in domestic affairs at such a time as this. And first I must tell you how admirable Mr. Riggs has succeeded in the domestic department & as an assistant or perhaps chief nurse even, during the night. For our babe has had no care at night beside what we were able to give it from the first. It will be a source of joy & gratitude to you, that you have as far as earthly protection is concerned confided one over whom you have watched often, & long to such a kind husband. And besides that we have such kind friends around us ready to render any needed assistance, friends that God has given us. Mrs. Williamson has daily & almost hourly during some days taken some care of me & the babe, & Dr. W. has been no less willing to perform the duties of a physician & older brother. Mrs. Huggins, & Mrs. Pond have also led us to feel that we all having one common interest, & being fellow laborers together, are a band of kindred.

Dec. 21

Last evening the long expected & despaired of messenger from Fort Snelling to Red River arrived & brought us a precious packet. We were just seated at the tea table when informed that there were letters for us below. Mr. Riggs brought them up & laid them upon the table. Our meal was suspended till each seal was broken & each signature scanned. Inclination would have led us to have substituted entirely the feast of affection for our supper, but the presence of Indians whom we were aware would not leave while the table was spread, led us to defer our letters until tea & worship were over, when we sat down & perused & reperused each message & reperused some of the most precious. That our hearts were full of gladness you will not doubt & though not entirely unmixed with sadness were our feelings of joy, it was still a happy evening, a precious feast.

Dec. 28

Yesterday our dear little babe was three weeks old. I washed with as little fatigue as I could expect, still I should have thought it right to have employed someone, was there any one to be employed who could be trusted. But the Dakota women beside not knowing how to wash, need constant & vigilant watching. Poor creatures, thieves from habit & from a kind of necessity, though one of their own creating. Nothing but the transforming influence of the gospel can fit them to live comfortably even while they sojourn & wander here. I think I mentioned some time since that several of the chief men of this tribe were on their way to the seat of government in order to negotiate in reference to a narrow section of land on the east of the Mississippi. They sold the land (as a matter of course provided the government had determined they should) for which they received ample compensation, but I fear their annuities will be a curse. The Indians here will be less affected than those on the Mississippi but very probably in a few years they may also dispose of their territory here, & fade away while following the setting sun, leaving their western as well as eastern border to the rapacity of Christian speculators.

Lac qui Parle, Dec. 30, 1837
Dear brother Alfred ,

A few fleeting moments this last Saturday eve of the expiring year shall be yours. Before this last hour I suppose you & the rest of our little band have thought of the distant ones, & remembered them before the merry seat, & now perhaps are sleeping quietly while guardian angels hover round. Sweet be thy slumber. May the God of Jacob guard you all & keep you beneath the shadow of his wing.

The last year has been a memorable one to us both. Surely then dear brother, we should look back upon it, that we may feel the goodness of our Heavenly Father who has gently led us through all its difficulties, & led us frequently to rejoice in peculiar manifestations of his unbounded love.

New Year's morn, 1838
    .... Next Sabbath is our communion season here, & I suppose it is also in H. Then two Indian women who were baptized yesterday will probably participate with us in the sacramental feast.... It will rejoice your heart that there are additions to the church here from this heathen people, who give as good evidence of a change of heart as would be expected. One of them has an uncommonly interesting & intelligent countenance & is one of the few who raise more corn than is sufficient for their own families, & consequently are expected according to Indian custom to support or partly support the many sick & lazy, who are indefatigable beggars and sometimes impudent also, particularly at this season when they are accustomed to receive many presents from traders & others during Christmas week. This custom I suppose may be traced to the influence of French Catholics who regard Christmas more sacredly than the Sabbath and by feasting the Indians on that day & New Years have led them also to regard them as the crowning days of the year. Then their bodies which they make their Gods, receive ample offering, and feasted to satiety they lie down as happy as such poor degraded creatures are capable of being.

With such ideas of the "chief good" & "the chief end of man" as they have universally, it is not strange that they should think that we who profess to love them very much, should give them food and clothes, & every thing they want. The Chief *Taktayme Mah* "Round Wind" who has been with us the last hour decked with feathers and scarlet for the traders' feast, asked why we did not give feasts & give the Indians plenty to eat, & when Mr. Riggs endeavored to tell him if we gave them paper, ink, and books, we could not give them food, he said if we would make much corn & potatoes for them, they would learn faster....

Last Saturday a son of Big Thunder a Dakota Chief "took a wife" by making her father a liberal present, which consisted of five guns, a cow, leggins, breech cloth, & blanket. The father, approving, accepted the present by firing the guns, & his daughter was a wife, or more correctly speaking, a servant, for they all think as one said in reply to Mr. Riggs' remark that girls were also good, in answer to congratulations in reference to our son, "women are good to wash & make corn." And he might have at least have added, to cut wood also for the poor women cut it all & this cold weather they might be seen with an axe & a load of wood larger than themselves fastened to their backs. Thus it will probably soon be with "Sparkling iron" the young bride. According to Indian custom *Eyongmahny*, the running walking man, must never speak the name of a *htoddootan*, & his son in law must never look one of his wives kindred in the face, at least his eye must never meet the glance of theirs. The first singular custom called *Tak-tay-mah-me* (Round wind) a chief here, to propose *Ze to-kah-dan-wash-ta* (Good bird) be substituted for another Dakota name Mr. Pond had given our little Alfred, because it was the name of his son-in-law which he would not speak.

We of course assented & he apparently quite proud of giving our little son a name. Probably a daughter would not have received this honor. . . .

Doubtless a kind Providence hedged up the way you thought open to the poor Indians. The more I thought of it, the more I rejoice that you are not laboring under government patronage, among any tribe that it has treated with & deceived. I should fear the curse of God would rest upon all efforts under the control & immediate influence of a government guilty of treacherous cruelty in reference to the aborigine of our land. . . .

Lac qui Parle Mission, Jan. 10, 1838
Dear sister Henrietta,

If the imperfect sketch before you gives you a more correct idea of our location, & thus affords you pleasure our design will be accomplished. Supposing it might aid your imagination, I have copied Mr. R's draught, about three or four miles of territory in length.

It of course is very far from being perfect, as you know, neither of us possess any knowledge of drawing, & but a slight one of this vicinity.

Lac qui Parle, only a small part of which is represented, is seven miles long, being an expansion of the St. Peters, which you will perceive, is a crooked stream. It is likewise shallow & narrow, & is navigable for only 120 miles except, by canoes, or at high water, although the river is 500 miles long. Notwithstanding its great length, the volume of water would not compare with the tributaries of the Connecticut or Hudson. One reason is, that little rain falls here, & consequently there are but few & small branches; another, its meanderings give it greater apparent length in proportion to the territory it drains, than in less winding streams.

If you do not understand all the words in our letters, or anything you read, do not fail to use "Uncle Noah's patent plough" or some other, until you have found the meaning. And if my spelling varies from your idea of correctness, try it by the same test, & let not any failure pass unnoticed, & if I can find no good authority, I will try "reform." In reference to musquito however, I will say, although Webster does not sustain me in that orthography, which is Italian, good writers do. I am very glad you noticed it, as it manifests a desire to spell correctly, & aid others in doing so also.

Jan. 1, 1838

This is *Ano patoo Wah-kahn* or "Spirit day" with the Indians here, not because they assemble together to pray as in Christendom for the conversion of the world, but because they are feasting their poor bodies at the fur trader's as is the custom here at New Year. And as they care more for their bodies than their spirits, it is not strange that they should so regard a day in which they are fully satisfied with eating which is infrequently the case with most of them. Neither is it strange with such ideas that they should wish us to feed their bodies rather than their minds. . . .

Monday, Jan. 15

Having learned this morning that an opportunity of sending to the Fort may soon be afforded, we obey the impulse of one heart in preparing letters for friends far away. Yesterday our little Alfred was dedicated to God in baptism. I hope we both renewably gave him to the Lord, feeling that as our first born son he was peculiarly His & only lent to us to train for usefulness here & happiness hereafter, if our prayers are answered in his early sanctification. Sister H's letter shall be forwarded the earliest opportunity after I have had time to complete another folio. Till then a "cheek chestnut" were very small indeed, a lock of her little blue eyed nephew's hair must suffice. And the reason it is so very small is, that he has but very little, though he is a plump healthy child weigh-ing nearly 10 pounds, & almost six weeks old. Henrietta would have been much interested in a scene from my window a few days since, & perhaps she can imagine two Dakota men & three or four women with their children returning from their hunt, having been absent some weeks. First came an Indian woman loaded with skins, whose greater speed or lighter pack enabled her to take the lead, & following her was another whose back was doubly laden with skins, & her babe mounted on the top & just peeping from its high nest over its mother's head. Then came the half clothed little children, & one little girl not as large as cousin Eliza brought a pack as large as herself.

The men were not far behind & one would have supposed they might have been first, for one had no load & the other but a small one, the women being their slaves "the bearers of burden, the hewers of wood & drawers of water." With the children came the little dog skipping along with his load fastened to his back like the rest & at the rear was a heavy laden tired woman who seemed unable to keep pace with the others of the company.

We find the winter quite comfortable & the air very bracing, the thermometer stand at the lowest at 23 degrees below zero. Thus far we have found the climate very healthful. I have had no coughs, no cold since our arrival & enjoy pretty comfortable health, though I probably feel less vigorous than I should have done had I not attempted doing rather too much too soon after the birth of our little son & perhaps less strong than I should do if my breasts were not still sore & one of them quite a tax upon my patience & power of endurance. If mother has any wisdom gained by experience that might be beneficial in healing wide spread & long "cranny's" I suppose she will truly impart it.

March 22, Thurs. eve

This is the evening of our mission prayer meeting, & we have just returned to our chamber, our happy home. Before leaving it two Indian women came & sat a little while, as is very common. One of them had a babe about the age of Alfred with her. You would have smiled to see the plump, undressed child peeping out from its warm blanket, like a little unplumed bird from its mossy nest. Last Monday the father & mother of this little one came together & passed most of the evening with us, talking & singing Dakota hymns. This was the first time we had received such a call, as it is very uncommon for a Dakota man to accompany his wife, or both to remain, if they happen to meet at our house. A few Sabbaths since a woman, now a member of the church, stopped after meeting, & soon her husband apparently not aware of her remaining, also came in. He sat a short time, & they exchanged a few words, then he rose saying, "Now I will go home, my wife will stay."

Mon., March 25

.... Alfred grows finely & can almost sit alone. He is very good natured & lies or sits on the bed the greater part of the day. He would like it very much if aunt Henrietta were here to talk to him.

February 16, 1838 [Stephen's tribute]

I copy my morning's gift — affection's Offering
 A year ago this was your bridal day.
 It seems but yesterday since we were there
 Upon your native mountains dear
 Where lives the snow, as here all winter long.
 Your parents, brothers, sisters all were there.
 There sat the aged sire whose hoary locks
 Proclaimed almost a hundred winters gone.
 But now those scenes are numbered with the past,
 Now you are far, far, far away from home
 A wife and mother in a heathen land.
 The poor, the maimed, the halt, the blind around.
 Yes here are poverty's most beggared sons,

Who for the bread of life are perishing
God keep you here and bless our little one
And keep us all and bless our dearest friends
And give us all a crown of life in Heaven
And make us shine as stars forever there.

Feb. 28, 1838

The thanks of Mary for affections' gift

A precious tribute, fraught with tenderness.
Accept, my dearest, simple heartfelt thanks,
For one so wholly thine can give no more.
Our marriage day I too remember well.
And all its scenes, its scenes of interest deep—
Our friends and kindred dear-the ancient church—
The messenger of God-the silent throng—
And music sweet, are fresh in memory still.
Again that day has dawned on us, so bright
And beautiful.
Let us give thanks to God.
For all the blessings strewed along our path
Since it was one, and I was what I am yr. wife.

Lac qui Parle Mission, Apr. 5, 1838
My dear Mother, & Father,

. . . . Yesterday afternoon Mrs. Pond & myself walked to the "lodges."
As the St. Peters now covers a large part of the bottom land, we wound
our way in the narrow Indian path along the side hill. An Indian woman,
with her babe fastened upon its board at her back, walked before us, &,
as the grass on each side of the footpath made it uncomfortable walking
side by side, we conformed to Dakota custom, one falling in the rear.
For a few moments we kept pace with our guide, but she, soon outstrip-
ping us, turned a corner, & was out of sight. As we wished for a view of
the lake & river, we climbed the hill that skirts the river & spreads itself
out into a vast prairie. There we saw the St. Peters, which in the
summer is a narrow & shallow stream, extended over miles of land, with

here & there a higher spot peeping out as an island in the midst of the sea. The haze prevented our having a good view of the lake, though the wide sheet of water we could see resembled somewhat the view on the Sound, some part of the distance between New York & New Haven.

The Indian lodges, pitched at the foot of the hill, & their summer bark houses at a short distance, surrounded by water, would look still more strange & wild when contrasted with the churches & dwellings of Connecticut & New York. After counting 30 lodges stretched along below us, we descended, & entered one where we found a sick woman, who said she had not sat up for a long time, lying on a little bundle of straw.

Another lodge we found full of corn, the owners having subsisted on deer & other game while absent during the winter. Most of it was [put up in skin sacks, & thus buried in the ground,] but some had been deposited on the cob, a part of which she had been beating off. The corn will probably not last long, as the Indians who wintered here are nearly destitute, & here one must be willing to divide, & subdivide, until the last morsel is gone, if she would not be called "mean & stingy." After calling at Mr. Renville's, which was a little beyond, we returned through the heart of the village, attended by such a retinue as I have never before seen, & such strange intermingling of laughing & shouting of children & barking of dogs as I never heard. Amused, & almost deafened by the clamor, I turned to gaze upon the unique group. Some of the older girls were close upon our heels, but, as we stopped, they also halted, & those behind slackened their pace. Some were boys & some girls of from four to twelve years, some wrapped in their blankets, more without. Quite a number of the boys were almost, or entirely destitute of clothing, and a large number of dogs of varying sizes & colors, presented themselves in an irregular line. As all of the Indians now here have pitched their lodges together, I suppose there might have been 30 or 40 children in our train, & some followed us for a considerable distance homeward. When we reached home, I found little Alfred happy & quiet in the same place on the bed I had left him more than two hours previous, his father having been busy studying Dakota.

Sat. April 15

Today has been one of weeping & wailing among the poor Dakotas here. This morning Mr. Pond, who has been absent nearly two weeks with some Indians on their spring hunt, returned unexpectedly, bringing the sad tidings of the massacre of D, with whom he had been a part of the time of absence, by the Chippewa. Providentially the Indian with whom he lodged, had removed the morning previous to the slaughter, & encamped about six miles distant. Three lodges remained, in which were two men, their wives & children, & the family of another, who also left in the morning to take charge of his traps at some distance from the tents. In the afternoon 11 Chippewa men came, apparently in a friendly manner, to these defenseless abodes. As they had often met while hunting peaceably in the same vicinity during the winter, no suspicions were entertained, but, as a mark of hospitality, two dogs were killed & eaten. After the feast they all lay down as if to sleep. Alas, to most of the Dakotas it was the sleep of death. At midnight the Chippewa rose & killed all except four, two of whom escaped severely wounded, & one unhurt. Another, the younger wife of the trapper who was absent, is missing & probably is reserved for a fate most ignominious—worse than death. When they had finished their awful work, breaking the guns of the murdered & taking their furs, scalps & one head, they departed. In the morning, the woman who escaped though wounded, returned to her desolate home, the abode of the dead. After covering the bodies of the slain with their blankets, & placing her scalpless little ones & the wounded boy on two poles, she fastened them to a horse & thus proceeded to the nearest encampment.

On her way she met a Dakota who returned with her to the lodge, & then in company with Mr. Pond, repaired to the field of slaughter. They found most of the bodies lying as if massacred when quietly asleep, though some of the children had evidently been killed in attempting to escape. After digging a hole in the ground, they hastily buried men women & children in one common grave. Mr. Pond left the Indians soon after returning from this melancholy task, & reached home before noon, having traveled about 40 miles since yesterday noon. Several Dakota men left immediately on hearing the sad message he brought, to meet their friends & aid them in returning, & I fear they will seek an opportunity of revenge. I suppose scarcely a Dakota can be found who has lost no friend or relative by the hand of a Chippewa, & often in answer to the question "Who is your father," the reply is, "He is dead, the Chippewas killed him."

April 30, Monday afternoon
The Dakotas referred to above, returned the week after this awful massacre, in a peaceable manner, though one intended to kill a Chippewa & his wife, but was unable to find them as he expected. I know not that the Dakotas are at war with the Pawnees now, though they are enemies, I believe. We are too far distant to hear of such affairs by report, & our earliest accounts are by Boston or Cincinnati, through the Herald & papers—the B. Recorder or Cin. Journal. Neither are they at open war with the Dakotas, Sauks, & Foxes or the Chippewas—but they regard each other as avowed enemies, & feel little security, if they suspect themselves exposed. Their vigilance does not equal what I had expected from my ideas of Indian cunning—at least in the case I have mentioned, as it is supposed by the survivors that most, if not all who were killed, went to sleep without suspecting any danger. Perhaps you will feel some fears for our safety—but they will be quelled, when you remember our lives are in the hand of the same Parental Protector, that keeps our friends in happy & peaceful New England. And I know not but we are as safe here as in a civilized land, where a man's life is jeopardized by speaking what he deems truth when it comes in collision with popular feeling. I hope the peacemaking influences of the Holy Spirit will restore order & harmony where confusion has reigned, & put to flight all bitterness & clamor, & evil-speaking.

May 2, Wed. eve
I cannot at this late hour answer definitely your inquiries in reference to our winter weather, as we made no note of observations at the time, & I cannot trust memory in particulars. The fall was pleasantly & mild—snow fell in December & remained till about the middle of March. During some parts of January & February the thermometer fell 32 deg.

below zero, still we were very comfortable in our little room, which we fitted up as well as we could by nailing cloth at the sides & spreading a tent over the loose boards above.

Pa'a remarked that grandpa'a wished to know how we live & what we live on. To answer it laconically, we live happily upon the bounty of our Heavenly Father. But to be more definite, I will give a specimen. If we do not rise with the birds, we do soon after them. After the room is put in order for breakfast, &c, the table spread with a brown cloth &c, we thankfully, I hope, partake of our frugal meal, which usually consists of some kind of salt, potatoes & weak coffee. During the winter corn bread has been our chief food of the bread kind, as all the flour is obtained from the states at great expense of time & money. At noon, milk & mush, or bread, is our common dish, & bread & butter & a glass of milk, our supper. As it regards dress, it is much as when at home in Hawley though we have little need for change, except for washing, as a plain, clean calico, or gingham for the Sabbath, answers for the week. Thus you will see we live very comfortably, though we do not have all the good & super comfortable things we might enjoy in the States, we have enough & perhaps more than enough. As for apples, though I used to love them so well, I can do as well without them as with, though I sometimes resort to our little stock of dried fruit as a substitute. Perhaps I may soon conquer this childlike propensity.

You mention the benevolence of our friends who have surprised us by fitting out so valuable a box, for which you will "greet" & thank "them all by name." It is very cheering, in this far off land, to feel that we are thus remembered. It melts our hearts in gratitude. I am sure a mother would rejoice with us, could she read the letters we receive from our friends in New England, Ohio, Indiana, & Illinois, inquiring what they can do to aid us, & how they can be co-workers with us in this heathen land. We need to make the most of every moment, in order to accomplish that which we can do without much knowledge of the language, & much more that we may make such progress in it as to labor successfully in future, if our lives are spared.

Mr. Riggs, I believe, has accomplished considerable towards a good beginning, but I cannot write so favorably of myself. Perhaps it is my own fault, though I do not feel that it is, entirely, for you know it is a "woman's lot" & especially that of a wife & mother, to take charge of domestic affairs—to do a thousand little things that require time & patience. I am as yet, unwilling, nor do I think it would be right, to relinquish reading, & writing entirely, though I do very little of the former.

As for studying Dakota, I find it a very different thing, with the present calls upon my attention, to fix it upon this unwritten Indian language, from what it was to prepare a lesson in history or mathematics. I fear it will be a long time before I shall be able to talk much Dakota—to tell them about Jesus Christ.

I am glad that you are pleased with "Phillip's writings." We have some of them, but none you named. And I am still more glad that the ladies in Hawley were disposed by furnishing a room in the Mt. Holyoke Female Seminary, to aid in preparing females for usefulness. For ought I can see, it is as deserving of patronage as Amherst was at its commencement, & probably even more needed, that is, if it is admitted, as I think it will be in Christian New England, that Seminaries for females should at least bear some proportion & comparison with those for males. But it has not been & is by no means thus at present. . . .

As I think Henrietta may feel interested in the names of our Dakota girls who are learning to read, sew, & most of them, to knit, I shall give some of them in Sioux & English. You will recollect a is always sounded ah, e like a in name, i like e in mete. H is used to denote the sound of sh as in Haice—as Shaise. Ç is always used for ch, as in the same example Ha-i-ce, pronounced Shah-ee-cha. Win, which you will perceive terminates most of the names, signifies female or woman, as many of the names are used indiscriminate of sex, without this termination. Ta-no-ge, Her, hers. Win-no-na, The first born when a daughter. Wa-kan-hndi-maza-win, Iron spirit that comes or lightening woman. Tan-hin-ya-ya-win, Her passing by woman. Stato-win, the woman on this side. An-pe-tu-o-tan-in-win, Day made manifest. Gi-a-kan-i-yo-tan-ka-win, the woman that sits on the house. Hax-ka-win, Binding woman. Ha-pan, the second child, if a daughter. O-ye-sna-sna-win, The ringing woman. Ma-za-to-win, Blue iron woman. These will serve as a specimen, & Henrietta must endeavor to think of them clad in their short gowns & petticoats, seated around, engaged in their work, some on the benches & some on the floor, for they often exchange the former for the latter when they grow tired. Some have tolerable clean hands & faces, & all have bright eyes & pearl white teeth, & generally look quite good natured & happy.

May 10

An Indian has just been here begging for pork & stockings. The moc-casins he wore were ornamented with small pieces of lead dangling around the ankle at every step. They are very fond of such trappings, & often wear half a dozen or more thimbles, or little bells, attached to their knee bands, & head dresses, "making a tinkling as they go." You would smile at their gaudy ornaments, could you see them dressed with blan-ket, curiously, though coarsely, painted, bracelets & armbands of brass, holes in their ears, & sometimes noses, through which bits of lead have been thrust & fastened. Add to these, paint, feathers & beads in abun-dance for the head & face, & I think you can conjecture the visage & garb of these sons of the prairie.

I believe I have mentioned in some of my letters the dreadful ravages of the small pox on our western & north western borders. The Mandans, we hear, are extinct, & the Tee-tones, the largest band of Sioux, report says, have also fallen victims to this desolating scourge. Thousands have died from this malady during the past winter. Several of them caught the disease by going on board a steam boat on the Missouri to obtain "whiskey," & 11 of the 14 who went on board, died. From these it spread far & wide, often making whole lodges its prey.

The Indians here have not been smitten, though one from Lake Traverse, who had it, was here a short time, but was soon put away. So destructive have been the effects of seeking "the whiskey," that the Da-kotas here call it the "contagious poison," & they say, when an Indian gives a man poison, it kills him only, but the white man's poison kills the man to whom it is given & his family & neighbors. And it is in part true, though not often is the work of death accomplished so speedily as in the case of the small pox. . . .

May 25

Mr. Riggs expects to leave on Tuesday next for Fort Snelling, & will probably be absent for several weeks. A trifling incident occurred this afternoon that will show how little we can depend upon honesty here. As the day has been warm I baked in a Dutch oven, or bake kettle, in the school room below. When it was nearly baked I heard a little noise below about the fire, & soon the door opened & shut cautiously. It diverted my thoughts a moment, still I continued writing, but on going for our supper, part of the loaf was missing, someone having cut out a piece very cunningly. As we had enough left for our meal, we could not complain, but congratulated ourselves upon the benevolence of the thief who was, doubtless, more hungry than we were.

Fri. morn, July 12

For a few days past we have had uncommonly fine cool weather, the thermometer stands at 51 above 0 after sunrise, & indeed, very few days this far have been as warm as last summer. Still our crops are very fine in prospect — & our peas from the 4th, inst. have afforded us quite a supply. If grandpa'a should be inclined to send a little token, a thimble marked MR (if a silver top no. 7 is right which I should prefer) if not no. 8 or a small cotton or silk shawl, or large neck handkerchief suitable to wear to the school room on cold mornings. I have seen quite decent ones of twilled cotton, or a few horn "twisting" combs, or a pair of shell side combs, or any such little articles would be acceptable — but I need not name more. If a box should be forwarded, send the remnants of your old cloak. It would make fine pantalets, & it is with articles of clothing that we pay for washing & other labor. Brown, black & indeed any kind of flannel is of use, if it is large enough to make a short gown, skirt or pantalets for a woman or even a girl. Of socks, also we have yet received a very poor supply, & unless we should receive more, we may need both to spin & knit before the cold of January. But I doubt now we shall be provided with all that is necessary for our welfare. We have not received any supplies from Boston, & if it had not been for Mrs. Burgess' kindness, I should have been almost without frocks, & as for shoes, I have but one old pair of boots & a thick pair of shoes, both of which I brought from Mass. that are comfortable to wear. But I can substitute moccasins, though they are not good in wet weather. It is possible we may receive our boxes from Boston, which have been unaccountably delayed, though it is not very probable, as boats are not expected up the St. Peters again this season.

Lac qui Parle Mission, Wed., May 10, 1838
Dear brother Alfred,

It is a lovely day, though not as warm as several days in March. The grass is beginning to look green & the trees are budding, but in this high latitude summer's adorning steps are slow, & its tarrying brief.

I have been unable to learn the origin of "echoing lake" or "talking lake," as it was given long ago, but the name perhaps will be sufficient to evoke the muse. Probably an echo might have been heard in the vicinity, & echoes are very uncommon in this open prairie land. They have not the hills & dells the rocks & woods in which echoes can play as in New England, & on this account the speaking of an echo might have been regarded as a voice from "the spirit land." Gladly would I welcome my brother to this native land. The providence of God toward this people is mysterious to mortal ken. Hundreds & thousands have died this past winter, unless the reports that have reached us have been greatly exaggerated. You recollect, perhaps, that we thought it probable we might eventually go to the Missouri but a report says the Tee-tones who were the most numerous band of Dakotas, & lived upon that river, are swept off by small pox. Mr. Riggs & Mr. Pond think of exploring some part of the Sioux territory next fall to ascertain the openings for missionary labor west of us, the number & location of the western bands, &c. That tour, if accomplished, may throw some light on our future location, & perhaps, yours too. I do not fear that you will be unable to brave these keen, but bracing blasts. Mr. Riggs has found the cold biting his ear & face, & then it was not a very unfriendly grip, at least it was soon forgotten.

May 14

Your friendly caution about dress & furniture, led me to suppose you will be willing to conform to our plain customs & frugal fare, will be willing to walk over prairie & through marsh & to sleep on the ground in order to reach us, & perform any missionary labors after your arrival. You will not forget however that teaching some 10 or 12 young men to read & write during a part of the day in winter is not like instructing a class of regular attentive & intelligent students in some high school in New England. And preparing fuel is not simply sawing it in a snug wood house but even if others bring the logs to the door it requires a considerable time & struggle to supply the stove when the thermometer is from 26 to 32 below zero & the wind blowing fiercely.

Mideiyedan, June 27, 1838

My dear Parents,

Thanks to our Heavenly Father our hopes & prayers in reference to "the war" party are realized. After a long tour of 27 days, & a fruitless search for their enemies, they have returned with a supply of venison and geese, sufficient for one or two feasts I suppose, but without a single scalp. The war party I alluded to is the one mentioned in our last letter which seemed thirsty for the blood of their fellow men, & determined to shed it in defiance of all remonstrances of man, or command of God. But this being, whom they call the Great Spirit, has I trust, showed them the vanity of their boastings, even if they are not willing to acknowledge his restraining & controlling hand. I hope this unsuccessful adventure may exert a happy influence on all. . . .

Some fine bunches of strawberries brought by an Indian woman, the first I have tasted at Lac qui Parle, reminded me very forcibly, of those days when I used to search for them on the knolls & dells which abound on the paternal farm. Another circumstance also, no less, spoke of the hills & valleys of New England & its busy industry taking from a rude press, a small cheese, my first attempt. Several of the members of our mission family have been very desirous of this luxury, & though none of them had been as much accustomed to it as myself, excepting Mr. Pond, who has left, I should not on my own account, merely have been willing to take the time & trouble. But I think I have succeeded tolerably, though it is several years since I have seen the process of cheese making, & even, if I had not, I congratulate myself upon the absence of judges of good cheese, for they make very little in the western states. . . .

Lake of Echoes, July 19, 1838
My dear sister Henrietta,

Never should I have been more glad of your society than during the last six weeks. Although I joined Dr. Williamson's family soon after Mr. Riggs left home, yet I have felt solitary, & particularly when alone in our little room, I have sat by Alfred when asleep, and when awake, he seems to miss the children to whom he has become accustomed of late. When we sit awhile in our little chamber, I think he would be very glad if Aunt H. were here to play with him. He is now a little more than 7 months, has two teeth, stands by the side of the house, & creeps about sufficiently fast to soil his clothes in a short time. Thus you will see his mother thinks him as promising as other mothers do their babes. Do you still keep rabbits & bantam fowls, or have you grown so old that you have no time to feed & take care of them? Little A would like your rabbits very much, though I fear he would frighten & hurt them too, for he pulls the cat most unmercifully. Two Dakota women have brought me some green gooseberries, which are the only fruit we have in abundance. They told me yesterday they would bring some strawberries, but they were unable to find any.

Sat. evening

I have lit a candle this evening, which I do not usually do these short evenings, as the mesquitoes are so troublesome, that I may finish this now, as I may not have another opportunity for several weeks. I thank you very much for your note & little presents. The apron & bonnet fit A very finely. You will believe I have had a busy Sat.

Mr. R. came last evening & besides some boxes which I wished to examine, we had about 30 letters & notes to read. We could not read them very attentively, but shall look them over again, & they will afford us renewed pleasure. . . .

The box which our dear friends so kindly filled out & forwarded, we opened yesterday. It was pleasant to receive this new proof of interest in our labors, to think it came from Hawley, from home. Nothing was injured. May God bless all the donors & make us feel more humble & more thankful as we receive such tokens of his loving kindness. Thank all those who wrote us letters. Last evening & today we have had a continual feast.

Lake of Echoes, July 23, 1838
My dear brother Thomas,

If you had been here when the large packet of letters was opened, you would have seen seal after seal broken & each signature eagerly sought, until I had literally a lap full of letters. Little Alfred too, as if conscious they were from a far country, sat ready at my side to catch any that might fall, & pay it the highest compliment in his power by putting it to his mouth. Fortunately none were devoured, notwithstanding he is so much of a "book worm," though several were in jeopardy while I was rapidly glancing at their contents. . . .

Fri. eve

I have so little time to write & so much writing to do, that I feel I ought to write something that would be interesting & useful, or my minutes would be misimproved & yours also. But for the want of anything more interesting at hand, I will give you a little incident that occurred yesterday.

In the afternoon Round Wind, a chief, sat with us an hour or two smoking or talking & fanning himself with an eagle wing. On my inquiring if many of the Dakota had them, he said, "A few," & asked if I wished for one. On telling I did, he immediately gave me his fan, notwithstanding I objected, fearing he had no other. In return I gave him one of some red cotton handkerchiefs brother J. Riggs had sent us to give to the Indians. He immediately folded & tied it round his head "a la Turk."

This shows how freely they give, & usually they beg equally freely. Although there are many Indian men who think they cannot dig, there are very few who would be ashamed to beg. When they, having nothing, are so liberal, they think it strange that we who have, in their estimation, so many things, should withhold anything which they ask us for. And when we say the Bible says we should love our neighbors as ourselves, they ask why then do we not divide what we have with them, "that would be loving them as well as ourselves." We of course do not think it our duty to meet all their demands for several reasons—it would make them the more indolent, & we should probably starve & freeze if we should reduce our comforts to their standards. Perhaps it ought to be nearer theirs, though I do not know that it should. Sometimes I think if we were more like them we should be able to do them more good.

It is almost too dark to see without a candle & we seldom light one as the nights are very short at this season in this high latitude, & what is still a more weighty reason, it draws such a multitude of musquitoes through the numerous crannies in the walls, that it renders it uncomfortable at the time & afterward. Thus far this summer we have not been as much annoyed as we were last, as we have a bar at our window, but the poor Dakota as have no remedy but smoke. This our cattle have also, as regularly as the night comes, for it would be almost impossible to milk without one.

Mideiye dans, July 28, 1838
My dear Henrietta,

.... I thank you very much for the articles you put in my trunk when we left home, & for those two you sent last winter. The little bonnet fits Alfred exactly, but it is so pretty he will not often wear it. . . . You must have taken considerable pains to dry the fruit you sent me. Did you dry the cherries on the rotary? I think it would be a good place for drying small fruit. Mrs. L. of Ind. dried peaches upon tin sheets laid upon bricks & covered them with the reflector. We have had quite a plenty of green gooseberries for several weeks, but no strawberries. A poor Dakota woman brought us some one Sabbath, which she found at a considerable distance from this place when she was out hunting tepsin, but we did not take them as it was on the Sabbath. We told her this, but she seemed unable to understand such a reason & continued saying, "You do not love them, you will not eat them." Though I have inquired several times for strawberries since, no one has brought any, all saying they grow a great distance off.

You will be sorry to learn very few Indian children come to school now. The girls who are old enough have to dig roots & pick berries, & frequently whole families go several miles distance where tepsin is found more abundantly. When the corn is ready to eat I hope more will come, & next winter I think we shall again have a full school. I think you would like to see the nice little cradle quilt sister E. Riggs sent me. All our friends are very kind. Be a good girl & write again to your own affectionate brother & sister.

Lac qui Parle Mission, Aug 23, 1838
My dear Mother,

A few moments ago I was sitting, solitarily engaged at my work, it occurred to me that I had not written to my mother for a long time. . . . The stirring thoughts of home & my obligations to my parents induced me to drop the needle for the pen, thinking when shall I have a better time for writing as no one is with me save little Alfred who is fast asleep. But before I had folded my sheet & minded my pen, our little "jewel," if I may be allowed the expression of the Roman mother, had finished his nap, & his mother must lay aside her embryo letter to his distant grandmother, of whom he knows nothing, till a "more convenient season."

Fri. morn

Again a few moments of quiet are mine & I may perhaps enjoy the privilege of answering your inquiries without much interruption. As for a description of the lodges & furniture — of the former you have probably received our rude sketch, & the latter can be briefly given. A kettle or two, a few wooden bowls & spoons, & pieces of skin, is all, & more, than many have, aside from their blankets. The wives of those men who have two or three, & most of the principal men here have at least two, do not live free from jealousy, though perhaps they dwell together as happily as could be expected. One Indian, who has been a frequent visitor, used often to say his wives were envious & sometimes beg something for his younger wife to quiet her jealousy excited by a present made to the elder. The Dakota men say sisters usually make the best wives, & several of them, & most, I believe, take sisters if possible. They frequently "make their corn" in the same field, but others usually have separate fields, & keep their things entirely separate, at least during the winter as each woman has her own skin or bark lodge, takes care of her own children, provides her own fuel &c. Those who can, frequently keep an old woman, perhaps their mother to assist them. If an old woman is able to work at all, it is apparently little matter how hard she works—how large a burden she carries. The wife first taken has usually the supremacy, I think, has the skin lodge, if they own but one, & is probably most be-loved, though with their ideas of the rights & privileges of women, I should suppose, & the affection felt, would be that of a mother to a faithful servant. If she fails to please him—or even lets fall his box of ornaments, he may beat her until his revengeful domineering spirit is appeased.

You inquire how many Frenchmen & Indians there are here. Of the former there are only those in Mr. Renville's employ & one or two oth-ers. The number of Indians is supposed to be about 400, & not far from one fourth of them are men. As it regards the number of the tribe, they have probably been over estimated, though they may perhaps equal 20 or 25,000. They are divided into seven principal bands, or council fires, & these are subdivided, with chiefs over the various subdivisions.

I will give these seven divisions according to our orthography in English: *Medwakanton* (Me-day-wah-kahn-tone-wan), those of the spirit lake; *Warpetonwan* (Wah-pay-tone-wan), Leaf Indians; *Warpekutamnon* (Wah-pay-ku-toy-wan), the Indians that shoot leaves; *Sisitonwan* (See-see-tone-wan,) *Thanktonwan* (T-hank-tone-wan), *Titonwan* (Tee-tone-wan), Ihanktonwan, or Yankton.

Sat. eve, Sept. 8

Another week has almost fled & now I can only rescue a few of the fast fleeting moments for writing to my dear mother, of whom I have been reminded today by an Indian pipe. You may think the association a singular one but it was no less forcible than singular. *Wah-kah-u-cho yu* Crying Spirit, an elderly Indian, was in a while this afternoon & smoked, of course, with all due gravity. The smallness of his pipe attracted my attention. I mentioned it and inquired if he had another. He replied he has a larger one also, & added, "Will you take this?" I was very glad to procure a pipe for mother, though I hope she does not use one much. It being unusually small is almost its only recommendation, & the stem is by no means such an one as I should prefer. Crying Spirit, after scraping the smoke off a little & polishing it with a little tallow from a candle, said he would smoke in it once more, & then it should be mine.

In addition to what I gave him in return, he begged a little "grease" for the hair assigning as a reason that his "women needed it," especially as they danced very much. And, why my dear mother do you suppose they dance more than usual at the present time? You could hardly con-jecture a reason that would reveal to you the heart of women in such a soul sickening light as the true one. You recollect, probably, the slaugh-ter of 11 Dakotas by the Chippawas last winter. The woman that was missing has been returned, but the United States government has done nothing to bring the murderers to justice.

Consequently some of those, whose friends were killed, were determined to have vengeance. A war party from this village left some time since, in pursuit of the enemy, & a few days ago returned with one scalp—that of a poor defenseless woman. They surprised a few Chippawas who fled. All escaped excepting one woman in such circum-stances that she could not keep pace with her companions. Later, cross-ing a small stream, she was overtaken by her pursuers, & her unborn babe ushered into the world by a murderous hand, that he might see it dashed in pieces & he might revenge the death of his children. It is the scalp of this poor woman that is brought home as a glorious trophy. It is this scalp around which the Dakota women may even now be dancing—shaking their rattles, drumming, & singing their fiend-like music. This is the only dance in which women engage, & I am told, it is frequently commenced by some old woman, who carries out the scalp & shakes it upon a pole.

Oct. 4, Thurs. eve
Writing this date reminds me that it is Lucretia's birthday. She is 27 years old & I am almost 25. How fast our days are flying & we as rapidly growing old. If I recollect brother A's question in reference to the hoes used by the Indian women has never been answered. I believe I stated

the truth, though it might have produced an incorrect impression. Mr. Riggs says they excavate a hiding place or more correctly speaking throw up an entrenchment around, to screen them from an enemy. The idea however which I received was that it was intended more as a cover for women & children from an expected foe, than aid in defense provided they were attacked. Indians seldom make an open attack or defense, but more frequently in the latter case "run away & live to fight another day."

We have had an addition to our mission family in the birth of Mrs. Pond's little daughter. Of course I have been very busy as I have taught all that we have both usually taught, & at this season, there are many more scholars than in the summer. One day 30 came, most of whom read & write, though they usually remained only a short time, & I am always glad to have them go as soon as they have finished their lesson for I cannot make them sit still or refrain from talking. If I could talk, I think I could teach them silence & order, but I am as a little child that can lisp a few words, & those, often, incorrectly.

Thurs. eve

As we must be closing our letters, I can only add that Mr. Riggs made his first attempt at public instruction in Dakota on the Sabbath before last. We had an attentive, though not large, assembly, as most of the men, who usually attend, have been absent some weeks. You will be rejoiced to learn that I have succeeded in obtaining assistance from a Dakota woman in washing. My health is now pretty good. I found my-self unable to wash & teach as much as was necessary, & though the others thought it almost in vain to try such poor help, I was unwilling Mr. R. should assist me, especially as a little of mother's pride, if I may so speak, flows in my veins, when none of the other sisters would think of having such assistance from their husbands. Fortunately I was very suc-cessful & very glad of the assistance. Thus we shall also benefit a poor woman who has 2 or 3 children & her husband, I suppose, has thrown her away. At least she has no husband now & is obliged to furnish food & clothing for herself & family, or be destitute. Since I have had her assistance my health has much improved.

Mide-i-ye-dan, Oct. 23, 1838

My dear Brothers,

Sisterly affection prompts me to write though I am by no means in-debted for letters. Your latest date to a letter commenced March 27, 1838, is a postscript of June 1837. This is the only communication received from brothers A & M written the present year. . . .

. . . . In reference to ourselves a kind Providence still bestows on us health & contentment. We try to make some progress in Sioux, although mine is very slow. Husband preached in Dakota for the first time Sabbath before last, & if Dr. W. had remained they were alternately to preach in Sioux & English. The one who led in the Dakota exercises on the forenoon, was expected to perform the English afternoon service on the following Sabbath. Now I suppose Mr. Gavin, a Swiss mission-ary who has just arrived & will pass the winter with us, will probably lead in the morning service occasionally, as he will have every facility for procuring translations from Mr. Renville, French being his native tongue. He talks English, though not perfectly & will probably assist Mr. R. in learning French this winter. Mr. Riggs is very busily engaged in com-pleting a first reading book which Mr. Pond has translated from lessons husband prepared. This, with Mark's gospel, & some other portions of scripture, we hope will be printed during the winter.

Wed. eve

The small pox is still raging in the Sioux country. Last winter it ap-proached us on the north, now it is on our southern border. A short time since, nearly 50 lodges of Sisitonwon & others from the north, pitched their tents near us. They dress almost entirely in skins; leggins, moccasins, hunting skirts & blankets, all of buffalo skins. The women wear a petticoat, which comes up round the waist but without sleeves, & when trimmed it is quite a curiosity to say the least. When dressed in a full suit of skins, they look like nature's own children. Perhaps you can imagine a woman wrapped in a buffalo robe with dark skin, eyes & hair, & teeth the very reverse, & you will have an Indian woman before you.

Last Saturday Mr. Renville returned from the Fort & besides bring-ing letters, he brought apples. I had five given me by one of his daughters, & I assure you they revived our recollections of old times & perhaps for a few moments we might, Isrealite-like have desired the leeks & onions of Egypt. But it was soon past. Your namesake is now learning to walk & will soon run all over our little room, though he now totters slowly from chair to chair, or to his mother when he wishes to move more rapidly he has recourse to his old method of creeping. One thing let me say in regard to preparing for usefulness among the heathen. Acquaint yourselves with the manner of manufacturing glass, powder, calico, &c, &c. The Indians often inquire how these things are made. Another thing I had thought of mentioning, though it may seem foolish, learn how to cure beef, pork, &c, if you do not already know. All such knowledge will be of practical utility among such ignorant people.

I know not as this will find but one of you at Oberlin, if either, but which ever receives it will, I trust answer it, for we are very desirous to hear.

Lac qui Parle, Mission Station, Nov, 8, 1838
My dear Mother,

Again I have commenced a folio for home, hoping we may have at least one opportunity of sending letters before spring. Dr. & Mrs. Williamson left, with two of their children, two weeks since, but the weather has been so extremely cold for the season, the thermometer at several deg. below zero, that we fear the Mississippi will be closed with ice & they will be detained at Fort Snelling during the winter. I have forwarded by them a small packet for you. The spoon, which is a part of a buffalo's horn, I intended for sister Henrietta. *The cho-tan-kan,* or Indian whistle, is the bone of a swan's wing. I have seen some, still longer than the one I forwarded, though I have never been so fortunate as to see a live swan except on the wing. Then they look very beautifully.

Dec. 6, Thurs. eve

This is our little Alfred's natal day. He, of course, has received no birthday sugar or earthen toys, & his only gift of such kind has been a very small bow & arrow from an Indian man who is a frequent visitor. The bow is about 3/8 of a yard long & quite neatly made, but Alfred uses it as he would any other little stick. I do not feel desirous that he should prize a bow & a gun, as do these sons of the prairie....

During Dr. & Mrs. Williamson's absence, we expect the continued pleasure of Mr. Gavin's society, which is a valuable addition to our little band. He is a missionary to this tribe from Switzerland, & is passing the winter here, to avail himself of the superior facilities for learning Sioux from Mr. Renville who translates from the French into Dakota. As French is Mr. Gavin's native tongue, we think the translations maybe more correct than any that have been obtained. Mr. G. breakfasts & takes tea with us in our little room, & last evening, for the first time, I invited three of Mr. Renville's daughters & Mr. Jeffries, another half breed, all of whom are my pupils. We had barely room enough, though probably more than might have been our share at some fashionable fête.

As I am introducing you to our home & our visitors, I must mention for sister Henrietta's sake Mr. Gavin's remark upon industry this morning at table. He said that he had been told that American women were not as industrious as foreign ladies—referring particularly to Christians. I replied that some even of professing Christians, thought idle hands if we might judge by the way they spent their evenings & afternoons if a few friends were present, a mark of wealth & fashion, but there were others who improved the moments even though they did not need the avail for their own support. He mentioned in answer that when at the seminary at Lausanne, he had frequently passed the evening at the house of a member of the committee for the institution, a man of great wealth, & his wife was not idle, but kept busily at work. Also that when he visited the seminary at Basil he saw stockings that had been knit by the mother of the reigning king of Prussia. Though an old lady perhaps 70 or more, she annually sent some of the labors of her own hands to this institute devoted to the education of pious young men.

Monday eve, Dec. 31, 1838

Nearly three months since my last date to my dear parents have fled, & left no written memorial of my unceasing remembrance. I hope to make ample amends for my silence, & I will rescue a few moments of the departing year, that it may not close without some record. We now have between 29 & 30 scholars in our morning school which, includes females, & lads, & children. Mrs. Pond teaches from 1/2 past eight till 1/4 past ten, & then it is my charge till noon. The afternoon is devoted to the young men & is smaller. Mr. Huggins teaches reading & writing upon slates, & Mr. Riggs arithmetic. A few also come occasionally to our room to be taught.

Last Friday a woman spent the afternoon reading with me. She came with her husband to hear some truths of the gospel, but as my husband was procuring translations of Mr. Renville, I gave her a short column of Dakota words to read. After reading them with assistance once, she was able to go through with only a few mistakes. And this she did again, & again, & again, times uncounted, as though she could not tire, & if for a moment she forgot, she called my eye from my work to teach her anew.

One little slip of paper containing three or four words, Alfred had pulled from her, unperceived, & wrinkling it thoroughly, had thrown it aside. When she discovered her loss she shook her blanket clothes, felt in her sleeves & under her girdle, (these places are the pockets of Dakota women) & seemed very sorry. When I found it, her face brightened & smoothing it out, she folded it very carefully & put it out of his reach.

She came again today & said that she had learned all that I gave her & wished for more, which I furnished. She did not stop long, as we were going up to attend the burial of a child, daughter of one of our church members, & occasionally a scholar. Most of the things were arranged by the relatives, aside from the prayers & hymns. When we entered the mother was wailing, & at intervals, repeated frequently "my daughter — my daughter — or rather *mi-cun kxi-mi cumkxi* (mee chume-kshee)." The corpse was wrapped in a new blanket, such as Indian girls wear, & then in scarlet cloth tied round in three places with striped ferret. I did not see the face or inner clothes, for no one looked at the corpse while I was present, but I suppose they were what she wore when living, as it is customary to bury the clothing with the individual, but the outer was a large bed blanket her mother had procured not long since by washing at the mission. Thus wrapped, she was laid in her rude coffin in which there was not room for the little kettle, bowl, & spoon that were tied over her head. Though I suppose they designed depositing them with the dead, for they were taken to the grave, & I suppose, left there according to the Indian custom. During the time we spent two or three hymns were sung, a few remarks made & then a prayer. We then walked to the place of internment where another prayer was made after the dust was consigned to its kindred dust, & then we dispersed. I suppose the services of this afternoon have approached the nearest to those held in Christian lands on such occasions of any that have been held here. The Indians do not need to pay the last tribute to the departed, but the nearest relatives leave it for some of the more distant connections to perform the requisite labor when it suits their convenience best.

Tues. eve, Jan 1, 1839

Again we have been spared till the dawn of a new year. . . . The morning was passed in common employments, but the afternoon we spent at Mr. Renville's where we were invited to dine. After a few hymns were sung & a prayer made, dinner was announced, & we found the table beautifully supplied with roast pig, pork, mutton & fish, sausage & raisins, also wine which I regretted. The table was spread in a manner quite creditable to those who have known so little of civilized life. The family seem desirous to learn the customs as regards many things, though the daughters do not make that progress in learning English which would be desirable. Indeed we cannot make much advances while they are surrounded, with a few exceptions, only by those who talk Sioux. They have learned marking & will learn knitting soon. Although Alfred has awaked, I must tell you of the New Year's present I finished yesterday for Mr. Riggs, namely a pair of pantaloons, the first I ever cut & made. Not long since I also made myself a dress which fitted very well, though it required much more time than it should have done. It would be pleasant could I know that the friends there are also enjoying the same mild weather that has smiled upon us the last of December & thus far in January. Today the thermometer rose to 44 above zero & several nights it has frozen but little. Our little room has been very comfortable

& some of these warm days we have been obliged to raise the window when we made sufficient fire to boil a tea kettle. Soon however we expect it will be as many deg. below as it is now above zero. Last night we had quite a rain which is uncommon here at this season & it melted most of the little snow the sunny days had left us.

Thurs. eve, January 24, 1839

We still have such mild & lovely weather that the winter is slipping by without our scarce feeling that winter is here. . . . You will not doubt we find ample employment in our school, which is in charge of Mrs. Pond & myself, and today numbers 45 in the forenoon.

As it was her day for washing, I spent the whole forenoon in school, & the noise & confusion compared with a well regulated school of young ladies in the states, made me resolve to make extra effort to tame these wild children. They are very quiet when they are singing or busy about any thing, but at intervals they show their Indian origin & that they are still little Indians. I frequently say to myself if I could talk Dakota as I can English, then I could transform our miniature Babel to the quiet regularity I always loved. But as it is, I must try to do what I can, though it is but little. . . .

Lac qui Parle Mission, Feb. 9, 1839
My dear Parents,

. . . . For a few days past we have had another spring-like season & though cold winter has resumed its throne tonight, we hope, ere a few more weeks, it will abdicate its northern territories, & give place to the smiling face & musical attendants of its successors. Then too the messenger bird comes back to our prairie land, with notes most sweet from the friends of our early home. We mentioned in our last letter the encouraging prospects among the Indians here. The forenoon schools, which are for misses & children, have some days been crowded during the past few weeks, & a Sabbath school, recently opened, has been so well attended as to encourage our hopes of blessed results. The children remain after school to the ordinary Sabbath exercises, & on the last Lord's day more than 80 were present, exclusive of the mem-

bers of the mission, a larger assembly than has ever met for divine worship in this land. The room we have occupied for a church, & schoolroom, & Dr. W's, had been previously arranged for being united on the
Sabbath, by a large door in the partition. It was a solemn & interesting
season. Ten women who, had been examined for admission to the church
the week preceding, presented themselves & their households for baptism, making the whole number 28. After signifying their assent to the
questions asked by Mr. Riggs, they received the sacred rite, & then dedicated their children to the Lord in baptism. There those Indian mothers stood without their husbands, covenanting to serve the Lord, to
renounce all trust in stones, & earth, & sky, & all their hosts, & trust
alone in the true living God. We hope they are truly Christ's disciples,
but God only knows their hearts.

Sat. eve, Feb. 22

The recollection of home & early friends are usually more vivid as we
draw near the close of the week, & allow our thoughts to fly backward
to past scenes, than when the pressing duties & cares of more busy hours
confine us more exclusively to this prairie land. Last Sabbath we were
again permitted to commemorate the dying love of our ascended Lord.
Nineteen native communicants were present, ten of whom there for
the first time enjoyed the privilege of sitting at Jesus' table. Several
members of the church were absent on account of the illness of Mr.
Renville's oldest son, which died during the service. It was buried on
the following day & we regretted that their example should be thrown
upon the side of heathenish superstition. Although they did not give
away all as is the case with many of the Sioux on the death of a relative,
they distributed very lavishly both clothing & provisions, killing a beef
expressly for the Indians. Besides there was a mixture of Roman Catholic ceremonies that seemed to me less natural than those of the Indians.
As we entered the room where the family & others were assembled
previous to the interment, we found the room darkened & candles standing each side of the coffin which was then closed, for what purpose I
could not divine unless it was to enlighten purgatory. The females had
their hair unbraided & flowing gracefully upon their shoulders, the

mother & grandmother wore clasped common Indian blankets instead of their usual broadcloth & all had the appearance of desolation. Within all was very quiet, but one or two without spoke a doleful wailing at intervals. The child's cradle or Indian board was deposited in the grave, & I was told by an Indian woman that the corpse was wrapped before it was placed in the coffin, first in white, then in scarlet, afterward in a broadcloth *Shrenah* or blanket richly embroidered with riband & again in white. While we stood at the grave the moaning and wailing was repressed but it commenced immediately after our departure.

The following morning also Mr. Riggs heard them very distinctly immediately after rising though we live nearly a mile distant. It is not strange that their prejudices should accord with those around for they are in many respects but little more enlightened. We hope however that God will overrule this chastisement for the good of his cause & for the repentance of the bereaved father who has been guilty of violating the 7th commandment since his union with this church.

This evening several who have been absent during the winter have returned in a starving condition. Fear of the Chippawas they say induced them precipitately to leave their encampment without furnishing themselves with venison & nothing eatable is to be found at this season upon the prairie. They traveled several days eating a dog or two, deer skins, & the like, until corn was carried them from this village to which they had sent a runner to appraise the Indians here of their condition. Several left immediately, but before they reached their camp they had suffered severely.

At an encampment some days previous they had left one to die of hunger, who was unable to walk. She had been long affected with a bothersome disease, & for this reason might have had a smaller share than most of their scanty pittance. Last winter she was one of our scholars, though she made but little progress. What must have been the feeling of her mother when she left her to die alone upon the bleak prairie! Two others are quite ill & perhaps may not survive. I am forcibly reminded of Matthew 24:19. The suffering of these Indian women are perhaps similar at times to those foretold of the Jews when their cup of iniquity was almost full.

Friday, March 22

The Indians have nearly all returned from their winter hunt & many have left to hunt otter & the like. Besides the little girl to whom I alluded in the foregoing, two old women were also left to die upon their return home. Such is Indian life. We have thought considerable of late, of taking an Indian girl into our family. The parents are desirous that we should receive her, but we know not what is best. On Alfred's account I tremble. . . .

If she could be brought early to see & accept the truth as it is in Jesus, we should rejoice. The same spirit that taught Catharine Brown, is able to teach the equally ignorant *Anpetnakitoninwien*, which means the "Dawning Day Woman" & is pronounced an paye-too-o-kee-tan-iin-ween. Her baptismal name is Isabella Burgess—named for Mrs. Burgess in Ohio. Her father's wife & mother's elder sister, professedly dedicated her & her motherless sister to God with her own children, when she united with the church last February. . . .

Dr. & Mrs. Williamson we do not expect will return as early as they had intended. They had a very tedious journey from Fort Snelling to "Prairie du Chien," the Mississippi freezing before they had proceeded more than 50 or 60 miles. They remained two weeks at the station of the Swiss missionaries, & then proceeded in a sleigh on the ice, were detained two weeks at a trading post, & finally reached "the Prairie" in December about six weeks after leaving Fort Snelling, a distance that a steamboat would descend in a day. We have not heard whether they have reached Ohio yet, or are still at "the dog prairie."

Although we experience many joys, we are not without heartfelt trials in this heathen land. Sometimes we fear most of the members of our little church know scarcely anything of vital piety. Early in the winter the room occupied for a church & school room became too small, so great was the apparent desire to receive religious instruction. And for a few Sabbaths after, the rooms were filled. Since our communion season however, Mr. Renville, the trader, his family & most of their relations have absented themselves from the regular exercises, so that one room was scarcely full. The church session wanted to know the cause of his absence & also why his men had drawn wood upon the Sabbath. The first inquiry he evaded by saying he wished to leave the room for the Indians, who needed instruction more than himself, & added that when there was a church built, he should attend. To the second, he replied that they were out of wood, & that he felt as much bound to observe Christmas as the Sabbath, without scruple, in order to observe Christmas & new years. We do not know the hearts of men, but it is confidently expected a Roman priest will be located here next summer, & educated as Mr. Renville has been in the Roman Catholic communion, it seems most probable that he will return to a church that has more to flatter a proud and ambitious heart than one which follows the simple truths of the Gospel. If Mr. Renville should leave, his family & relatives will of course follow, & what will be the fate of this little feeble church we know not. . . .

Thurs. eve

The Indian girl that I mentioned we thought of adopting, came this evening with a letter from her father which Mr. Riggs has translated as follows: "Ta-ma-ko-che-Pa-yu-ha My friends, My daughter, An-paye-too-o-kee-tan in-win, 'Appearing day', whom you asked of me, you will keep well for me, therefore I give her to you. We shall always live together & for that reason I do this. But my daughter says she wishes to wear Dakota clothes. For four winters my daughter shall be yours. She is very sad, but I will see her often & thus she will not be sorrowful, & so I also shall not be sad. If she comes home to my house, & then goes to yours, she will not be sorrowful" signed, "Wamdiokiya, Wah-mdee-o-kee-ya, 'Eagle help.' Thus you see we have this little girl committed to our care before we had fully decided what would be best. If she is contented to remain, I hope we may be the instruments of leading her to God. She is 10 or 11 years old, I suppose, & quite interesting. . . .

Please write if you think it probable a box will be sent next year, as I should love to send for some little articles that I think you or Henrietta could procure. Has grandpa'a Milnor's Church History? Does he read it much now, & prize it very highly? Have you ever received the box of 'barnibians', or moccasins. I hope to send pa'a a pair this spring, provided grandpa'a received those I sent last fall. I think he will find them very comfortable.

Lac qui Parle, March 18, 1839, Monday eve
My dear Sister, [Lucretia Cooley]
Your kind letter, mailed in November last, reached us on the 12th instant, with two letters from home, from Ohio, & Indiana, & Missionary Heralds & newspapers in abundance. Now I feel the reaction occasioned by such an excitement. . . . You will present our thanks to the Maternal Association for the favor of the Mother's Magazine, they have so kindly voted to confer. . . . I think your resolution "to leave undone those things which can not be performed without complete exhaustion," a very good one, but the difficulty will be, I think in determining that point, if we are inclined to go as near as possible to that boundary.

My husband said when he read it, "That is just such a resolution as you need to make, Mary Ann. I hope you will adopt it." Tomorrow is my washing day, or "thanksgiving day" as Mr. Riggs calls it, because I am so heartily glad when its duties are finished. Perhaps I shall make a trial. I now have an Indian girl who renders considerable assistance. She also comes every morning except the Sabbath & sweeps the school room &c, for which a few turnips, or potatoes are her reward. The success we have met with thus far, in teaching them to wash, knit, & sew, leads us to hope they may not only be valuable assistance to us, but that they will imbibe a love of neatness & order, to which they are utter strangers, & which will render their own homes more comfortable & happy. . . .

I am quite alone this evening, which is quite an uncommon occurrence, as you know our sitting room answers the quadruple purpose of kitchen, parlor, study & sleeping room. Mr. Riggs is with the church session consulting what his duty in reference to some of our church members whose recent conduct has been quite a trial. During the early part of the winter the prospects here were uncommonly favorable, though very many of the Indians were absent on their hunt, our place of worship was so crowded, that an adjoining room, was united to it by a large door. At our last communion season which was in February, ten women openly renounced their trust in their own idolatrous worship & professed their faith in Jesus Christ. The same day on which they received the baptismal seal, they presented their children, making the whole number baptized on that Sabbath by Mr. Riggs, 28. Several of the fathers & husbands of this interesting group, witnessed the solemn scene, but not one stood with that little band to vow to be the Lord's. Both rooms were full. The next Sabbath also a large number were present, since that however Mr. Renville, & family & all those under their immediate influence have absented themselves for the four succeeding Sabbaths which are past, & now one room is sufficiently large for our lessened congregation. What can have led Mr. Renville to pursue this course we know not, but his desire to be esteemed the greatest, & his early predilections in favor of Romanism perhaps have considerable influence. He talks very much of a Roman Catholic priest whom he says he expects next summer. If one should come, our little church in this wilderness would probably be sundered, for most of its members are relatives of Mr. Renville, & he was the son of a French Romanist. This is a specimen of our trials, but God can & will overrule all things for his own glory. Perhaps he designs to purify this church of its "dross & tin," that it may be sweeter for the worship of the upper sanctuary. . . .

Thursday, March 22

During the winter the school averages 30 daily, but the past week it has been much less, as the women are now making sugar & the boys fishing. We are now abundantly supplied with pike, which I think the best fish caught here, but it does not compare with our New England trout, shad &c. I believe it is also considerably common there, though I do not recollect seeing any before our arrival here.

The ducks & geese, for whose return the Indians have anxiously watched, are now coming back from their winter retreat, but as yet they are but few. Though a notice of this may seem childish, you would doubtless think more of it, if corn was your only food from November till March or April, & even that was nearly, or quite, exhausted. And besides the interest we catch from the Indians, the return of birds is the welcome harbinger of Spring, after a winter of four months. The past season, however, has been remarkably mild, & has slipped rapidly away. A kind Heavenly Father has tempered the winds to these half clad children of the prairie. Last fall when they left us miserably clothed, some having no coats, others with battered gowns & pantalets, & but one blanket, & that in many cases an old one, we feared their parting remark, "We shall die with the cold," would prove too true. But a merciful God preserved them from cold, though they suffered from famine. Fear of their enemies the Chippewas, induced them to leave the "big woods," as they call the place of their encampment, without any supply of provisions for the jour-ney, & before the snow had left the prairie. Finding very little game, they subsisted on a few dogs & dried deer skins, until corn was carried them from this village as soon as their friends were apprised of their arrival. Two old women & one girl exhausted by fatigue & want of food were left to die upon the prairie. It is said the girl, when unable to proceed farther was covered by her mother with snow. . . .

Monday, March 25

We shall be quite alone this summer, if Dr. & Mrs. Williamson do not return till fall, which we think probable, as they were detained by the freezing of the Mississippi, until December between Fort Snelling & Prairie du Chien. We have not heard from them since. Mr. Gavin, the Swiss Missionary, will return home when Mr. & Mrs. Pond leave. Husband & myself have taken a little time to read French with him during the winter. French is spoken more than English by traders, & others dwelling among this tribe.

Home, Wed. April 4, 1839
My dear Mother,

This evening little Alfred & his mother are the sole occupants of this mission house. Last night we were alone, but I slept very quietly, though I awoke once under the impression that the Indian boys had unseason-ably taken possession of the school room which is under our chamber & found it but a dream. Mr. Riggs left home yesterday, intending to accompany Messrs. Pond & Mr. Gavin on their route to Fort Snelling, nearly two days journey by the river, which they descended in a large canoe or pirogue. The chief object was to visit a spot which some of the

Indians say is quite an Eden, & a very desirable place for an Indian village. A few have even proposed removing there provided Mr. Riggs
will accompany them, but I do not think the plan will succeed for several reasons. One is there will be some danger of its decreasing the fur
trade at this post. If so insinuations will doubtless be made that husband wished to obtain the land from the government when treaties shall
be formed. In truth this rumor has already reached our ears, & probably
originated with one who thinks his interest at stake & knows full well
how to prejudice an Indian mind. We trust God will lead us to that part
of this vineyard where we can do most for his glory.

Monday Afternoon, April 5

Fortunately our expected messenger to Fort Snelling is so unlike an
eastern steamboat, that I have an opportunity of writing today, as the
Frenchmen's tomorrow is still to come. So uncertain is the word of these
Canadian French, & so poor their calculations that we can with considerable safety expect they will not leave on a journey until a day or two
after the time they specify. Hoping that I should be able to write today, I
went to rest Saturday night as soon as I had finished the pantalets for a
little Indian girl who lives with us, thinking I should encroach upon the
Sabbath in spirit by sitting up much later than usual. Saturday's work
witnessed the wedding ceremony husband alluded to. . . . Anna which
is the English name of the little girl who is now with us came on Friday
in as tattered & dirty condition as you can easily imagine, though not so
much so as many we see from day to day, as her parents are perhaps more
industrious than most, if I may.

Thurs. eve April 17

Again my dear mother, Mary & little Alfred are alone. I feel quite
lonely during even a short absence of Mr. Riggs from home, though Mr.
Huggins' house is but a few rods distance, & our intercourse is of course
frequent & unceremonious. But it is unpleasant for a female to be even
so nearly alone. . . . My health which was not good a week since, is now
quite restored its usual tone, & though I always feel the effects of much
hard labor, yet I hope by prudence, industry, & economy of time &

strength, to do what I can in the service of our blessed Master.

Monday eve, April 22

Your letter commenced on Sabbath eve, Dec. 30th & mailed Jan. 12th reached us yesterday afternoon. A son of *Wamdiokiya*, the man who accompanied Messrs. Pond & Gavin came in while Mr. Huggins was reading a sermon in Mr. Riggs' absence. . . . For several days past, the Indian children & our own also have been attacked with vomiting & purging attended with a high fever. Last night Alfred was very restless, tossing to & fro in such a manner as to make me quite solicitous about him. I gave him some rhubarb & he is now better, & also gave a dose to an Indian child whom its mother brought here quite sick at sunrise. I have been asked very frequently for medicine since husband left, & though I have confined myself to castor oil & rhubarb, I believe they have been quite efficacious. I should now find some knowledge of medicine very useful, & indeed there is scarcely any kind of knowledge that is not requisite, or could not be called into action in a heathen land, where you have not the counsel of an aunt or a mother, or a few but any one in whose wisdom & experience you can rely. . . . I think I have mentioned in some of my letters, that Mr. Renville & family had absented themselves from worship on the Sabbath & our fears that a Romish priest would be sent as has been proposed next summer. Mr. Renville's family have recently attended & nothing is yet developed in reference to their intentions for the future. . . . Last evening the mother of our little adopted girl came nearly a mile bringing her babe but two days old, because as she said, she heard that her daughter was *cante yiia* literally of a bad heart — but meaning in this case "home sick" I suppose. We told her it was not so, that she had not cried at all, but had a *canta waxte* that is a "good heart" or is happy. We are all enjoying one of the most beautiful spring seasons. The trees are already clothed in their delicate green & the wheat & peas are promising us an abundant supply, & what is to us a great blessing, we have as yet but few muskitoes.

Thurs. eve

We have just been up to the encampment of the Red River emigrants.

Fewer families than last year & these were mostly French & half breeds. A man who has passed down & back several times gave me a very beautiful pair of moccasins which I should like to send to some of my dear Massachusetts friends. We saw two fine buffalo calves that were about two weeks old. Their mothers were shot & these taken by the company. They are larger than the domestic calf, the hair is finer & thicker of a light brown color. We are expecting several of the men to supper & shall probably procure some pemmican & buffalo tallow for candles.

Mideiyiedan, June 14, 1839
My dear Sister Henrietta,

As our adopted Anna has gone on a visit to her mother & little Alfred is asleep, I improve this precious opportunity for writing. From some little unpleasant circumstances I felt additional fears that our Indian girl might not return & they excited perturbation & anxiety of mind. But I tried a better antidote than yesterday & it has proved more efficacious. After being quite tired with continued begging for a little milk & bread, by those who I had paid abundantly for services performed, taking my work I went to sit with Mrs. Huggins awhile, feeling considerably discouraged by new manifestations of the pride & laziness of the men & boys. An Indian woman may hoe & chop, or pack burdens large enough for an ox or horse while her lord & master walks near with his gun & possibly some other trifle. Some of the Dakota women pack upon their backs burdens such as the men could not lift, so little accustomed are they to labor. Last week Mr. Huggins weighed a load of bark of 127 pounds that had been brought about a mile, & was to be carried nearly the same distance farther. A lady, educated in a civilized land, would never dream that a sister woman could be so inured to hardship & toil, as to become so much like a "beast of burden."

Offer a boy of 15 an ax to carry to his mother & he is ashamed to carry it, or give him a few potatoes, as Mr. Riggs did one yesterday for assisting him a short time, & ask him if he likes them & he says "perhaps so," or a term equivalent to that, & proposes to his little sister of 8 or 9 years, to lay them away for her to carry home in the morning in a clean white blanket that I had given her not long since. Thus did the brother of our little girl. I objected to that course, telling him it would soil her blanket as much as his, & that if he would bring a kettle in the morning, she might help him carry them and, too proud to do even this, he gave them away rather than to be seen carrying them home, notwithstanding the family are very fond of them & not abundantly supplied with food. Proud of what he is! Ashamed of what he ought to do & not ashamed to steal. At least I have every reason to suppose he & another boy who had seen me take food for Alfred from a closet just before leaving the house, forced upon the window during my short stay & helped themselves without shame, I suppose. The use of such terms as glory, honor, bravery, & their opposites, is peculiarly perverted among this heathen people. A man who has a heart of stone & can stab women & children, if Chippawas, is a brave man, & a man who refused to go to war is a mean coward, in the estimation of the Sioux. And if one who asks you for a favor that you cannot grant, for even a fish hook if you have none, as was recently the case, he may kill a hog or a calf, & not be ashamed. If you disapprove his conduct & he is angry & kills cattle, it is not theft, according to their ideas of morality, but justified by their code of honor that demands retaliation, if one would be deemed a brave man.

I feel quite desirous that you should cultivate your musical talent, as I feel daily that I might be more useful if I could teach these little Sioux some of Zion's songs. There are few Dakota hymns that I am able to sing & just before going to rest at night Anna frequently says, *Sing Marpeya kin ekta &c.* Write me what progress you are making in music as well as other branches of study, & also respecting all your pursuits.

Thurs. morn, June 20

. . . . I cannot plead guilty to the charge of having my house & its affairs in too good order, though perhaps I may devote more time to such duties than their comparative importance demands. This is not, however my intention, & I think as far as our friends are concerned, they cannot justly complain. . . . It is true that I can obtain more assistance than formerly in domestic duties but they are also increased. The woman who assists in washing also churns for the buttermilk, and can now wash floors tolerably well, though I usually help her, or at least do the finishing part. Our little girl also wipes dishes, picks up chips & sweeps some, but I never supposed an untrained Indian child of 8 or 9 years would be as much assistance as care & trouble. If she should re-main with us & become a child of Jesus, we shall be repaid a thousand fold, for all our anxious & wearisome hours.

Alfred is so fond of playing with Mrs. Huggins little ones, that he frequently slips away in a moment & is gone, & his mother must send for him, or go herself, or both, for Anna frequently forgets her first errand, when she finds someone to play with. When I see Alfred run-ning as fast as his little feet can carry him, I often think his grandmother would love to see her little grandson, & almost wish for a moment that he could run up the elm shaded lane to the home of my youth. You would not recognize in him many lineaments of Mary, though you might perhaps in the developments of character. He has not over much pa-tience, & has the same untiring industry at play for which mother used to give me credit when a child. Still he talks a very little, or rather, says very little in an intelligible tongue, which is rather a matter of surprise to me, as you know his parents are neither of them "slow of speech."

But enough of us & ours — I write thus particularly that you may see us as we are, & know our every day affairs, & I wish that I could cheer your hearts by recording our spiritual as well as temporal prosperity. The war party has not yet returned, but is daily expected. During their absence, those that are here have been ready to tremble at every shaking leaf, proving this truth, "The wicked flee when no man pursueth." A few nights since several lodges who had gone out 10 or 12 miles to dig tepsin, which is now their principal dependence, discovered at a dis-tance at the north encampment which they surmised to be 200 Chippawa warriors. Of course they were in the greatest consternation, & returned by night homewards. These emigrants from Red River which were doubtless the cause of their alarm we expect will arrive today. I think I have written something respecting the Red River, or Lord Selkirk's Settlement. It was commenced some years since under the pa-tronage of this English lord who has expended time & property for its advancement. The colonists are a mixture of Scotch, English, & French. Many of the latter, & also some of the others, have intermarried with the natives. The laboring class, according to their own statement, find very poor encouragement, as there is no market for produce, & all articles which they purchase are an enormous price. This is the cause of their immigration, & if they continue to flock to the United States, as they have done every summer for four years past, this settlement at Red River must be depopulated.

Home, Aug 1, 1839
My dear Mother,

I doubt not that you felt a lively interest in our little adopted Indian girl & that you will regret her departure. Last Friday she went home on a visit & returned on Sat. morning requesting her clothes, saying that her father & mother commanded her to go back & live with them. Knowing that expostulation would be in vain, & not doubting that it originated with her father who, it is said, declared at the time of leaving for the war party that he would take her away, I gave her the garments such as little Indian girls wear, retaining her new dresses that she had just made in *Isantankay* (American) fashion. Telling her that we were sorry she was about to leave us, & that I hoped she would fear & obey God, & continue to read, she took up her packet to go. Husband told her we would shake hands & she turned back. As I took her hand & pressed the lips of our adopted, I could not avoid weeping at the thought of her returning to her heathen home & habits.

Thurs. afternoon, August

For several days past, we have been in the furnace, perhaps I should not say of affliction, but of painful experience. The elder of the war party, to whom I have so often alluded, has been repeatedly demanding a remuneration of Mr. Riggs for making them angry last spring by endeavoring to dissuade them from making war. For several weeks he only requested or intimated that if the war party were invited to a feast here all would be well, but last Sat. he demanded powder & lead, stating that if it was not given, our cattle & horses should all be killed & we be sent away. Mr. Riggs consulted Mr. Renville who has been very friendly of late, & who said nothing ought to be given them. Wishing to conciliate them as much as possible a feast was made for the principal men, hoping they would declare their determination to protect our cattle & forbid their being killed. Mr. Riggs wishing to draw out their opinions requested them to say whether it was a crime according to their customs, to speak one's own opinions & tell what God had commanded. No one except the leader of the war party, pretended it was while they were here, but through his influence after leaving they determined, that Mr. R. should pay a keg of powder & a box of lead or leave the country & wrote a letter to that effect in the name of one of the principal members who was not of the war party, so as to give it the appearance of requesting a decision, to the Indian agent, Major Taliaferro-pro (Talifero). Since however we have ascertained that the letter was a forgery & probably the work of *Wandiokeya* the leader of the war party and the man whose signature it bears says he knew nothing of it; nor does not approve its contents. The chief also had no evil, but I greatly fear *Wanmdiokiya*, who probably has more knowledge of gospel truth than any other Sioux, is given over to the service of Satan, & that it will be ye knew your duty & did it not will be his final sentence. I know not what the decision of the Indian agent may be, but I should very much regret, if to appease the clamor of the Indians he should recommend the payment required.

Sept. 2

Mr. Necolett whom I mentioned has endeavored to persuade the Indians to pay for the cattle they have killed the past season & last Saturday proposed to them to pay what they were able & he & his assistant, would pay the balance — Indian like, they told him they were poor & he was rich & wished he would pay it all. To this he assented saying he would furnish them with means to cancel the debt today. If he should do so I suppose it is with the expectation of being repaid by government. He has been in their employment for more than a year & spent two summers exploring the Sioux country. He will probably prepare an account of his observations discoveries &c the coming winter. He leaves in a day or two. Remember us particularly to grandpa'a if he yet lives, & also to our other relations & friends.

Home, Sat. eve, Sept. 14, 1839
My dear sister Henrietta,

It is a source of regret to us that our younger brothers & sister write us so seldom & briefly. You are now past 13 & surely ought to be able, & willing, often to write us a good long letter.... I hope you will be able to attend Miss Lyon's school in the course of a year or two. But there are studies with which you should be familiar before leaving our native town. Instead of studying Natural Philosophy, Chemistry, Rhetoric, &c, as I did before I was 13, become well acquainted with History. Perfect yourself in review of your Geography, & systematize your knowledge of it, so that you would be able to tell most of the principal cities, rivers, mountains, &c, their situation & comparative size, & above all neglect not what I most of all neglected, Arithmetic. Make yourself skillful in figures, at least to the rule of three on Hawley hills. If you have resolution enough these winter evenings that are approaching, you might accomplish considerable. Thomas or Joseph will assist you, if at home. Oh, how much time have I spent at Ipswich, & Amherst, & Buckland, plodding away at this simple yet fundamental branch of education, that might have been saved if I had acquired a taste for Arithmetic by early practice. Oh, it looks as foolish to set a little girl studying Rhetoric & Philosophy that does not know the abc's of Arithmetic. And yet it has been often done. Profit by my experience, & do not let a preference for other branches lead you to neglect those which should be foundation stones. Improve the talents which God has given you & do not trouble that you are not like the pictures of romance in beauty & grandness. Cultivate a mild & quiet spirit, a dove-like disposition & it will impart a charm to the plainest features.... I do not wish to undervalue personal accomplishments, but the surest way for their attainment is to have a higher aim than simply to please & be admired. Seek to make others happy— feel at home & others will naturally feel so too. Be frank & open hearted, & ever practice the true heartfelt politeness enjoined by the apostle Paul, & you will need no other. Be willing to be seen & known as you are, & that will relieve you from embarrassment & awkwardness if you should be surprised *en deshabille.* May God bless you....

Lac qui Parle Mission, Sept. 15, 1839
My dear Parents,

As we have heard nothing recently from home & I have written such a short time since, there is very little to write. If it were not that you may see an account of the Indian mode of worshipping the sun, I should endeavor to describe a scene Mr. R. witnessed last week at the Indian village. Some years since *Waanatan* performed this dance to the sun three days in fulfillment of a vow, with the additional torture of passing thongs through his flesh to the pole around which he danced as the sun revolved. He continued this worship until completely exhausted, & since that time his eye sight has failed him until he is nearly blind, which is probably an effect of this torture of the eyes & whole system.

Sat. eve

As husband, if nothing prevents will leave on Monday next, I have but a few moments at command & those must be divided between three letters. Notwithstanding it has been a windy afternoon, as my husband invited me, I have taken a short ride on horseback. Alfred accompanied us, & evidently enjoyed the novelty of such an excursion. It seemed pleasant to me also, once more, to look out upon the smiling earth & sky.

Lac qui Parle Mission, Wednesday eve, Oct. 2, 1839
My dear Mother,

Again I commence you a letter not knowing but it may remain a long half year, unable to take an eastward flight. On the 24th Sept. husband left home for Le Blanc's, where we had some supplies, & we expect his return tomorrow. The weather has, however, been so warm for the last two days, thermometer at 83 in the shade, that I shall not feel much disappointed if he should not reach home until the following day. This morning, while busily engaged at my work, an old woman came in & showed her ragged gown, wishing, as is usual, for at least an old gar-ment to make her another. As a reason why it should be given, she said she came here on the Sabbath & also attended meeting at Mr. Renville's on Sabbath evening. Her poor, sick daughter would come too, but she could not walk & bring her so far. "I carry her to Mr. R's," said she, "but

I am unable to bring her here." Can you picture this aged mother carrying her daughter, who is at least of my years, upon her back?

Monday eve, Oct. 14

Today if you had been here, you would have seen a specimen of Indian character—women busily engaged at work—men marching or
sauntering about as if they were a superior race of beings. Their better
dress, their proud idleness, both indicate their self esteem & the low
condition of the women. In the morning most of the native church members were called to aid in gathering turnips, & afterward the Indians
generally were invited & between 30 & 40 bushels were given them.
As most of the older men were receiving their supplies of powder &
lead, the young men & the women with their children, were sent as
their representatives. A great number went to the field, & you might
have seen old & young women returning with nearly a bushel of turnips slung very carelessly or rather, dexterously, upon their backs while
the young men came twirling one on their fingers or eating it as they
stepped proudly by. The turnips given the Indians were brought by the
women & thrown in front of our dwelling. Then the representative for
each lodge sat on the ground in a large circle & the task of distribution
commenced. This was performed by a man & occupied more than an
hour, & then the women & children packed home their treasures to
share with these self esteemed "Lords of creation." Perhaps I do not feel
right, but I cannot endure such slavery as we see from day to day. Not
long since, I gave an old man a few potatoes which he had begged, & on
receiving them he wished me to lay them away until he could go home
(a mile & a half) & send his wife for them. To this plan I objected, telling
him I had determined not to give a thing to a man & have him send his
wife for it, & if he would not carry them, he need not have them. This
seemed at least to have some effect upon his pride, for he took them in
his blanket without further hesitation, & replied that what I had said
was well. Such circumstances are by no means infrequent. You need not
fear that, in our liberal distribution of turnips & potatoes, we have not
reserved enough for ourselves, & some for the sick & needy, as occasion
may require. The Lord has truly blessed us in our share.

At a low, & safe estimate, we probably had not far from 175 bushels potatoes, 100 of turnips & also of corn, 40 of wheat, & 6 or 8 of beets, one of which weighed 5 pounds. Thus we have repeated & continued manifestations of the kind & Fatherly care of him whose cause we have espoused, & in whom we trust.

Last Thursday eve, Oct. 10,

We received a packet of letters, two of which were from home, the earliest marked no. 3 or 4, & the third received this year, mailed in July & the other in August. The following morning these pleasurable feelings were put to flight by a shocking suicide. Whether intentional or not, we know not, or whether as has been reported, it was occasioned by drinking whiskey that an Indian had just brought up from Fort Snelling we cannot tell. The man was intending, apparently, to clean his gun, & standing near the fire, blew into the muzzle, when it discharged & in an instant he was in eternity. Indeed he has seemed to think that Satan had a peculiar claim upon him since the death of his father, who was the high priest of Indian witchcraft & superstition here, & who died soon after officiating at a "wakan feast" last fall.

And, as we supposed, in consequence of exposure to the cold in a state of nudity, seated on the bare ground for several hours during the ceremony a cold day in Oct.

Tuesday eve

Please write the charge for making a coat, vest, & pants in Greenfield. In Ohio, even in the small towns, the charge for a coat is 7 or 8 dollars & other garments in proportion. This has led to the query if they could not be occasionally purchased to better advantage in Mass. You mentioned some had proposed making a bed quilt. Such articles as quilts, comfortables, blankets, &c, we always find of use, though I do not now need a quilt excepting a small one for Alfred's bed. For two winters I have conformed to western custom, strange as it may seem to you, & slept next to a blanket instead of an upper sheet during the winter. The blankets generally used are not much heavier than a flannel sheet & the custom is not to change it during the season. I cannot quite like this, but it is so inconvenient for us to dry bed clothes that by using two, I make them suffice till spring, & it saves washing. I am not sure however, that I shall not use cotton sheets this winter.

Thurs. eve, Nov. 5

As you are ever interested in the advancement of these poor Indians towards civilization & Christianizing, you will rejoice whenever progressive steps are taken or encouraging effort is viewed. And surely in a country so inclement & among a people so poorly clad & so ignorant, a few yards of rude cloth, manufactured by Indian women, would at least be an encouraging omen. Last Tuesday the first piece made in the Sioux country was completed, the warp having been furnished by friends in Ohio. It was not more than 5 or 7 yards, but we hope to have a longer piece ready for the loom in the spring. One of our pupils, a girl of 15 *Morpiyaxkanxkanwin,* Moving Cloud Woman, claims the honor of completing the first short gown of Dakota manufacture. When she had finished weaving it, it was cut from the loom, & she came to our room several days after school to make it, though I suppose if she had been beyond inspection it would have been sewed (or basted, rather) in half the time. Two women & two girls share their proportion of the first effort in cloth making, & are indeed the only ones who have tried learning to weave, & among the best of the 8 or 9 who have learned to spin tolerably. We hope the numbers will be doubled during the winter, as the oldest of our school girls spin alternately during the hour for sewing. Had we a supply of knitting needles, we should also hope to number at least 29, instead of 11 knitters who learned last fall & winter, but a donation including them from friends in Galena, Ill. has never reached here.

A few Sabbaths since, Nov. 24, we observed about 8 o'clock a singular phenomenon, at least it was singular to us. The moon had risen but 30 or so minutes before & the sky around seemed dimmed by haze, making more apparent the broad stream of light extending from the moon to the horizon & another crossing at right angles & extending over the moon's disc. The outlines were so perfect & the form & proportions of the cross so like the one imagination has often pictured as that on which our Savior suffered & died, that the circumstances of the crucifixion as narrated by the Evangelists, came forcibly to mind. An illiterate Romanist might easily have believed the representation super-natural.

And this is not the only memorable circumstance which has occurred of late on the Sabbath. The last one in Nov. a cold blowing day some men returning home to the Red River Settlement joined our Sabbath assembly & gave us a packet of letters & one was from home mailed Oct. 5, it having traveled from New England hills to Lac qui Parle in 48 days. If I have not already answered all of your queries in reference to this settlement & its immigrants to the United States I will add that the colony was founded by Lord Selkirk & is by a regal grant under the government of the Hon. Hudson's Bay Company. The original settlers were Scotch, English, French, &c but by their alliances with the Indi-ans many of the present inhabitants are of a mixed race, though quite a number that I have seen, evinced that they were true descendants of Scotia's sons.

Most of those who go to the United States go with the intention of remaining or of seeking a place for future location while others, as was the case with some of the present party go, for the purposes of trade — such as selling cattle, pemmican, &c, or "to spy out the land."

Home, Nov. 9, 1839
My dear Parents,

This is a quiet Saturday eve, & tomorrow will bring the 26th birth-day of your absent daughter, or perhaps more correctly the 26th recur-rence of that natal day. Had you been within the sound of an old Indian woman's voice yesterday, you would have had a fair specimen of the customary inward or return often made by the Sioux on receiving even a small present. On returning from school in the morning, I found seated on the floor, a living witness of the sad union of poverty, rags, & age, who, for the first time, had found her way to our chamber. As she seemed truly an object of charity, I gave her an old garment with which she seemed delighted & doubtless, wishing to reward me as far as in her power, she explained at the top of her voice to those in the room below,

"Women, do you hear me? I came here to the *wantan tipi* (high house) & they gave me a short gown, needle & thread." Although I was amused at her earnestness, I requested her to say no more. She replied that the Sioux did thus, & that when she returned to the village, she should again proclaim the favors received.

Friday, Dec. 27

During the past week our morning school which is composed chiefly of young women & girls has averaged 33. Miss Huggins & myself are busily employed in teaching them to read, write, & sew from half past 8 until nearly 11, when we close by singing, & return to our room to make some preparations for dinner, or perform some other duty. The Indian woman who assists me in washing & who is probably 35 or 8 years of age, is quite a constant scholar & can read spelling lessons very readily. Several others considerably advanced in years, are learning to read, but they do not attend our morning school.

Both men & women are usually too proud to learn the alphabet in the presence of their children, & some are unwilling, when any other Dakotas are present, to make any attempts. It is not strange they should feel some reluctance, & in their first efforts we are willing to indulge them when consistent, by hearing them alone. . . . The winter thus far has been very mild & pleasant, the coldest days, Nov. 24 & 25, the thermometer sinking only 10 deg. below zero.

28th, Sat. eve

Another week is almost finished & I seem to have accomplished little except the ordinary school & domestic duties, & yet I cannot reproach myself with idleness. Even the little time that I can rescue from such labors is so broken, that I am unable to seat myself for sewing, mending, &c, without a strong probability of being interrupted almost as soon as my work needle & thread are taken. Today I flattered myself that I should complete a garment that I have had on hand two weeks; but I have been unable. After our morning meal & work was over, until afternoon, our room was crowded with men, women, & children. The children troubled me by flattering or vexing Alfred as best suited their different humors,

& the women delayed him by their sociability. For when I listen to, or try to talk a language I understand so imperfectly, I often find an undivided attention necessary, eyes & ears must both be wide open. Perhaps you may be amused with the lesson they gave this morning. One of them wishing for a measure for Mr. R's Moccasins, asked me "Why do you not unloose them?" I told her, "I never do it. I don't know how. If he is sick, I should do it, but not when he is well." "I can teach you," she replied, & continued, "The Dakota women always do thus & so when their husbands return from hunting. One of the wives goes out to meet & help him, taking his pack, whether game or furs, she carries it home. Then she unloosens his moccasins, & taking them off, & also his leggins, washes his feet & anoints them with a mixture of oil & paint." Is this being a "help meet" or a servant?

Monday morn, Dec. 30

We have risen betimes this morning to add a few lines to our letters, & as I must be in school at half past eight, I will take a few moments while breakfast is cooking. Sat. eve, while we were writing, we heard crying a long time at some of the lodges a few rods distance, on the opposite bank of the river, & supposed some woman might have been whipped by her husband. Yesterday, however, we learned that a child had been born, & its mother had been thrust out of doors, according to Indian custom, the thermometer standing at 12 deg. below zero. Mrs. Williamson, hearing that the woman intended throwing away her child, carried her some clothes, as was probably expected by those who circulated the report. On her return she said she found her sitting out of doors, with a small, old buffalo skin stretched on some poles behind, & a little fire on front, & the child wrapped in old blanket with its naked face open to wind & sun. When I thought of her exposed condition, I determined to go over & tell our wash woman, who is a church member & has no husband, that it was her duty to ask her to her tent. On going I found Mrs. H.[uggins] returning from the same errand. She said at first that "It was hard but the Dakotas all did so, not only at such times, but at others." It is the same referred to under the ceremonial law of Lev. 15, when they must build & live in a house by themselves, & cook

& eat alone. She added that "When it was dark she would ask her to sleep in her tent, & that the reason she was cast out was because she had no husband," (he having left her, I think, last fall) "If she had, he would pity her, & because it was cold, ask her into the house." Finding, however, that I wished to see that the woman was invited, she sent her little girl with me on this errand. We found the young mother curled up in a fragment of an old buffalo robe in what I should suppose a most suffering condition. One of the women from the lodge which had been her home, said, in reply to my inquiries, that the child was within & that its mother should also sleep in her tent. And when I asked why she did not go in now, or else go with the little girl, she said, "The young would laugh at me," & seemed to choose remaining still longer out in cold that made me shiver, though I was much more comfortably clothed. Thus I left her, pitying her not so much as I had done on account of her present suffering, but more on account of her bondage to superstition.

Home, Sat eve. Dec. 28, 1839
My dear sister H,

....Some time since you inquired respecting the children of the traders & other white men in the Indian country. Having Indian mothers their early training is in most respects like that of Indian children. Their dress is as nearly like that of white people as they know how to make it, still they are not ashamed to lay it aside for the leggins & petticoat when they join in playing ball, even after they are men & women. The girls do not learn to chop & pack wood as do their darker faced playmates, & if possible are more useless & idle than Indian girls & their brothers are still more lazy & proud. They can join the feasts & the amusements of the Indians, but some of them would think it a disgrace to chop a stick of fuel, or even lay it on the fire. Such consider themselves gentlemen & yet they would make their mothers, wives, & sisters their servants, almost as much as do Indian men. And in truth in many of their habits & feelings they are more than " breeds." Our morning school is now so full that most of the boys attend in the afternoon. The class most advanced are bright, dark eyed girls with the exception of a blue eyed trader's daughter. They can read a little without spelling out the words

& write some without a copy on their slates. Anna is the youngest but the foremost in reading & perhaps in writing also. The class agree in the opinion that the scissors which some time since I promised to any of them who would learn to write some without a copy & to read without spelling before New Years, belong to Anna alone. She does not think I suppose that her superiority is in consequence of her stay with us last summer. I hope they will all be good readers before spring. As my writing indicates, I am too tired to guide the pen, but I could not refrain from sending you a few lines.

Lac qui Parle Mission, Sat. eve, Jan. 18, 1840
My dear Parents,

This is my first date in this new year, one month of which will soon have fled... my husband, who is very unwilling that I should write less than before our marriage, is very desirous I should complete, within six or seven weeks, a small English & Sioux vocabulary commenced a short time since. I have been over to the Indian lodges this afternoon to see our washerwoman who is unable to walk, in consequence of a fall while packing wood. She complained very little for two or three days after, & came constantly to read & spin, but yesterday, after passing the day carding & spinning, on going home tired at night, she found they had nothing to eat, & went for corn half a mile distant, & returning with a sack of two bushels, hurt herself again & I fear will suffer a long time in consequence. In most of the lodges in which Miss H. & I called we found the women quite busily engaged making moccasins & dressing skins. In one I noticed with surprise a young woman wearing a short gown that I gave last fall to a poor old widow with a sick daughter. But the probable way it came into the possession of its wearer soon occurred to me. Her husband has been officiating as "powon" practicing his "charms" over the widow's sick daughter, & for such Satanic conjurations he must be paid. Although his incantations are unavailing, decrepit age must be disrobed of charity's offerings, if no better reward is afforded. The conjurers among the Sioux do not labor gratuitously. Almost every other supposed favor may be begged, but this must be paid for liberally.

Fri. eve, Feb. 7

Mr. R. commenced praying in Sioux about a year since, & for some time past has thought it the duty of the female members of the mission to add their example, thinking it might have a happy influence in teaching our Indian sisters to pray social, as well as secret prayer. And I have felt that it would be a privilege to meet with them, but so imperfect has been our knowledge of the language, that it has been postponed from time to time, & even now my "spirit groans being burdened" when I think what a field of usefulness lies open before us & of our inability to enter in and labor. I feel more then ever that I must learn Sioux, & I hope that I may be so assisted from on high that I shall ere long be able to perform duties that seem now reproaching my tardy stupor. I do not now feel, as I have some-times felt, that the wives of Indian missionaries have less opportunity for direct efforts to do good than those in other fields.

Lac qui Parle, March 25, 1840
My dear Mother,

Our little daughter is now nearly five weeks old, & generally a good babe, & as I have nearly regained my usual health, I hope to find some moments for writing to my dear friends. Little did we think last Sabbath when our little one received in baptism the name of Isabella Burgess, that our friend Mrs. B. was not a tenant of earth. But on Tues-day following, we received intelligence that she died in Nov. The par-ticulars we have not learned, though in death, as in life, she evinced her love to the cause of missions by bequeathing $500 to this mission.

Sat. eve, April 4

Spring has come again, & its harbingers, birds of passage, have once more returned. The last of February was uncommonly mild & the ducks & geese, to our surprise came back from their winter retreat. Some cold days in March frightened them back for a few days, but the unmusical sounds "quack, quack" are again heard, & soon we hope to hear the songs of more melodious birds. Apparently no one rejoices more in sunny days than Alfred after having been shut up in our little chamber a long winter, he would delight to run with the older children or gambol with the lambs till his strength & good nature are more than spent. I fear he will love play better than his book. We have taken but little pains yet to teach him to read, & took none till he was two years old, as I have never been ambitious that he should be a wonderful boy. After we commenced giving him a letter or two daily he learned the alphabet in about its number of days, but as yet he has made little progress in spelling. I think he is affectionate, though rather rude sometimes. He evidently loves his "little sistit Bella" notwithstanding her nice eyes, fingers &c. are in danger, if her little brother is near & unwatched, & I hope vanity will not whisper to him that he is the prettier because the fairer. Husband has often said why do you not write about our little daughter? One reason perhaps is that I have waited to know what to write. At her birth & for three or four weeks, she was a yellow babe, as yellow as in severe cases of jaundice. The Indians said she was a Dakota, & I almost feared the yellow hue would be permanent. Now she is not much darker, if any, than her mother, has dark hair, somewhat curly, & blue eyes. I think I am truly grateful that God has given us another sweet babe, which I hope we may be enabled to train up for heaven.

Monday eve, April 13

In our last letter husband mentioned I think, the death of Mrs. Renville Feb. 16th. She had been ill for some months with insidious consumption, & as its victim, often flattered herself that she was recovering, while the disease was making sure & rapid progress.

The Sabbath on which she died, she calmly conversed with her family in reference to her departure, some account of which was written by themselves & translated by Mr. Riggs. I will transcribe.

"On the morning of the Sabbath her husband being with her alone said to her, 'Today you seem to be failing much.' She answered, yes. 'Today, God calls me. Jesus Christ who suffered for me I have in remembrance as my only trust. This day I shall stand before God & supplicate mercies for you & my children & relatives who do not believe. Of a truth today my afflictions & troubles will be at an end. God call me, I shall rejoice in his presence & joy in Jesus Christ."

She said these things, when her husband, overcome with sorrow,

begged her to cease, to which she assented. Then her children & relatives all came & sat around her weeping. She looked upon them & said,
"It is the Sabbath, sing & pray to God & pray to him." Her children &
relatives all sang crying & prayed. They stopped & spoke to her but she
answered them not again. They kissed her and she looked upon them.
Her husband then said to her, "You are now about to die & they have all
kissed you." With difficulty she said, "God, it is so, I will sit up." She sat
up & looked upon them all. Her husband then fixed a pillow for her on
which she laid her head & died. The Indians who witnessed her death
acknowledge that she died differently from other Dakotas, & the
contrast between her last hours & those of a young man who died shortly
after with the same disease was very striking. She seemed willing to go
when her Savior called, he having no Savior on whom to lean, had recourse to powwows & at last, weary with suffering & vainly hoping to
put pistol into his mouth which however contained only powder &
afterward attempted hanging himself. Poor man attempting to rush into
the presence of his offended judge, to escape the sufferings of earth.

Lac qui Parle Mission, April 20, 1840
My dear Miss Hallock.

The chief passed this forenoon with us, & in reply to Mr. Riggs inquiry why he had not listened to God's word said if he should listen his
people would not, & changing the subject as soon as possible to temporal maters, expressed a wish that we should teach them to make powder, it was well to learn how to make coats & blankets, but it would be
still better he thought to learn to make powder. They are slow to believe & put in practice what would be for their happiness here & still
more faithless in reference to the future. Many seem to live heedlessly
from life. Within a few months two instances of suicide have occurred,
or rather one & another attempt made by a young man who had been
suffering from disease for some time previous, but "consumption" he
deemed too slow, too severe, & would have hastened the torment of
another world in exchange for the sufferings of this.

April 24, 1840

.... You will not infer from this that we are not forming attachments here. I hope we are, & those too that will survive death & the grace. Some of the native church members give cheering evidence of having passed from death unto life and are we think making progress heaven-ward. I have felt quite desirous that they should understand more fully the nature of prayer, both social & secret, & for this purpose proposed to some of them to join our female praying circle & present their own requests.... An Indian woman left her husband four or five years since in consequence of his taking a third wife, & for more than a year past has clothed herself & children by assisting me in washing & supplies them with food by cultivating corn. Having no husband she regards herself as she says, as more dependent upon God, though in reality she is not, for her circumstances are more comfortable than if she had a hus-band for whom she must toil to raise food as is the custom here. You are aware that Indian women are too much slaves of their husbands & broth-ers, & they seem peculiarly so among this tribe. It is a disgrace for a man or boy ordinary to chop wood or raise corn, labor which in their estimation is emphatically "woman's work." The woman above alluded to wishing to visit a distant sister a few days since inquired of her daughter's husband if he would assist his wife in the cultivating of their field during her absence. The reply was "am I a woman that I should hoe corn, I thought I was a man." And the women many of them would be ashamed to receive such assistance lest it should detract from their own reputation or draw ridicule upon their kindred. We hope however a change is commencing, & that the day is not far distant when the hoe & the axe will give place to the wheel & the distaff, & the men will exchange the war club & tomahawk for the implements of husbandry. Already a good beginning as we hope has been made, six women have woven a few yards each & 20 including a number of girls have learned to spin.

Mon eve, May 4

This evening as we sat at our little mission band have as we fondly hope visited with the Christian native land & the whole world in petitions for the enlargement of Christ's kingdom. At such times it is natural for the inquiries to arise how our monthly concerts at home regarded by those who profess to love our blessed Savior. Are they becoming more fully attended than they often used to be? Could we feel assured that they were witnesses of more interest in the world's conversion, of more importunate prayer in behalf of the perishing heathens, our hearts would rejoice with exceeding joy. But the remembrance of the thinly attended monthly concerts, & the cold formal prayers sometimes leads me to fear that God's people are not yet fully awake to duty. Oh that we could all feel that we are not our own, that we are bought with a price, the precious blood of the Lamb.

Sat. eve, May 23

It is now seven months since the date of your last letter received by us.... We have scarcely anything to write except exhibitions of the folly and superstition — and wickedness of this heathen people. They seem more determined this spring than heretofore, to hold fast to their superstitions. Two weeks ago this evening they made a *wakan* dance and feast. As it was at night, we could not witness their wonderful feats in killing each other with the "medicine sack," and coming to life again. They have lately commenced dancing what they call "no flight dance," the object of which is to prevent flight in battle. A few days ago I witnessed this dance for a short time. It did not then differ materially from their common dances for food. Most of them were boys, stripped naked except their breechcloths, with their bodies painted and their heads ornamented with feathers, and in their hands a stick of rattles. I asked a young man whether it was true that those who thus covenanted together did not flee in battle. He said it was not. They all fled, notwithstanding, very rarely one that stood his ground.

Fort Snelling June 19

This date may surprise you, but here we are with Messrs. Ponds, who are now residing near the Garrison in consequence of the removal of their band of Indians from Lake Calhoun & waiting for their location. We left Lac qui Parle June 1 & reached Le Blanc's the Sat. following, having enjoyed as pleasant a journey across the prairie as we could ex pect, or hope. Perhaps you will think me less courageous than formerly when I tell you I chose to walk rather than ride through some of the swamps & small streams. We rested on the Sabbath at Le Blanc's, but were some disturbed in the afternoon by the Indians playing ball, & in the evening, by those dancing near us. We had hoped to find a barge, but we could not even procure an Indian canoe. With no other alterna-tive, we mounted our horses on Monday with no other saddles than our baggage. Mine was a buffalo robe & blanket fastened with a trunk strap, but Mr. R. was not as well furnished. My spirits sank within me as I gave over little Isabella to an Indian woman to carry perched up on her blanket behind, & I clung to my horse's mane as we ascended & de-scended the steep hills, & thought a journey of 70 miles by land was before us.

I rode nearly 10 miles & then walked a short distance to rest myself, at the place where our company were taking a lunch. There, to our great joy, a Frenchman exclaimed "le grand canoe, le grand canoe," & we found that the Indian who had been commissioned to search, had found & brought it down the river thus far. I gladly exchanged my seat for one in the canoe with two Indian women & Mr. Renville's daughter, husband proceeding on horseback. Our progress was quite comfortable though slow, as some of our party were invited to Indian lodges to feast occa-sionally, while the rest of us were sunning by the river bank. On the fourth day we had an addition to our little party. The woman at the helm said she was sick, so we went on shore, perhaps half or 3/4 of an hour on account of the rain, & when it ceased, she was ready with her infant, which was born in the interval, to step into the canoe & con-tinue rowing, although she did not resume her seat in the stern until the next morning. This is a specimen of Indian life.... About a mile & a half below the fort on the west of the Mississippi, a Dakota man & his wife were killed, as is supposed by Chippewas. The man & woman were ascending the river, bringing bark home for their house on the St. Peters, a few miles above. The report of guns was heard & examination made. The bodies were found scalped & disfigured but the perpetra-tors had made safe their retreat. Their trail was discovered, but the Sioux were afraid to pursue them far, fearing there might be a large war party in ambush, as these were so daring as to cross the Mississippi & commit such a deed so near the Fort in mid day. A steamboat has arrived by which we send this letter. Do write often.

Banks of the St. Peters, July 2, Thurs. morn, 10 o'clock
My dear Mother,
A few moments since we were gliding up the St. Peters as fast as our bark canoe & oars would carry us. Now our baggage is laid upon the bank & our frail bark turned upon the sand. You will surmise the truth, a snag caught the canoe which our Frenchmen are now repairing with birch bark, gum & willow. These canoes, which are made by the Chippawas & other eastern tribes, are truly a specimen of skill, & were we to judge this in comparison with the "dug out" canoe of the Sioux, we should be obliged to acknowledge the latter as holding a lower place in savageism. True the bark one is more frail, but it is peculiarly suited to imperfect water navigation. For example, yesterday when crossing the rapids, our canoe was unladen & then, without the least difficulty, carried over & notwithstanding our delays in consequence of its frailty, we have as yet made good progress, being more than half way to Traverse des Sioux from Fort Snelling which we left on Thursday morning. Sister Henrietta, could she see us in our canoe, would like a seat. It is more than 20 feet long, & near the middle, is sufficiently wide for two persons, so that with my babe I am much more comfortable than when descending the river. In the "dug out" there was no room to move, scarce an inch to the right or left.

This kind of canoe is made with ribs about 2 inches wide and half an inch thick which are bent round from one side to the other and placed about three inches apart. Over them is a kind of very thin lathing placed close together, running lengthwise of the canoe, and over all this the birch bark is placed, one piece being sewn to another with a kind of osier, and the seams pitched over with gum which, in the absence of a better way, may be made as shoemaker's wax of rosin and tallow. The bark is sown to the side rails, which are formed of two slender pieces of cedar and wrapped tightly with the same kind of willow. Thus there is not a particle of iron about it.

July 4, Traverse des Sioux

The canoe we have praised so highly in the foregoing failed us about 5 miles below this place, in consequence of not having a supply of gum to mend a large rent made by a snag early this morning. Not thinking it was quite so far, I chose to try walking, husband carrying Isabella, the Frenchman having hastened on to find our horses to bring up the baggage. We reached the river & found there was no boat here with which to cross. Mr. Riggs waded with Isabella, [five months old], the water being about 2 1/2 feet deep, & an Indian woman came to carry me over to where our horses were brought up. Husband mounted without any saddle & I, quivering like an aspen, seated myself behind clinging so tightly that I feared I should spill us both from our horse. I do not think it was fear, at least not entirely, for I am still exceedingly fatigued & dizzy, but I have reason to be grateful that I did not fall into the river from faintness, as husband thought I was in danger of doing. I am so exhausted & lame that it is with pain that I walk across the room. Isabella's face is near to blistered & mine almost as brown as an Indian's. We do not forget that this is the anniversary of our country's independence, though we have been so far removed from 4th of July scenes that we think little of them. Husband says, tired & worn out as we are, he cannot write even "limpingly," but if you could see us you would think we both limped. Love & remembrance to all. Grandpa'a of course.

Lac qui Parle Mission, July 27, 1840
My dear Parents,

.... Now the repetition of that parental injunction "Mary do be careful of your health," recalled your watchful case most forcibly. How often have I heard those words, & perhaps too often deemed necessary for my highest welfare. And even now were it not that the experience of a few more years may correct my present notions about health, I should be so unfashionable as to affirm that necessary exposures such as sleeping on the prairie in a tent drenched with rains, & walking some two or three miles in the dewy grass when the water would gush from the shoes at every step, & then continuing our walk until they were more than comfortably dry, as we did on the morning our canoe failed us in ascending

the St. Peters, are not as injurious to health as the unnecessary exposures of fashionable life. And perhaps even less so than the sickly fear of
wind rain & snow. The query has sometimes arisen in my mind should I
not have possessed a greater capability of endurance, if my early discipline had been more severe. I think I hear your reply, "You would have
been in the grave ere this, had it not been for the vigilant & restraining
care that with God's blessing preserved your life in childhood." And
sometimes I feel a strong conviction that it would have been thus, having often seen that a Heavenly Father even in the events of my own life
has so caused some circumstances of trial & discipline to precede
others, that they seemed to have been in kindness intended to fit me for
subsequent scenes. At other times I feel I am ashamed to say almost
impatient that I cannot endure more hardship & perform more labor
with less fatigue.

Lac qui Parle Mission, Sept. 12, 1840
My dear Parents,
    Mr. Riggs left home on the long desired exploring tour to the river
Missouri on the 2nd inst. & may be from home six or seven weeks.
    He was accompanied by Mr. Huggins. They were expecting to pro-
ceed slowly with a party of Indians going out on a Buffalo hunt a part of
the distance, after which a guide was to travel with them as rapidly as
they wished. . . .

Tues. eve, Sept. 22
    The children are again in bed but not asleep. They are very pleasant
company during their father's absence. A. is learning to read slowly. He
does not give his mind to it, & I fear will not be able to read much in the
bible his great grandfather has sent him, should it reach us this fall, which
is barely possible. We have just received letters from Boston, stating
that through mistake the box did not leave there until July 1st. So I
hope it will yet come safely. Although we are enjoying many blessings,
both temporal & spiritual, yet the native members of our little church
are not without afflictions. Two of the youngest members who are mothers have been called to part with their babes in one instance an only

child, & both of them during the absence of their husbands on a war party into the Chippawa country. But thanks be to him who is Lord of Hosts, they returned without a single scalp. This is the third unsuccessful war party including Wamdiokiya's, at the time they killed our cattle, within a little more than a year. Their want of success some of them are ready to attribute to the influence of the mission, & even request us not to pray against them. Others say they could not kill Chippewas, they suppose, because there are missionaries among them & consequently the Chippewas will not be able to kill the Sioux, should they come here. We have enjoyed the luxury of fruit this summer to an extent we have never before in this country. We raised some very good melons & there have been wild plums in abundance. Twice I have enjoyed a ride of about four miles & once the pleasure of seeing once more trees laden with fruit. The first time I think we brought home a bushel & a half—the last was after they had fallen to the ground & many of them decayed, of course. The late frosts usually destroy them & this is the only season in five years in which they have been abundant.

Thurs. eve

Some of the Indians have just killed a fine calf for us. It was found nicely jointed & cut up ready for packing by some boys who came & gave information. It has most of it been brought home (a few choice pieces had been taken) but having lain so long exposed to the sun & flies, it is doubtful whether it is of much value. But such things do not move me as they did at the time the enraged war party were threatening. . . . I know not that I mentioned a young horse having been stolen from the mission by some roving *Warpakutes*, a band of Dakotas. If the prediction about the *Itonawa* stealing the horses Mr. R. & H. took with them we should have none left but good old Kate to go down to the Traverse. We have oxen however & if they are spared they can do our carting over the prairie. . . .

Mon. eve

The day following we saw Indian women packing by putrid meat which on examination proved to be another of our calves shot at the same time with the first which was brought home.

Home, Wed., Sept. 23, 1840
Dear brother Alfred,

. . . . . You have of late written us much less faithfully than formerly. Thus I lose one by one of my hearts correspondents. In this case I hope we shall not eventually be losers. I hope the reverse for I am anticipating a letter from a new friend—a perfect specimen of letter writing, neat, elegant & full of soul. I should love to receive such a testimonial of affection—it might be beneficial to myself, for most of my correspondents have rather a tendency to make me contented with a lower standard than I once was. Just before husband left home he completed a Sioux vocabulary of 5450 words, which kept him closely occupied a little more than a month when he was not assisting at the hay. . . . I tried to dissuade him from it during the hot weather, but when he commences anything he can take no rest until it is accomplished. . . . It is really a neat pretty volume. . . . I should love to bind it as neatly while he is absent, *tuka awakitpani* (but I am unable). This is a trait in husband's character which I hope will enable him to accomplish something for God in the moral waste. If he does not ruin his health by too close study, as yet it has not suffered much. As far as health is concerned, we certainly seem to enjoy peculiar blessings. Who would have supposed when we were children— that a pale sickly girl, coughing wheezing girl would have become healthiest of the group, & yet it is I suppose so. At least your last letter led me to this conclusion. . . .

I have written the last half page as its appearance indicated, alternating taking the pen for a moment & laying it aside to attend to the wants of little Alfred or Isabella. Now A. is sweetly asleep & Bella lying quietly smiling herself to the same region of forgetfulness. But I have other letters that must be written before next Monday, besides having to do the work we used to do in New England early in the week, in consequence of the failure of my washerwoman. Sometimes they work very cheerfully for us & then again, if we have it not in our power to pay them just as they wish, they think the favor they confer upon us can scarcely be canceled & although we are conscious of paying them well and are very careful about our arrangements with them, they sometimes think we deceive them.

. . . It requires patience — much patience.

Lac qui Parle, Nov. 10, 1840
My dear Mother,

For several days past we have all been suffering with influenza & husband is still quite ill, & I am fatigued too much to write more, but I could not let my birthday pass without some record for the eye of her whom I thank our God was given me for my own dear mother. Good night mother, good night father, grandpa'a, brothers, sisters all, though you cannot hear my voice a birthday kind good night.

Mon. eve, Nov. 16

. . . . Sat. eve came, & as husband was still ill & it was not certain that the Indians had returned, no one went to Mr. Renville's, so that our letters might not be an interruption or an encroachment on the Sabbath, supposing Mr. R. would bring them down on coming to church. As I have sometimes felt doubtful about reading those which have repeatedly come to hand on the Sabbath, I felt a desire these might reach us on a week day, still sanguine in my expectations that we should at least receive half a doz. letters. As I had wished the "precious packet" was forgotten & not brought at the morning service, but in the evening was brought home by the members of the mission who attend meeting Sab. eve at Mr. Renville's house. I looked early for my share, but not one letter from New England was there.

Thurs. eve, Dec. 10

Since our last date we have been tried both with afflictions & miseries. A week this evening our little Alfred seemed on the confines of eternity. The night previous he had a high fever attended with diarrhea, but in the morning he said he was "big well & little sick." At breakfast however, he ate nothing, notwithstanding his favorite rarity "white bread" was on the table & afterward took a dose of rhubarb. About ten A.M. he left my rocking chair, where I had pillowed him up & fastened the rockers, just as you, my dear mother used to fix our easy chair for me when I was sick, & asked his father to take him on his knee, where he sat but a short time when he was seized with convulsions, which Dr. Williamson pronounced an attack of Epilepsy. You, my dear parents who have seen birds from your own household snapped & withered in a day, can realize our feelings as mutely we gazed upon our firstborn, or raised our hearts to him who so suddenly, so unexpectedly had stricken us. I think I felt submission, indeed it seemed to me I dared not feel other-wise & if by touching life's pendulum, which was vibrating so uncer-tainly, I could have decided between life & death, I could not have presumed to raise a finger. After a second paroxysm about three in the afternoon, the fever sunk & the next day he was evidently recovering & is now nearly well. He has not yet, however, had for some weeks past that healthy countenance he used to have. We hope by close attention to his diet with our Heavenly Father's blessing, he may be fully restored to health, though we know not how long any of us are to be spared. Loss of sleep watching with Alfred & the excitement occasioned by his distressing illness, which wound up the nervous system too high for sleep when the danger was over, produced such a reaction on my frail strength, which for some time past had been too greatly tasked to leave any in reserve, that I was prostrated for several days, though I did not suffer much severe pain. Isabella, too, participated with me in the ef-fects of my illness, losing her accustomed food, she was also quite un-well. But God in his great mercy has so far restored us all that we can declare his kindness & sing his praise.

Lac qui Parle, Fort Snelling PO, Upper Mississippi, Jan 20, 1841
Dear brothers T and J,
    Perhaps you will be surprised to receive a letter from us when you are so remiss in writing.... We suppose Harrison is elected, & pray that his administration may be as prosperous as his friends anticipate, but it is with feelings of deep regret that I read accounts of the popular excite-ment — party enthusiasm & expensive pageantry that have attended his election. I think the friends of temperance have dishonored them-selves & the cause by following in the train of "Hard Cider" even though

it was but an empty barrel. I am ashamed to think there is so little of moral principle in our native land, as to require rousing & enlisting by "Log Cabins" "Buckeye poles" & "Cider barrels" for watchwords & songs. I am grieved too, to find in the midst of such "hard times," such a reckless waste in useless trappings, of that at conventions, of that which might have supplied many perishing heathen with the bread of life. I suspect the expenses of the Bunker Hill convention alone would exceed the annual expenditures of the A.B.C.F.M.

The query has also arisen whether my own dear father & his family have not devoted more, including time etc., to Harrison's election than to benevolent objects? I hope God has not been robbed to place Harrison in the Presidential chair, but I fear he has, & if so can we expect a blessing as a nation? Have not the people forgotten that it is God that setteth up one & pulleth down another, & felt that they by their own strength were to rule a nation's destiny? . . . Our schools are crowded & some are making rapid progress — others can do so little about instruction that it is trying to try & teach them. Eight women & girls have woven themselves flannel short gowns this winter & three are weaving blankets. The youngest who spun the filling & wove a short gown, I suppose was not over 13, & the oldest perhaps 38. Your little niece Isabella is 11 months old, but she still prefers "all fours" in her races over the room after Alfred, who usually likes to play better without her troublesome assistance. We hope he will become less selfish & love his little sister's company as much as she seems to his.

Lac qui Parle, Feb. 24, 1841
My dear Parents,

As has frequently been the case we received a packet of letters from Fort Snelling last Sab. eve. . . . The bearers of our precious packet brought up whiskey to purchase horses from the Indians, & though but few at this village own one, they found those who were willing to exchange as they wished, & intend returning tomorrow. . . .

Last Sabbath was Isabella's birthday. She does not walk yet, nor even stand alone & seems rather afraid to test her strength, although she has been a healthy child for which we have cause for gratitude. But this was not our only, our principal cause of joy on last Sabbath. Five adults received the baptismal rite preparatory to the celebration of the Lord's Supper on next Sabbath. One of these was a man, the first in this nation a full blooded Sioux, that has desired to renounce all for Christ. . . . Three years since he was examined by the church session, but then he acknowledged that the 6th & 7th commandments were too broad in their restrictions for him. Now he professes a desire & determination to keep them also. His wife, whom he is willing to marry, with her child & three children by two other wives he has had, stood with him & at the same time received the seal of the new covenant. As they all wished English names we gave "Hetta" to a white, grey eyed orphan girl, who was baptized on account of her grandmother who has adopted her. . . .

Little Alfred often speaks of the bible that his great grandfather sent him that is coming on in a box. Our hopes are strong that we shall see it in the Spring. A. is learning to read pretty fast, in proportion to the time we can spend teaching him. I admire the persevering energy manifested by grandpa'a's widowed mother in teaching her children to read. With a family dependent upon her, it would have required no small amount of energy & pains to have performed her duty so well.

Last week on Wednesday quite a farce was played here. One of our pupils, a young woman of 20 perhaps who had been neglected by a former husband in consequence of his taking another wife, was secretly given by her relatives to another, while reports were in circulation that "Fearfulface," the hero of my story, was too much of a coward to resent it. With natural impetuosity & bravery, ignoring all danger, he went to the lodge where she was secreted & while her relatives & those of her new husband sat around, dragged her forth to the tent of one of his relatives. Magnanimously, in the morning he at first determined to make a feast & call his rival & give to him his wife. But hearing that his other wife was to be taken from him, he declared he would take vengeance upon his unfaithful spouse by cutting off a piece of her nose &c, as is the custom in such cases, but yielding to the entreaties of his mother, he desisted. Taking his bow & arrows, he went & killed a horse belonging to her sister that stood in sight of the camp & then, calling the name of his rival with a loud voice, repeated several times, "If you are a man, come here." From motives of safety he did not make his appearance. As night drew on all the relatives of "Fearfulface" expected their horses would be killed in retaliation. His brother brought his to our stable for secretion. At this moment the discharge of fire arms was heard & we supposed an attack might have been made. The children fled in conster' nation to Mr. Huggins & the women were screaming. As it was dark it was not thought safe to venture to their tents while the commotion lasted, but all becoming quiet, Mr. Huggins & Mr. Riggs went & learned that a young man who was connected with both parties had attempted to kill himself in consequence, it was said, of Fearfulface, his particular friend wishing him to aid in avenging his cause. This served as a quiet' ing & as the contents of the pistol passed above the head no harm was done. This is the fifth Sioux here who has attempted, or pretended to attempt suicide since we have resided at Lac qui Parle. We have had remarkably mild weather during most of February. Several days so warm that sufficient fire to boil a tea kettle in the afternoon caused us to raise a window for cool air. Quite in contrast with the thermometer below zero in our room as it was several mornings in January.

Mission House, Lac qui Parle, Sat. eve, March 27, 1841
My dear Parents,

Can it even interest mother to know that I have become such a prac' tical housewife & chemist that I can transform lye & grease into good soap! & that the Indian women & girls have been so busily engaged at their sugar camps during the week now closing, as to afford me time to experiment in the laboratory of the kitchen? Until this the seasons for sugar making have been very unfavorable since we have resided here. But this spring the Indians brought us a little maple sugar which, after melting and thawing was excellent, & forcibly reminded us of "home sugar." Sugar is a luxury for which these poor women are willing to toil hard & often with but a small recompense. Their camps are frequently two or three miles from their lodges. If they move the latter they must also pack corn for their families, & if not, with little in hand they go to their camps, toil all day, & often at night return with the syrup, or sugar, & a back load of wood for their husbands' use during the next day. Sugar is to them a dear & hard earned luxury. But they have others also, which they sometimes offer us, such as muskrats, beaver's tails, & tortoises. I have never tried rat, but husband says they are as good as polecats, another delicacy. Beaver's tails are said to command a high price in London market, ranking with Buffalo's tongues, which are also exported by The Hudson's Bay Company, but I was not pleased with the trial we made of one last winter. And for tortoises, who would think of eating such frightful, loathsome looking creatures? So I thought last summer while we were traveling on the prairie, when I saw the Indians putting the smaller kind, the common mud turtle, alive, into a kettle for boiling. As the water grew uncomfortably warm, the poor sufferer tried to escape, but one stood watching with his knife to push back the head or paws until it ceased writhing. After the feast was over, & we had all again started, among other things which a black Indian dog was packing, I saw the poor turtle shell that had been saved for a dish. But notwithstanding all this, a part of a well dried & properly killed tortoise found its way to our table not long afterward, & had it not been for unpleasant associations that I could not overcome, I should have pronounced it good. The external appearance of a live tortoise would lead me to class it with "unclean animals." Not so with the swan, & I was rather surprised, on reading again what I had forgotten, that the white & graceful swan was included in the list of unclean birds recorded in Leviticus 11.

Monday, May 5

May has come again, but has brought no flowers & green fields. Smiling & frowning, April has left the earth & trees as bare & desolate almost as she found them. The poor birds that came back to their summer home those warm sunny days in March & early in April, have since then repeatedly "found no place for the sole of their feet," except the cold pure snow, but soon we hope they will have green branches & trees for shelter & home. And our little ones will I think sing & rejoice with them. Alfred loves to be out in the air, gamboling like a lamb, but repeated snows have obligated me to confine him very much as he has worn out his only shoes, & moccasins are little better than nothing when the ground is wet.

Tues. May 13

For the last few days Mr. Riggs has been busily engaged in preparing, with the help of some of the native church members, the foundation of a building we hope will be erected this season. It is designed to answer a twofold purpose of church & school house. During the week the two rooms will be separated by folding doors which are to be thrown open on the Sabbath & will probably be built of unburnt brick, as timber for building is very scarce & difficult to be obtained here. Contrary to Sioux custom, which makes it a disgrace for a man to dig or till the ground, the two men mentioned above have been quite active in the work. Most of the female members of the church have also helped a part of the day & several more. Others have showed their indifference by neglecting to accept our invitation to work even half a day, & partake of dinner afterwards. This has been something of a trial to my faith & patience although I cannot but hope God will aid & bless all our efforts to rear a house to his praise. . . .

Not long since our washerwoman, in consequence of my reproving her daughter for eating some of our chickens that had been stolen, stayed away from meeting two Sabbaths, coming to wash regularly in the meantime. For her first absence she made some trifling excuse in reply to my inquiry, but after fulfilling her vow as I suppose, she said she was angry with me & so she did not attend meeting for two Sabbaths. I told her that she had offended Him & not me by disobeying His command. I also asked her why she came to wash if she was so angry, but I knew though she did not say it, that she was afraid of losing her place if she should revenge in such a way, & thus she would suffer more than I should from the effects of her anger.

Thurs. May 19

I shall endeavor to present before you your little grandchildren. Perhaps the scene which would amuse you most would be "the babies morning ride." The little wagon in which Isabella & my namesake M. L. Huggins are drawn by the older children, even Alfred ambitious to assist, would be in complete contrast with the royal princess cradle, yet I doubt not it affords them as much pleasure as a more elegant one would.

Alfred's was made by his father & Hetta, Henrietta's namesake, an Indian girl living at Mr. Huggins constructed a canopy, which gives it a tasteful though somewhat rude appearance. Mrs. Williamson's son John draws his sister in a wagon of his own, so that the whole troop of 10 little ones with their carriages form a miniature pleasure party. Isabella is quite short still. Now nearly 15 months, but runs under the table with impunity. She manifests an irritable temperament as she grows older. We thought her a very mild babe. She is good natured still, excepting when the trait to which I have alluded betrays itself. I find daily the need of patience, great patience to govern & train our little ones aright. On one hand are rocks, on the other quick sands. It cheers me to think their grandmother cares for them & prays for them & their mother. I think Isabella's irritability may be partly owing to teething.

Lac qui Parle, April 28, 1841
Dear brother Alfred,

Your letter presented to my "mind's eye" our mountain home. I entered the lower gates, passed up the lane between the elms, maples & cherries & saw once more our mountain home embowered by the fir trees & shrubbery I loved so well. How many times have I watched the first buddings of those rosebushes & lilacs, & with what care & delight have I nursed those snowballs, half dreaming they were sister spirits telling by their delicate purity of that Eden where flowers never fade & leaves never wither. Perhaps I was too passionately fond of flowers—if so, it is sufficiently blunted, if not subdued. Not a solitary shrub, tree or flower rears its head near our dwelling, excepting those of nature's planting at no great distance on the opposite side of the St. Peters, & a copse of plums in a dell on the left & of scrub oak on the right. Back of us is the hill, which shelters us from the furious wind of the high prairie beyond. Until last season we have had no enclosure, & now we have but a poor defense against the depredations of beasts & still more lawless & savage men. . . .

Little Bella already creeps to her father, & if granted a seat upon his knee, folds her little hands, although, as Alfred says, "She does not wait till papa says Amen."

Sat. July 3

I have delayed answering your query respecting the new emotions &
responsibilities exacted by having become with another, one flesh, that
I might feel more at leisure than I usually do when I take the pen. But I
am now less so than usual & probably ere this, your experience may
have superseded the necessity of my giving you a leaf from ours. If so
you have realized the meaning of those passages of scripture which por-
tray the nearness of the marriage relation, & have also felt a peculiar
beauty & power in those in which the cherished is spoken of as the bride,
"the Lamb's wife." What love, what condescension is manifested by such
endearing, though figurative comparisons? I suppose you have hardly
found how much of conscience is mingled with your ideas of a married
state. You will find real life much the same that you have ever found, &
with additional joys, additional cares & sorrows. I have realized as much
happiness as I anticipated, though many of my bright visions have never
been realized, & others have been much changed both in outline & finishing. For instance our still winter evenings are seldom enlivened by
reading, while I am engaged lulling our little ones or plying my needle.
Although I should greatly enjoy such a treat even occasionally, I cannot,
in our situation, expect it, while it is often almost the only time husband
can secure for close & uninterrupted study.

You know the time of a missionary is not his own. I might multiply
instances similar to this, but it is unnecessary. In sickness, perhaps more
than at any other time, we feel there is no romance in our circumstances.
Instead of the exquisite pleasure of alleviating the pain & weariness of a
sick companion, you are worn out by the additional burden thrown upon
you, & have barely strength to perform necessary duties, leaving undone those acts of kindness & delicate attentions that throw such a
charm over the sick chamber, & tend to alleviate the weariness & con-
finement, if not the pain occasioned by disease. I had hoped husband
would have time at hand to write, but his heart is bent upon helping
erect a building for a church & school rooms this summer, & "Whatever his hands find to do, he does it with all his might." He is in the
brickyard today as Mr. Huggins is absent....

An Indian man who joined our church last winter has worked at the brick regularly for a month notwithstanding the ridicule & abuse that is heaped upon him by men & women, "for being the slave of white men." We do hope he is truly a Christian. Pray that God will sustain him & make him a "burning & shining light." He has apparently quite a desire to lead others to Christ & God is able to make him instrumental in the salvation of his tribe. Should husband go on to superintend some printing in Sioux next summer, we should wish to see as many of our friends as consistent. I say we for I cannot think of staying here alone, & I hope some way will be opened for my going, without expense to the Lord.

Lac qui Parle Mission, June 14, 1841
My dear Mother,
I cannot express our joy on the arrival of the long & anxiously looked for box. We thank the generous contributors, & we thank God that our hearts have been gladdened by so many tokens of affection for us & love for our work. We were happily disappointed in finding every article uninjured. Notwithstanding the time that had intervened, owing to your care in packing & the providence of Him who remembered even the hair of our head, neither mildew nor moth had tarnished the valuable contents of the precious donations from Hawley & S. Deerfield. . . . Thank them for us individually. I suppose owing to an intimation that grandpa'a had given little Alfred a bible, we inferred it would be forth coming in the long expected box, and raised his expectations exceedingly.

Immediately on its reception he asked for his bible. As it was nearly his bedtime, I told him to go to rest & he would awake early & then he should have the bible his great-grandpa'a had sent him. He went to sleep, but we searched in vain for the expected treasure. Anticipating it would be a sad disappointment to Alfred, unless a substitute was provided, I selected for him a small testament hoping it would satisfy his expectations. On awaking in the morning his first inquiry was, "Where is my bible, I want my bible." I told him the bible did not come, but here is a pretty testament your papa gives Alfred. "Did it come on?" he rejoined & with my answer yes. He seemed satisfied, & pleased with the little testament, although it is too fine print for him to read readily at present. I hope he will soon be able, though we do not teach him as frequently & systematically as I could wish.

Owing to the relaxing influence of the weather or some other cause, my health has not been quite as good as usual for a few weeks past. Still I hope I shall not neglect Alfred, as I am in danger of doing in consequence of the various duties devolving upon me & the interruptions to which I am exposed by the habits of this people.... Late newspapers or rather those lately arrived apprise us of the death of Harrison, though we did not receive them until past the time appointed for a day of fasting & prayer....

Lac qui Parle, Oct. 2, 1841
Dear Mother,

Your letter mailed from Hawley Aug. 9th with one from brother Moses mailed at Oberlin Aug. 4th reached us this morning. As a specimen of the petty vexations to which we are often subject from this selfish people, I will mention one connected with the transportation of our letters. These Indians here know nothing of the value of money, many of them feeling as one of them who remarked that "If we had a handful of small money he would throw it away." And although we have often paid them more than the ordinary postage in the states, they apparently feel not half rewarded. Perhaps they were 20 days they say coming from the Fort & Frenchmen are allowed a dollar a day. Their own bill is in round numbers $20 for bringing a small packet of letters & newspapers. The one which reached us today was less expensive, but the circumstances connected with it occasioned more unpleasant feelings than usual.

An Indian brave, to whom a cart had been lent by the mission with the condition that he should bring up our packet of news, reached home day before yesterday without any. He had apparently avoided calling on the Messrs. Pond for the bundle, & his brother, who did call with much hesitation, consented to take it, but passed it over to some Red River travelers who lost it on their way up, & pretended they had forgotten it at the trading post at Traverse des Sioux. It was found & consigned to the son of a chief who arrived with the party whom we supposed would bring us good news from a far country. But when it was called for this proud heir of a beggar's throne, refused to deliver it unless we would give him, in return, our faithful watch dog, Jacko. The manner as much as the request demanded it to be declined, & he, thinking to force sub-mission, kept the packet until it was called for the third time by Mr. Riggs, who went with witnesses to offer him the full amount of postage & if he refused intending to state it to the agent & have the loss deducted from his annuity. But happily no such course was necessary, he pretended that he was only sporting & gave up the packet at once, after keeping us in suspense a day & night. I did not intend occupying so much space with this but my power of abridgment seems to have failed me. It will be in vain if you look for us in New England this year. Husband has a hard winter's work before him, ere the books which we hope to get printed will be in readiness for the press, & there are two very good reasons why he could not complete his preparations in Mass. One, that you have no Dakotas there who could correct them, & an-other is, I fear, he would find his time as much interrupted by callers there as here. You would be rather more polite than are our unceremo-nious visitors, & perhaps for that reason, it would be more difficult to find time or inclination to shut ones self up to hard study in the midst of friends unseen for years. Here in an emergency we can fasten our door & without telling that fashionable "white lie" that we are "not at home," secure an hour from intrusion, if not from interruption. Henrietta hopes we shall bring our little ones, but the expense & inconvenience of trav-eling with children is so great, that we have thought it probably would be best to leave one or both with Ohio friends. I should feel unwilling to defray their traveling expense to Mass. with the funds of the Board unless we expected to leave them there. Indeed the happiness I should hope to enjoy in once more seeing sweet sweet home & its loved ones, would be lessened by the thought that I was thus depriving some famishing heathen of "the bread of life." It is unpleasant to beg especially for one's self, still I cannot but hope we shall not need to draw greatly from the fund of the Board on my account.

Mon. eve, Oct. 11

In your last letter, sister L. mentioned that Mrs. Wheat might perhaps be willing to take as her own one of our children. I almost fear I have not moral courage & firmness enough to resign one of our little ones at so tender an age to the parental care of another. The thought that they would scarcely remember their own parents, & that their adopted ones would secure the affections which should be ours, is extremely painful. And the idea that they will call any one else mother is peculiarly so. When it first occurred to me I was busily engaged at work, & for a few moments I could not restrain the gushing tears, but now I can think of it a little more composedly, though I should still love to retain exclusively to myself the title to which God has given me claim. The Dakota custom of calling all their mothers' sisters *Ina*, "mother" & their fathers' brothers *Ate* "father" never pleased me. And I think the effect upon the children bad. It nullifies the authority of the true parents & weakens their poor attempts to maintain family government, in proportion to the number of *Ate* & *Ina*'s that must be consulted & obeyed.

Alfred L. R. is learning to read without spelling, & it evidently affords him great satisfaction to be able to master the short words. I often tell him he must learn to read before he goes to Ohio (of which all the children love to talk as the Utopia of their day dreams) that he may be able to read in the New Testament to his grandmother. He often talks of his grandparents & sometimes of enlarging our table that you may eat with us.

Isabella is rather ill this week in consequence of cutting teeth, I suppose, & very troublesome. For two evenings past I have taken my pen after she was asleep hoping to write, but her disturbed rest has obliged me to lay aside the paper. And during the day I have accomplished little else than the most pressing ordinary duties. Owing to the partial failure of the corn crop, more of these Indians have left on a fall hunt than is usual. Among the number is the woman who has washed for us nearly three years. I think it would have been far better for her to have remained at home & economized in the use of her corn, & helped clothe her family more comfortably by her industry, but she thought otherwise. Although in present circumstances it was unpleasant for me to part with her, not knowing what I could obtain, yet I am already provided for and feel that I ever shall be. This, I am aware, is very far from being a good missionary letter—but I have no cheering news to write.

As far as most of the Indians are concerned I could only tell you of theft. We were obliged to pull our half grown turnips to secure any share for ourselves. Our potatoes were taken by bushels. Still we have a plenty both to eat & exchange for corn, of which we raised none this year in consequence of the care it requires to prevent the blackbirds from stealing it all. Perhaps I should not say stealing as they only take what they eat in the field & this was not accounted theft in ancient time. We give two bushels of potatoes for one of corn. Pa'a, I suppose, would like to exchange thus. This would have seemed more fair to me had I known only the comparative volume of potatoes & corn on Hawley hills. The greatest loss that we have met with as a family theft was a fine little patch of melons just ripening which husband had cultivated with peculiar care. Our vines were nearly stripped in one night & all our fair anticipation blasted most suddenly. I endeavored to console myself by thinking that we were much happier still than the thieves, & that perhaps we might have indulged our appetites too much had all of our fine melons been spared to us. Little Alfred felt the loss as severely I suppose as Hetta did that of her rabbit. I have scarcely room to beg a kind remembrance to all that are dear to us.

Oct. 7, 1841
Dear Sister Riggs,
    Please get a plain bonnet suitable for me to wear on the Sabbath during our journey, if we go east. A plain straw would suit my taste, but perhaps some other kind would be less expensive. You can of course judge best, and I shall feel satisfied with your judgment.

The collar with but little work upon it, is such a one as I wish, and stockings of a quality that will not exceed at most $1. I do not wish to wear articles more expensive than I ought to, or than people will think a missionary's wife should wear, lest it prove a "stumbling block." Whatever others may think however, I wish most of all a clear conscience. It is of little use to apologize for troubling you, when we still intend, while you are willing to perform such favors, to trouble you most of all with ourselves and a troop of little ones. You will do well to treasure up a large share of patience in readiness.

Lac qui Parle, Dec. 10, 1841
My dear Parents,

The last two Sabbaths we have assembled in our new chapel. Only our half is completed, though husband & Mr. Pettijohn have been very diligent & successful. You can scarcely imagine what a task building is in a land where there is such a scarcity of suitable material & men. During the summer great exertions were made to prepare plank, & two men were employed about two months in sawing with a ripsaw. The woods were searched & researched for two & three miles for suitable timber & the result was about 3,200 feet, which is not enough, at an expense of $150. I might mention other hindrances, but notwithstanding them all, the Lord has evidently prospered the work, & our expectations have been fully realized, if our wishes have not.

Most of the Indians from this village have returned from their fall hunt, alarmed & distressed by an attack from the Chippewas. Two Sioux men were killed & two women were wounded, the men mortally. One of the women was a daughter-in-law of one of the former & perhaps saved his life, as he is said after reviving the first man to have placed himself before her saying "I am shot, but I value highly my daughter-in-law."

Mon. eve, Dec. 12

This afternoon Mrs. W., Mrs. H. & myself invited eight old women here to receive their share of a donation in flannel sent by a factory in Ohio to our poor who attend meeting & school. We do not often see such a group. Wrinkles, rags, & dirt, told more eloquently than words their need of charity. To me it was a high source of pleasure to be an almoner of the bounty of others. Could those who bestowed it have seen the cheered countenances of withered old age, & heard the unanimous & hearty *han* (yes) when I told them by whom it was given & that she wished them to wear it themselves & to attend meeting whenever they were able. We thought it necessary to charge them not to give it away, as the old Sioux women seldom wear a comfortable garment long even if they have one given them. Some granddaughter or niece begs it, & they must then give it away of course. I also told them we did not wish them publicly to praise us, as is customary, by singing through the village of the gift & giver, but to thank God. We then sang a hymn in Sioux & as they said they were unable to pray aloud I endeavored to lisp our thanks to the Giver of all good. It is still a trial for me to attempt prayer in their native tongue & I sometimes feel tempted not to try again. My time for the past year has been so engaged with family cares &c, that I have made little sensible progress in learning Sioux, & especially in the language of prayer.

Friday eve, Dec. 17

There are several questions in reference to our little ones that often are suggested by some slight occurrence, & as often lead me to ponder our duty to them as parents & missionaries. One is, what affect will the habits formed in early childhood exert even should they at length find homes among our friends? Another is at what age ought we to give them up, if there could be found suitable persons willing to adopt them & train them up for us & for the Lord?

Such inquiries as these have been suggested this afternoon by Isabella's fondness for "packing." If she has a piece of cloth or paper or picks up a pair of scissors, as if by instinct, she places them on her neck behind, & then tries to fasten them with a pocket handkerchief. If unsuccessful she holds them in place with one hand & parades the room with evident satisfaction. But her favorite pack is the chair cushion you gave me before leaving home. This she holds by the valance with both hands on her breast & the cushion nearly half as large as herself hanging behind. When she commences walking I could not but smile to see her totter along with such a load, but now I am endeavoring to correct the habit, at least of packing the cushion. Mrs. H.'s little daughter of seven years delights to pack her little sister of two, holding her by a blanket as do the Indians. I do not suppose this habit will be as injurious as many I could name, but it shows the influence of "fashion," & you will see by it that our children are in danger of becoming little Indians in their tastes, feelings & habits.

If Alfred should be at home when you receive this there shall be a probability that an answer will reach Fort Snelling early in June. We wish him to state the necessary expenses from Oberlin to Hawley. Should we go east next summer, we have thought of taking the tour home by way of Oberlin, if the expenses of traveling would not exceed those of a Southern route. A. will also please mention at what place passengers on the Ohio canal leave for Oberlin & how far the latter place is from the canal. We do not regard it as certain that we shall see our friends next summer even should our lives be spared, as we have received no answer from the Board, but it is necessary that we should act upon the supposition that we may go & make all necessary preparations. Mr. Riggs is busier than ever in transcribing translations, teaching, preaching etc, & I am, I think as busily engaged as my health will admit, though I have not assisted in teaching thus far this winter. The most that I can hope to accomplish before spring is to finish copying two small tracts for the press, which Mr. Riggs has translated in consequence of my suggestion & promise to prepare them. They are No's 128 & 293 published by the Amer. Tract Soc.

I think it rather probable that we shall leave Isabella here. Brother J. Riggs wrote us to bring our children, intimating that they should not be any expense to the Board. But if God gives him the means & the liberality of heart, perhaps he will be as benevolent if one is left, as he would if both were thrown upon his generosity & consequently something will be saved for the printing of books which we very much need & which I fear the Board will not be able to grant in their present embarrassed state. And for one, I am ready to economize for their sake & the sake of the heathen, though it has never seemed plain to me why Christians in the enjoyment of the privileges & comforts of a civilized land, should expect of their missionaries, who are their representatives & who are necessarily deprived of these greater economy & greater self denial in other things than they are willing to practice themselves. We have talked considerably on relinquishing tea & coffee entirely. Now we drink it in the morning only, & as I have never become convinced that if used temperately it is injurious to health, I should dispense with it as a matter of economy. Hitherto I have justified myself in the use of it by supposing that the fact of our having become missionaries did not make it requisite to deny ourselves every comfort or luxury, when there were so many in which we must necessarily practice self denial. And in this case we have seldom ordered tea or coffee—they have been abundantly donated by friends, sometimes too abundantly, more than we used. . . .

Mon. eve, Dec. 20
This evening Katharine, one of the native church members, called. She has recently abandoned her pipe, though as much addicted to smoking as any other Indian. Not long since she washed for me, & among other things we spoke to her of the habit of smoking. Mr. Riggs told her he thought it injurious & also mentioned that only one animal beside the tobacco worm would eat it, & that many people who were once smokers had relinquished their pipes, & that she, by so doing might save something to send the gospel to the destitute. I perceived that the subject was taking deep hold on her. Suddenly, raising her head while washing, she asked about something which had been said that she did not well remember or quite understand. I remarked to my husband that I should not be surprised if Katharine should abandon tobacco, & the next time I saw her I learned that she had from that day ceased smoking. This is the second instance among our church members. The first which I may have mentioned, was that of Simon, one of the male members of our little church who also, upon Mr. R. suggestion, said decidedly after a few inquiries & a little thought *amdugtan Kta*. (I will stop.) But Katharine is the oldest & was more confirmed in the habit. Her influence will, I think, be greater than Simon's. She says that she has said very much to one old woman, but her reply was "It will make no difference. I shall die soon." I mentioned the circumstance & Katharine asked if my mother still smoked. I told her I thought she did not.

Lac qui Parle, Feb. 26, 1842
My dear Parents,
. . . . Before your letter reached us containing the remark of mother

Clark about taking "the little girl," we had another little daughter added
to our family & had concluded to leave Isabella here with Miss F.
Huggins, as it is probable that we shall return to this region instead of
ascending the Missouri. Our little Martha we shall of course not leave
behind if we are permitted to go east. Alfred, we intend taking with us
only as far as Ohio. . . . Possibly however should our journey be delayed
so long as to require us to take the shortest route, we may bring Alfred
as there will be no relatives with whom to leave him in case we go from
Galena to Chicago. You must have misunderstood us about the length
of time we hoped to spend in Mass. "Our Master's business" requires
diligence & dispatch. If we receive a letter from Boston granting us permission sufficiently seasonably, we hope to see Hawley hills, if Providence permits, by July or August. Mr. Riggs hopes to get a part of the
printing done in Boston, & to be prepared to return west in October or
early in November, as the greater part of the printing will be done in
Cincinnati. It is our wish as much as yours, that we could make such
arrangements as to make the season one of profitable enjoyment, if we
are permitted to revisit home once more I should regret to add to your
cares & labors instead of relieving & lightening them, & trust that my
health will be such that I shall not. I cannot, however wish that Thomas
would seek a wife at present much as you might like her aid. . . .

Tues. eve, April 11

On Saturday last we received the anxiously looked for letter from
Boston, granting our request in reference to the printing of books, &
the consequent visit to Ohio & Mass. May the Lord permit us once
more to see each other face to face & prepare us for the meeting. We
hope now to leave Lac qui Parle on, or near, the 17 of May, but we may
be obliged to make a canoe at LeBlancs, & wait for a steam boat at Fort
Snelling, so that we cannot calculate with any certainty of being able to
go from the latter place before the middle of June, though I hope we
may rather sooner. An agent of the pope has at length reached us here.
For the last two months a priest from Lyons has been residing with Mr.
Renville the trader teaching his family French & enticing his daughters
by his pictures, smiles, etc. Their father was I suppose unaware how

much he was exposing them to be led astray ignorant as they are, by receiving into his family a young & insinuating Romanish priest. We still hope that they are not determined to reject the pure gospel for the traditions of the fathers, & forsake Jesus as an all sufficient Mediator, for saints & angels. I have felt wrong about this matter—almost indignant to think the wolf would force his way into our little fold, & by his sheep's clothing deceive the lambs of the flock. His repeatedly praying to & kissing the virgin almost led me to forget that she was as the mother of our Savior entitled to affectionate respect, so abhorrent is worshipping her to my feelings. The priest called here last week a short time before he left for Fort Snelling—dressed in a singular garb, a cassock perhaps, almost touching the ground & buttoned from "top to bottom." He would be an interesting & intelligent looking man, were it not for the continued squinting & smirking which I have often conjectured concealed the dark designs of Romanish priests. I know not however as they are common characteristics of their countenances, as I have seen very few, but so much apparent servility & levity seem inconsistent with the sacredness of the office as ministers of the gospel of Christ Jesus. I never think of the Apostles as possessing such traits, or of the Reformers of the Puritan fathers. Humble dignity doubtless beamed in their countenances, & calm sobriety masked their demeanor.

Our children enjoy very good health. Martha robs me of strength by her haste in growing. Isabella is a picture of health. Alfred is rather poorer as he runs too constantly to be equally plump as his sister, & for myself—my health is not as good as it has usually been when nursing our other children. I sometimes look upon our proposed journey as a laborious task when I think of our tour to Fort Snelling in 1840, but I would not be excused from attempting it, & I trust the Lord will enable us all to accomplish it with joy.

Lac qui Parle April 13, 1842
Dear sister Henrietta,

This evening an Indian woman brought in a pair of moccasins, her donation towards procuring a small bell for our mission chapel. Some time in 1840 I wrote to a friend in Galena inquiring whether we could dispose of moccasins advantageously there, provided our church members would forward them, & received an encouraging reply. But it was so long in reaching us, that I fear we shall be unable to obtain very many pair. You can easily see that, where families have neither watches nor clocks, a bell or horn or something of the kind is almost necessary. Mr. Huggins made a large wooden horn which has answered a good purpose on still days during the winter, but when the wind was high it could be heard only a short distance. *Anawaangmani*, or Simon, who assisted in building the church last summer, has made rails & is about farming a lot near the mission which he intends cultivating himself!! He is willing to be a byword if his example will be of use in inducing others to do right. I suppose many think he has very much degraded himself by working like a *Woxiann hotixidan* (Canadian French boy). And this may have exerted some influence upon his wife causing her to leave him. Her father's family are very proud & self-righteous & very hostile in their feelings towards the innovations we would make and the doctrines we teach. Last Sabbath afternoon I perceived Simon's tent, or rather his wife's, as the women own the houses here, had been removed & was surprised that he should consent to it. In the evening we learned that his mother & sister-in-law had come & insisted upon his wife's going to live near them, some two miles from his new field, saying there would be danger from the Chippawas &c. Simon made such proposals for safety as he thought consistent, but she left him & two days after sent for their two children, so that he is truly bereaved. I hope his affliction will prove a blessing, indeed I am half inclined to think it an indication that he should prepare himself to be a preacher of the blessed gospel to his tribe. He might perhaps become a Wesley. His remarks, in reference to the departure of his wife, are similar to those Wesley entered in his journal on a similar occasion. "I did not forsake her, I did not dismiss her, & I will not recall her."

    With love,
    Mary Ann Longley Riggs

CHAPTER 4

Mission at Traverse des Sioux

1842-1846

Edmund Longley built this house in 1781 and the Thomas Longley family lived in it until Martha's death in 1858. It was later known as the Longley-rood-bellows house and stood until 1975. The artist Everett Longley Warner, Mary Ann's grandson, made this drawing. He was a member of the Impressionists from the Old Lyme, Connecticut, art colony.

In 1842 Stephen, Mary Ann, Alfred, and Martha journeyed to Hawley, Massachusetts, for the summer, leaving Isabella with Fanny Huggins at Lac qui Parle. The family spent the winter in Ohio, and Stephen attended to the printing of the New Testament in Sioux. While in Hawley, Mary Ann convinced her younger brother, Thomas, to join her family in the west. He drowned shortly after his arrival, and this tragedy permeated Mary Ann's emotional and physical life for the duration of their stay at Traverse des Sioux.

Mary Ann gave birth to her fourth child, Anna Jane, April 13, 1845, attended only by an Indian woman. She continued to teach English, knitting, and sewing.

Taoyaticuta, a chief of Little Crow's requested a preacher of the gospel to live in his village near Lac qui Parle. For a variety of reasons no other missionary was able to respond to this request except Stephen. However, the sacrifice was a difficult one for Mary Ann because she had become attached to her home at Traverse des Sioux. She finally had some basic conveniences which she never had before, and according to Stephen, "She has just gotten things fixed somewhat snugly about the house." In addition they had a small yard where her beloved brother, Thomas, was buried, and where she had planted a vegetable garden, roses, and a cedar tree.

Portsmouth, Ohio, Wednesday, Nov. 15, 1842
Dear Parents,

My husband with his brother Joseph left yesterday for their father's. I am as pleasantly situated as I could expect & if Mr. R could remain here & at the same time be accomplishing his work, it would be as delightful if not more so than I have any right to wish. But when he is separated from us, we are sometimes lonely. . . .

While we were traveling incidents frequently occurred, that I thought might be interesting, but having passed by they seem hardly worth putting on paper. My sympathies were very deeply enlisted in the case of a very decent looking man with his wife and child who had not money to pay his passage to Pittsburgh on the packet. On the Pennsylvania canal many of the line boats are simply for freight & have no cabins or accommodations for passengers. Being ignorant of this he paid for himself & wife on one of these boats, but found them too filthy & uncomfortable to remain upon & left it for the packet. After making the exchange he found his cash would not carry them both to Pittsburgh & he was about making arrangements to send his wife on alone, until some of the gentlemen offered him aid. He was going out as a teacher or lecturer & if he told the truth as he apparently did, he had not a cent left to sustain himself & family until he could get into business!

. . . . Our children are quite well now & I do not regret bringing Martha back with us. May the Lord show us what is our duty to do with them all, & give us hearts to do it.

We found a letter here from Miss Huggins. Isabella was well & a good girl—Very few of the Indians had any corn left when the letter was written. Poor creatures—famishing both for temporal & spiritual bread.

. . . . I am endeavoring to rest here & acquire strength for future labor. I don't mean however that I am not as industrious as ever, for I think it a sin to do nothing. I hope Hetta will always keep plain knitting & sewing at hand. They are no interruption to conversation if not followed too closely, while knitting lace & ornamental needlework require too much attention for animated conversation, excepting some of the less difficult kinds. . . .

There is a female prayer meeting on Sat. afternoon's which bro. J's wife & I attend alternately as we also do other meetings as there are so many young children which need our care.

Portsmouth, Jan. 27, 1843
My dear Brother & Sister, [Alfred & Julia, in Hawley]

My husband has sent me this sheet to finish for you. I fancy while I am seated at a side table in our back parlor with a small fire in the grate, you are sitting quite closely around a large one in the cold north room. I know not that there is much difference in the climate here & in Hawley as I am wont to imagine, but we have not had more than two inches of snow at once during the winter here & that hardly remained long enough for us to see how white & clean was a new snowy carpet. I imagine too you are trying the independent yet somewhat confining life of house-keeping. I presume you have or can have very easily, as many cooking utensils as we had the first winter we kept house, namely a sauce pan, & a stove pan & coffee pot. I washed at home but went abroad to boil my clothes, & when they were rinsed, hung them like tapestry around the low walls. Our cabin was rude & plain, our cheer, still it was home, & there's no place so dear. . . .

Little Alfred is attending Miss Corsel's school. He was very much pleased with your letter. I hope sister J. will find or take time to tran-scribe ma'a's letter containing our account of Grandpa'a's last illness.

Much love to all our friends, but I need not add as I have so long & often done especially to Grandpa'a, "Be of good cheer" looking unto Jesus for guidance.

Galena, May 9, 1843
My dear Parents,

It is so long since I have taken the pen, that there is danger letter writing will be neglected & regarded as a task instead of the pleasure with which I have regarded it even from a child. If I wished to be ex-cused from corresponding with you all, it would not be difficult for one who is traveling with two little ones without a nurse, to find or make an excuse as plausible as some whom I love are not ashamed to offer me.

But I have no wish to be excused. Although I know I must exert un-wanted energy & economize time more carefully. . . . Still you will not suppose that benevolence will prompt me, no it will be its opposite, as I shall be looking for the reward of my labors in the answers I shall receive. . . .

At Ripley, where are a large number of husband's friends, I had no time that I could call my own. The spirit of the Lord had increased their interest in our mission in such a manner that prayer was almost con-tinually offered for us & the poor heathen. In answer to prayer, Miss Julia A. Kephart a member of the Ripley church consecrated her time for the Lord's service among the Indians for a few years. She is the fifth member of the Sioux mission that has been a member of the church in Ripley, Ohio.

Our visit at Sardinia, where Mr. Riggs' parents reside, seemed rather hurried & brief as Presbytery was in session during one week of our stay. I was much gratified with an interview I had with a Rev. Mr. Bardwell, son of the Mr. Bardwell of Goshen who was one of the early missionaries to the Choctaws. Mr. Howse of West Hawley is an uncle of his. Mr. Bardwell received his early education in an Indian country, & was allowed unlimited intercourse with Indian boys, & yet has been preserved from ruin, & is now an interesting preacher of the gospel. He regards his salvation temporally & eternally as a peculiar miracle of grace, & says he would not dare try such an experiment with a child. He still remembers the native language & contemplates returning to the Choctaws.

Kindness from friends has met & followed us wherever we have been. At Red Oak the ladies made me a good rag carpet. A more acceptable gift could hardly have been presented. . . . The roads were just breaking up during our visit at Mother Riggs'. This gave me an opportunity of practicing on horseback with Alfred behind me. One ride was of seven miles through mud so deep that I expected my horse would any moment be fast, and that I shall not soon forget. We accomplished the fatiguing journey of seven miles in three long hours, & man, beast, & children were all exceedingly tired. . . . I would have left Alfred at Father Riggs' during this visit. . . I did not regret taking him, although the roads were so very bad. I could hardly divert him enough from his "aches" to prevent his joining Martha in crying.

Thursday, May 18

It is a year yesterday since we left our Isabella at Lac qui Parle. We have heard nothing from there since early in November. We hope that Isabella has been taught to remember her parents with affection. But my heart aches just now when I think of her.

We are now expecting to leave for St. Peters on "The Otter" on Monday next, the 22nd of this month. We did hope Thomas would reach here previous to our departure, but fear is beginning to dispossess hope. . . .

Mississippi River, Wed. noon, May 24

We have just passed Montreupalean! I do not know how to spell it, but you, I presume can determine its correct orthography by its signification which is a mountain in the water, as the Mississippi divides & passes around its base.

I have felt quite solicitous about Br. Thomas, but I still trust the Lord will bring him safely to St. Peters. . . . The kindness manifested to the Indian youths with us, was very grateful to our feelings. Summer coats & hats were given to each one, also shoes, & two of them had summer vests given them.

We passed the first Indians yesterday, poor wretched whiskey drinking Winebagoes. Shortly after we saw Sioux & I must confess I thought them more interesting & intelligent & my heart went out towards them, as toward old friends. We are now in the midst of God's handiwork — mountain like bluffs o'erhung with craggy rocks & trees of every form & shade of green, environs our pathway as we plow along. And lest any should be unbelieving still, the lightning is leaping from crag to crag & the loud thunder rolling, while the rain falls soothingly upon our roof.

St. Peters, June 1

There is now a prospect of our being able to ascend the St. Peters next week. We brought several grafted apple trees, & a plum, currants

& gooseberry bushes from Ohio. They were placed in a box & with care are now in a very flourishing condition. The pleasure of anticipating fruit I fear, may surpass that which we shall be permitted to realize, but I shall be rewarded for nurturing trees that revive such pleasant recollections, even though I may not pluck the ripe fruit from their boughs.

June 6

With a heavy heart do I date this again without being able to add that brother Thomas has arrived. Where can he be? God knows the answer. We expect to go up the St. Peters day after tomorrow. I shall leave directions for him to follow us should he reach here soon.

May the Lord bless you all. How my heart longs to hear from you. Much, very much love to sister Julia & all our friends.

July 18, 1843
My Dear Parents,

What shall I add, my dear parents, to the sad tidings my husband has written? Will it console you in any measure, to know that one of our first & most frequent petitions has been that God would prepare your heart for the news which we feared would be almost heart breaking? I feel that this affliction, such as I have never before felt, is intended to prepare us who are left for life or death....

I spent but two Sabbaths with him [Thomas] after his arrival. The first was at Saint Peters & we went together to the Episcopal service at Fort Snelling. Mr. Riggs was going to an Indian village to hold a meeting. The last Sabbath he was with us all was after my return from Lac qui Parle. I reached here on Saturday, having passed through distressing scenes on my way to Lac qui Parle occasioned by an attack of the Chippewas on some Sioux who were coming to meet us. I felt uncommon forebodings lest something had befallen the dear ones I had left here. But I endeavored to cast my cares on the Lord, remembering that while we were houseless & homeless we were more like our Sioux....

With such feelings as these, as we came in sight of husband's tent, I pointed it out to Isabella when she asked "Where's papa's house?" & soon I saw Mr. Riggs & brother Thomas & little Alfred coming to meet us.

Not quite one week from that joyful hour, Mr. Riggs came home from the St. Peters groaning, "Oh Mary, Thomas is drowned. Thomas is drowned." I did not believe the full impact. I still thought his body would be recovered & life restored. I still flattered myself after search for the body was given up for the day, that it had floated down upon a sand bar & he would yet live & return in the dusk of evening. But when I lay down for the night & the impossibility of my illusive hope's being real-ized burst upon me. Oh! If it had been one of our own little ones, could I have had the same hope in their death? I felt the trial could not have been more severe to us for we suffered both for ourselves & for our dear parents. The hand of the Lord touched us & we were ready to sink, but the same kind hand sustained us. If brother T. had gone home to our father's in Mass. I should not have grieved so much, & now he had gone to his Father's & our Father's home in heaven why should I mourn so bitterly.... One thought comforted me not a little. I saw his mercy to me in sparing my husband a little longer, when he was but a step from the eternal world. Still I felt that I had lost a brother & such a brother....

On my return, recounting the scenes I had passed through, the kill-ing by the Chippewas of the eldest brother of one of our young men as he was on his way to meet him & another young man, the shooting of one of our horses by a Sioux man who pretended to be offended that we did not pursue the Chippewas when we were more than three miles from the Mission, & that I carried Martha in my arms. Thomas said "I see you have grown poor." I replied that I expected to while I lived in a tent & led such an Indian life. He spoke of the cabin they had com-menced & said, "I expect you will improve from this time."

Day after day he labored at our little cabin, prompted by affection, hoping to enjoy the Sabbath in it before Mr. Huggins & his sister, who kindly came down with us, would return home. On Saturday morning, as we were busily engaged near each other, he sang "Our cabin is small & coarse our cheer, but love has placed our banquet here." Soon after-ward he went to bathe & of course our roof & floor remained unfin-ished, but we finished in sadness what had been to us a happy feast of tabernacles, by moving into our humble dwelling on Sat. evening. For a little while on the Sabbath his remains found a resting place beneath the house his hands had reared. I kissed his cheek as he lay upon a plank resting upon that large red chest & box which were sent from home, but, owing to the haste & excitement, I did not think to take a lock of hair. It curled as naturally as ever although dripping with water, & the countenance was natural I thought, but it has rather dimmed my recollections of him as he was when living. I felt so thankful that his body had been found before any great change had taken place, that gratitude to God supplanted my grief while we buried him. Mr. Huggins & Fanny sang for us an Indian hymn made from the 15th chapter of 1st Cor. & then "Unveil thy bosom faithful tomb." We came home just after sunset. It is but a little distance from our dwelling & in the same garden of roses, as Thomas termed it but few days since, where he now sleeps. . . .

Pray very much for us as well as yourselves. The death of our dear brother is not our only trial. It would only pain you if I should attempt to write what we frequently hear from lazy Indians stung almost to madness with want of food.

Traverse des Sioux, Aug 18, 1843
My dear Sister Hetta,

The precious letter for brother T. from our mountain home reached here Aug. 1st, but it came too late, alas too late for him to read. I took it to the grave & read a part & wept over it there. I know he could not hear your entreaty to return in Oct. '48. . . . Since his death we have experienced a variety of trouble, light in comparison with the loss of our dear brother, but following in quick succession it seemed accumulating as if to overwhelm us. . . . You know it is not a very common fault of mine "to hold my peace" when I might, with propriety, give my opinion. When the plan of bathing was first proposed I was at work near, & thought it was unwise, when all were so desirous of completing our cabin for the Sabbath, to leave for bathing in the middle of the forenoon. The idea "it will not be finished" darted through my mind, but a second thought of T's devotedness in laboring for us, made me ashamed of my selfishness, & I said nothing to dissuade him from going, but told him where he would find a towel which, alas, he did not live to use.

Another circumstance which seemed noticeable, was Mr. Pettijohn's cutting his hand the day previous. Mr. P. thinks he should have been able to have swum with T. into low water, while Mr. Huggins & Mr. Riggs were neither of them strong enough to effect anything. Owing to the wound Mr. P. had received, he did not go with the others to bathe. There was evidently an overruling Providence in all these little events . . . . Another mercy that I would not fail to acknowledge was that T. himself let go his hold of Mr. Riggs' hand when they both sunk together. It seems to me that the thought of my own husband disengaging himself from the death grasp of a drowning brother & indeed, I think it very doubtful whether he would have done it, & then I should have been doubly bereft.

I have often asked myself why Thomas should be taken & the rest of us left. His disposition, health, & habits both of mind & body bade as fair for happiness & usefulness on earth, & perhaps more fair than any other one of our number. . . . I felt that he would make all my burdens & cares light, he was so kind & ready to assist us.

Traverse des Sioux, *Sept. 15, 1843*
My dear Mother,

Just eight weeks after the death of brother Thomas, his trunk was brought from the trader where our goods had most of them been stored. It was placed on the same red chest where his corpse had been laid not two months before. During the last week we have aired & repacked it & shall send it this fall (probably at the same time with this letter) to Joseph Riggs, Portsmouth, who will wait until pa'a writes. Whether he shall ship it to Oberlin or to Albany, Troy, or Boston should be specified that you might know where to call for it.

When I first began to unpack the trunk my feelings almost overcame me, but I soon became calm. . . . I have looked over his things—his character is manifest in the care & judgment evinced in the articles he had supplied himself with for his intended stay with us. At the time of his death he was using a basket of mine to keep some of his clothing in. The mice took possession of it & spoiled a pair of socks & a waist coat. His calico shirts we gave to the Indian men who assisted in searching for the body, & we buried him in one of the new, fine ones which perhaps you, or Hetta, made for him without thinking to what use it would be appropriated.

The flowers in the little testament he gathered during his journey & stay with us.

Tears often come gushing forth when I think how solitary the old family mansion must seem to you since grandpa'a & Thomas are both gone. Six of your children are in the eternal world & five of the remaining six are widely scattered from the place of their birth. I feel that you cannot well be alone, & were I at liberty, I should love to take Hetta's place at home while she could go to school.... I have copied the traveler's hymn which he also carried in his pocket book & replaced it as I thought you would wish to see & keep it.

So you will see by this my dear mother that we have not been destitute of Christian sympathy although we have been alone. Mr. S. W. Pond & Mrs. Delia Pond were here on their way to St. Peters from Lac qui Parle when we reached this place. Brother Thomas left our party, who came by the river, on Friday, with Him for a guide & companion, and a horse & yoke of oxen in his care. At the time I felt anxious about him lest some accident should befall him, but it seemed best for him to go as we could confide in his judgment & management of the yoke of half tamed oxen. Mr. Riggs took the precaution to advise him not to cross the St. Peters with the cattle until he had procured assistance. As is often the case, he had a fatiguing journey, his horse being twice frightened by Indians when they met & Henok, who was riding, flew to the woods scattering blankets & saddle to the four winds. You will find his account of this in a note book. He reached here on Saturday & spent the Sabbath with Mr. & Mrs. Pond just four weeks before he was drowned in the same stream which he then crossed in safety....

I find Isabella a very affectionate child. When I reached Lac qui Parle she said "Is this my mother?" and immediately owned me as hers. When I took her in my lap she seemed overjoyed & repeated again & again "This is my mother," & "You are my mother."

Traverse des Sioux, Dec. 6, 1843
My dear Parents,

Whenever I take the pen to write to you, the memory of one in whom we all trusted & whom we all loved, demands a fresh tribute. During the past summer I have been severely tried by various imagining & feelings about his present state. I suppose the excited state of my nervous system may have been the cause. Of late I have felt usually a calm hope that it was well with him. Previously I had been so very much distressed by nightly visions that robbed me of sleep. . . .

This is Alfred's birthday &, as you wished me to write what he did & said one day, I commenced this letter to tell you something about him. He rose, as he often does when we do not rise before light, the first of the family, & was soon dressed, washed, & combed ready for breakfast. After this he put on a clean apron & read in one of the Eclectic readers & recited a lesson in Paley's Geography to Miss Kephart. And then his father gave him a note which he had written for him, & he read it with some little assistance.

Dec. 13

I commenced giving you a day in Alfred's birthday, but I was obliged to lay aside my pen before I had finished. I will complete it by a sketch that might suit almost any day excepting Sabbath. Alfred, finishing his morning lesson, plays till noon with Isabella & Martha & often wishes there were boys here for playmates so that he could play ball, or that our floor was not so full of cracks that he could use the marbles he had given him. Sometimes he tries jumping the rope, but there being no one of his age to practice with him, he soon tires of this. After dinner he reads a chapter in the Bible to me & then writes with a slate & pencil. I think he is making good progress & will soon be able to write you a short letter. Towards night he fills a large box which stands in a small porch near our door with wood & brings in most of the wood & chips which we burn, washes potatoes & is learning to be useful in various ways. After supper he studies in Peter Paley till seven, which is the time he goes to rest. Isabella & Martha usually go to sleep an hour earlier at this season of the year.

Isabella is both plump & rosy, with a broad face. Her father thinks she is rather slow of comprehension, but she is learning to read very well & can spell words of one syllable quite readily, & can sing one or two tunes. She does not enunciate all her letters very distinctly but I think she will eventually.

Martha is as rosy as Isabella but less plump & quicker in her movements, but she is very slow in learning to talk. Her sentences are very brief, sometimes not more than a word or two. At others she is very careful to say, "Mama will-you-me-water." She would interest her grandparents with her prattle I know, & were not the distance between us so great, I would love to take her in to cheer you now & then in your loneliness.

There are very few Indians here at present so that our school is very small, not more than three or four & those quite unregularly. We hope that when they return from their fall hunt that our school will be greatly enlarged. God keeps us from desponding amid the trials & discouragements that surround us. We often feel the need of more & more grace. And we need too, the influences of the spirit upon the heathen around us to incline them to receive the truth. And for these things the Lord "will be inquired of by the house of Israel." During the past summer when almost ready to sink, I have felt that all our efforts would be in vain, unless the church would arise & call upon God in our behalf. He alone can incline these poor ignorant Indians to receive instruction. . . .

Our last letters from Lac qui Parle state that her [Mrs. Hopkins] health is improving & we hope she will be able to come down when the river opens in the spring. We were quite disappointed in not having their company & assistance. Mr. Riggs has been unable to procure help since Mr. Pettijohn left us, but he has good health & is becoming quite accustomed to driving a one oxcart a mile & a half for wood. When the river freezes, wood can be obtained nearer. It is very late in the season to have the river but partially frozen here, but December has been as mild as October & November often are. . . .

I do not recollect whether I suggested in a previous letter that the property of our departed brother, excepting the clothing, be appropriated to Henrietta's education.

We have ascertained that there are no grave stones to be procured at Galena. They may be obtained at Quincy, Illinois, but we do not know at what price. Ought we to exceed $12, which is, as we suppose, about the value of the articles we retained?

Traverse des Sioux, Dec. 15, 1843
My dear Sister, [Henrietta]

The date of this reminds me that it is just five months today since our dear brother was drowned. The rude enclosure which is around his grave & the leafless oaks which bend over it, are in sight from our door. Very seldom do I go out without noticing that sacred spot, & thinking, there lie the remains of my precious brother Thomas. . . .

At present the Indians seem favorably disposed towards us. Our school is small, but we hope the Lord will incline many to attend when they return as they soon will from their fall hunt. They often bring us venison & ducks & wild fruit, for which we give them an equivalent in something they can eat or wear. Although as a manifestation of kind feeling I greatly enjoy their offerings, it is sometimes no small inconvenience to have such an unstable market. Were we entirely dependent upon it, we should like these poor Indians, have a feast alternated by a fast. And the latter I fear would be longer than we would well endure.

Traverse des Sioux, Dec. 20, 1843
Dear brother Joseph,

Your kind letter reached us in Oct. Some of your inquiries I may not be able to answer, but those which I can, I will with pleasure, for I love to think upon him we all loved. Most of your questions I can answer as well by copying from our Family Journal. "It was in a deep, deep channel where he was drowned, rendered deeper than usual by previous rains, but how deep I know not. It was not far from shore, if it had been, Mr. Riggs would not have been able to have reached it as the current in that place was strong & setting out from shore." Referring to the week before my return here my husband writes "We commenced cutting logs for a cabin, which we purposed to build in a small oak grove near the traders establishment. Still owing to wet weather & other hindrances, we progressed slowly & when M. with our two little girls, Mr. Huggins & Fanny & Mr. Pettijohn reached this place July 8th we had only laid it up to the square.

The next week we were bending all our energies to get a roof & floor in our cabin, but on Saturday when we hoped to have so nearly accomplished it as to be able to spend a pleasant Sabbath in it, God saw fit to blast our joyous hopes. The 15th of July is a day long to be remembered by us, for then our beloved brother Thomas was taken suddenly from us to the eternal world."

. . . . As you are my own dear brother, I will also transcribe a part of what I wrote in our Journal, dated July 23rd. Just a week since the corpse of our dear brother Thomas was brought into our unfinished cabin which his own hands had assisted in rearing. It was laid upon a plank which rested upon a chest & box brought from our mountain home in Mass.

" . . . . I passed my fingers through his curly hair dripping with water. I laid my hand upon his forehead, & took his hand in mine, but he heeded me not. I knew that he must be dead as his body had been lying in the St. Peters more than a day, but I now saw & felt that he was. The most robust, the tallest & manliest form of my father's house lay motionless & still before me. I thanked God that he had heard our prayers, & granted us the mercy of beholding the remains of our dear departed brother before a great change had passed over them. There was no time to prepare either a coffin or shroud. A grave was hastily dug & lined with rough boards, & there at sunset we laid him to rest, as a weary pilgrim reposes with his blanket around him.

Three dwarf oaks mark the consecrated spot, which perhaps may be the mission burial place, if we are permitted to remain & die here. To me there was a solemn warning to be also ready, in being called just at the commencement of our mission, to select a burial spot for one of our family & he the youngest & healthiest of all save our little ones. . . .

Would it not be well for Hetta to have the avails of "the note" as we know her education has been too long neglected & I think T. wished to assist her if his life had been spared. Before I received your letter I had almost hoped you were going home to comfort father, mother & Hetta.

I feel anxious about them. We have received no letter from home since pa'a & Hetta were apprised of brother T's death . . . . If your health should not improve, what course do you intend to pursue? Oh how I could have welcomed you here, but on account of pa'a & ma'a I cannot propose your joining us. But whatever you may feel is duty do it & wherever it is duty go.

If you & Moses are together I wish you would fill a folio sheet soon. Remember we were once a household band. May God bless you & give you such a measure of strength as shall be for his glory & your best good. Much love from husband, Alfred & myself.

Traverse des Sioux, February 2, 1844
Dear Sister Julia,

Husband has so benevolently filled a whole sheet to brother Alfred, that I shall direct this part of one to you. And another reason I do so is that you may not excuse yourself from writing us a longer letter than you have hitherto done. Your short paragraphs, inserted in some crowded corner of brother Alfred's letters, only makes us wish you would write us more at length. We feel some after reading them, as a very hungry child would after having devoured a small bit of good bread & butter.

I wish you would acquaint us with your every day life. Tell us how large the parsonage at Lafayette is, & with what comforts surrounded in the state of society & your prospects of being a blessing to it. And among the trivial things which I hope you will not fail to write, do not forget to mention the care of little Charles' eyes. I always think of him as a black eyed, dark haired boy. Our children all have blue eyes & rather light brown hair when small, which becomes darker as they grow older. But I sometimes have some four or five black eyed girls as scholars towards who I would gladly sustain something approaching to the parental relation, if their parents were willing.

A few of the Indians, not members of the club have, notwithstanding, learned to knit during the winter. We feel the need of a female assistant & yet are almost afraid that such an one as we would wish might feel that she would be more actively useful elsewhere.

I have spent from eight till nine in teaching reading to our little

Dakota girls for several weeks past, & Mrs. Hopkins has taught them to sew the hour following. While I have been engaged in teaching Sioux, Mr. Riggs has been occupied with the lessons of our own children. We hope to keep them with us until they are of suitable age to send from home to school. If you & Alfred should then be so situated as to extend to Alfred parental care we shall rejoice. I am so inclined to put far off the evil day of separation, that I do not realize that it may soon be here. As it regards Martha, I am afraid you would hardly be willing to take her too, if you should see her now. She is very frolicsome & mischievous, very different from Isabella in those respects.

Much love for you all, yourself, Alfred & Moses & little Charles, from your affectionate sister.

Traverse des Sioux, April 5, 1844
My dear Mother,

Of late my evenings have been occupied in endeavors to improve my knowledge of Sioux, but this evening I have redeemed for letter writing, by finishing last night the task I assigned myself in Sioux for this week. A few days since I assisted Mr. Riggs, who is still without help, in turfing T's grave & in setting some wild rose bushes in the little enclosure sacred to his memory. We placed two, one on each side near the head, & two more, near the foot. This will be T's "garden of roses." By his side there is a new made mound. It is an Indian's grave.

Monday, April 22

. . . . You mentioned that a Mr. Eastman is preaching in Hawley. Is he an Amherst Eastman? Has he a family? Are the people & the church united in him?

. . . . Just before the river opened this spring, Mr. Riggs was again providentially delivered from danger. He went with an ox & sled for posts for bars, which he had thrown upon the ice a few days previous. I feared the river was unsafe, but husband thought my fears groundless until the ox broke through the ice in the middle of the river. It being a shallow place the ox touched the bottom & regained his footing upon the ice, but in his efforts to do so the ax which T. handled & called his, was drawn into the hole & sank immediately. This however Mr. Riggs recovered with a pitchfork.

Sat. eve

Again I take my pen on a Saturday evening to add a little to this letter. How I should love to look in upon you in your loneliness. It makes me feel sad when I think of you as living entirely by yourselves in the old family mansion. It did not seem large when we were all at home, but I am sure it must now all of your children are absent. I think sometimes it would be well if you could shut up or rent a part of it, & then again I remember that it was not made for two families, & that in Hawley few if any wish to rent houses. I hope you will write to me how much of it you ordinarily occupy, & how each apartment would compare with home as it was when I last left. Does grandpa'a's room retain the same furniture which I have looked upon when a child, or is the tall clock & the writing desk & book case moved? Thomas's chamber too, is that unchanged?

The turf is now green on his grave, & it is a spot where we all love to go. Even Martha speaks of "Uncle Thomas's grave." Isabella had scarcely learned to acknowledge him as an uncle when he was drowned, for she seemed at first rather to fear him, & I thought it best, as we were all in one sense strangers to her, not to constrain her, thinking she would soon know & love him. When he was drowned, Alfred wept & made many inquiries. Isabella only looked sober because she saw I was sad. But when the body was brought home it arrested her attention. The face was bloody from the nose, & afterward when I told her I wished her to be a good girl so that when she died she might go to heaven where I hoped her Uncle T. had gone, she said she did not wish to die & go to heaven & have her face so bloody. I find some difficulty in leading her to understand even simple truths. Her mind is more childish than was Alfred's at her age. Still she is making tolerable progress in learning to read & her "Aunt Julia" as she calls Miss Kephart, has taught her to sing several pretty hymns very well.

I think sometimes I should love to send her to you for a few months or a year, that you might hear grandma'a & grandpa'a very frequently, if you do not often hear the pleasant words father & mother from the lips of your children.

Tuesday afternoon, May 21

Husband intends leaving tomorrow & will probably be absent two or three weeks. We do not know well how we shall succeed with drunken Indians while he is away, but we endeavor to put our trust in the Lord. Still it is trying to be surrounded by men maddened by whiskey, who not infrequently have knives & firearms brandishing about. Sometimes their threats & gestures make us rather fearful, but we have been kept in safety thus far, sheltered by an Infinite Shield. Mr. Riggs will add a line at St. Peters I presume, that you may know of his journey. He takes down our Mackinaw boat, which is but little removed from condemnation as not "seaworthy," with only one Indian to assist him in going down. He intends refitting it there, & bringing up the supplies for Lac qui Parle & for ourselves. Good bye, dear mother.

Traverse des Sioux, Saturday, July 13, 1844
My dear Mother,

I feel quite solicitous to hear that the trunk of our dear departed one has reached you in safety.

.... I suppose sister Henrietta will be at home when this reaches you. I am often reminded of her & dear Thomas by my beautiful dew plant from the seed she sent by him. Does the sweet scented geranium grow from the seed? If so, H. could send me one, & a flower pot to plant it in, I should love to watch its progress. I find my fondness for flowers as I have nursed my dew plant, the only one remaining of some half a dozen. The Indians, the babies, the chickens, & the mice seem in league to destroy them, & they have well nigh succeeded. Perhaps you will wonder why I should bestow any of my precious time upon flowers when their cultivation is attended with so many difficulties. The principal reason is that I find my mind needs some such cheering relaxation. In leaving my childhood's home for this Indian land, you know, my dear mother, I left almost every thing held dear, & gave up almost every innocent pleasure I once enjoyed. Much as I may have failed in many respects, I am persuaded there was a firmness of purpose to count no necessary sacrifice too great to be made. I do not think I have made what should be called great sacrifices, but I am using the phrase as it is often used, & I am conscious that in some respects I tasked myself too hard. I feel that I have grown old beyond my years. Even the last year has added greatly to my grey hairs. You were fully aware when I was at home that I was spending my strength too rapidly.

. . . . Mr. Riggs is very busily engaged assisting in building a small frame house for school & meeting. Under the front half of the building there is to be a walled cellar or basement, which is to answer a double purpose of cellar & workshop. If you could look into our garret & see how it is filled, in addition to our own supplies, with Indian packs, tents, buffalo skin, mats or beds, guns, kettles &c, you would think we needed large accommodations for storing. But if you knew how much trouble it occasions us, you would perhaps doubt whether it was wise to try to accommodate this unsettled & unthankful people. Not infrequently packs are brought or called for on the Sabbath when we neither give nor receive. Sometimes a pack is wanted when Mr. Riggs & Mr. Hopkins are both away, it must be searched out & if at the bottom of a heavy pile, lifted & put down to the lower floor, when perhaps all that is wanted is a little tallow, or a pair of moccasins, & then it must be lifted & replaced.

July 15

Again this day has dawned upon us. In 1842, the 15th of this month we stood in awe on Niagara's shore. But in 1843 when we stood on the bank of the St. Peters, so suddenly bereft of dear Thomas, over whom its deep current rolled, God spoke to us in a louder & more solemn tone than the cataract's voice. The turf upon his grave is very green.

July 17

The children often speak about grandma'a. I am sorry to see Martha manifests so much inclination to domineer over Isabella. I see faults in them all, one is rather obstinate, another sullen, & another irritable. Perhaps you might guess that I have begun at the bottom of the steps which our three little ones make when standing in a row. I think Miss Kephart succeeds pretty well in teaching the children. Alfred & Isabella both sing very well for such young children.

Traverse des Sioux, Sept. 10, 1844
My dear Mother,
   We had intended leaving home today for Lac qui Parle, but it rains, & we are glad to enjoy the shelter of a roof during the storm. Perhaps you may wonder why I should take such a journey, and I almost wonder myself. Still I think the influence upon individuals so secluded as we all are of an occasional visit, even though attended with care & toil, is salutary. . . .

October 10
   We returned home in safety after spending a week very pleasantly & I hope profitably at Lac qui Parle. Meetings were held on several days during our stay, & on the Last Sabbath, the Lord's Supper was adminis-tered. I had not enjoyed a communion season before since leaving Cincinnati, as we have not yet organized a church here. We hope to soon however. . . .

Friday eve, Oct. 11
   . . . . Sometimes I feel very sad, & I fear we are doing little or no good, & then again I am somewhat comforted & hope brightens the dark future. The Indians here have been drunk less since our return than for a long time before. For several weeks previous, we were almost daily annoyed by drunken Indians. At one time quite a number of men came together & demanded powder which they knew Mr. Riggs intended giving them. I battened the door to prevent their entrance as Mr. Riggs was not in, but the batten flew in pieces as the sinewy arm of *Tanka* came in. . . .

Oct. 16
   Last week husband assisted me in fitting up the little room we used during the summer as a kitchen, for a sleeping room. Now we have more room in our family room than we have ever before had, & beside the luxury of a bed room, a comfort I have never enjoyed since our

residence in an Indian land. The children seem puzzled what name to apply, & Martha often calls it ma'a's kitchen room, blending in one its former & present name. I was apprehensive Martha would manifest fear on going to bed alone in a dark room, having been accustomed to sleep where we were sitting, but she has not apparently noticed this difference, & has seemed much pleased with the change. We have an air tight stove, which was given us, in the room & use it every morning while the children attend Miss Kephart's little school. The time which she proposes remaining with us will expire next spring, & then what can we do, and how can we teach the children & perform all other du-ties, are queries that often arise before me. If I should step into your room & talk with my dear mother, it would be a great comfort....

Traverse des Sioux, March 15, 1845
My dear Mother,

We are uncommonly solitary at present, as our Indian neighbors are absent, some at their sugar camps & others hunting muskrats &c. Thus far the season has not been favorable for making sugar, & we have purchased but a few pounds, giving in return flour or corn, of which we have but little to spare. Last spring we procured our year's supply from the Indians, & for most of it gave calico in exchange.

Sat. March 22

Yesterday was a lovely day, & what is stranger still to one who is such a constant "keeper at home" as I now am, I rode out about two miles to a most lovely yet wild ravine. Apropos of rides, this is the third I have taken in about six months, & even now I could have found several ex-cuses for remaining as sentinel at our mission cabin, but husband offered to fill that post that I might go with the children to the Cedar Glen, in company with Mr. & Mrs. Hopkins & Miss Kephart. If I had just arrived at "the far west," from "the east," our carriage & horses might be worthy of a description. But I am so accustomed to oddities, that nothing seems as grotesque now as it would have done ten years ago. So black Nig & bay Daubigue, with their shaggy, uncurried manes & with sides made hairless by the trace chains of our carriage harness, scarce deserve a passing notice. And "the carriage," as Martha called the skeleton of a two horse wagon, might be a source of mirth as a western contrivance, but to us it has well nigh proved far otherwise. As a substitute for a wagon bed & a spring seat, some boards were laid down for the bed, & on one side, one board was placed perpendicularly for the back to our seat, which was hay, covered with a buffalo robe. On descending a hill this board slipped forward, & one of those in the bed to the side, & Martha came very near slipping between. Indeed we all felt fearful that we should find ourselves under the horses heels, but God took care of us & no accident happened during our ride to Cedar Glen.

There I remembered the "cedars wave over Lebanon" & there I thought too, of dear T. & of New England, as I sat upon a point overlooking the narrow vale below with Mrs. H. & the children, who were too small to ramble in the woods. There rippled the clear, pebbly brook that brother T. said was like a New England brook, the most like one he had seen since leaving Massachusetts. The rocks too, at the spot we visited yesterday, are like New England rocks, over one of which hung a congealed cascade. But the rivulet —I still see its crystal waters, so unlike most of the streams in this prairie land. I still hear the tripping of its silver feet as it meanders through the glen. We brought home, as mementos, a few raspberry roots, some white birch bark, which I peeled as I used to do when a child, but the prettiest thing was a beautiful cedar of Julia's selection, which is now planted in front of our porch, & which we are to call her tree.

Tuesday, April 22

Again my dear parents we have occasion to record God's loving kindness to us. I had intended the Saturday evening, before the birth of our babe, to have added a little to this memorandum of passing events. But after finishing making soap which occupied most of my time Thursday, Friday & Saturday, & putting away my sewing, & my basket work box, etc. in order for the Sabbath, I was glad to go to rest, & slept very quietly till midnight. As Mr. Riggs was very tired having been ploughing Friday & Saturday, I did not awake him until about three o'clock & our little one was born before four. Mrs. Hopkins who is but a little older than Henrietta, & whose experience in such cases extended only to her actual participation in this part of the cause, at the birth of their little & only daughter, performed for our babe what the Indian women think is worth a new suit of clothing when they perform such a favor for a white woman. By the way she did it gratuitously, although not exactly after their fashion, as ablution is not considered necessary, by a Dakota.

Husband mentions our feeling some anxiety on account of having no physician, but I must say that I have been a wonder to myself, that I, who am often so excitable, so "careful for many things," should be so free from anxious care respecting this event during the past winter. I have felt almost invariably a cheerful trust in the kindness of the Great Physician of body & spirit in reference to this, & He has been better to us than we had even hoped. Although I suffered more after the birth of the nameless one than I have ever before, I never, I think suffered so little before the birth of any of our children. Truly God has been very good & merciful. Mrs. Hopkins & Miss Kephart have been very kind & indefatigable in their efforts to render us all comfortable, & my greatest fear is that they will make themselves sick as they are neither of them enjoying good health. There is always danger of this if any is sick, where every one has as much to do as they can perform when well. I have written thus particularly because mother, I know, loves to have me definite.

Sat. May 30

We now expect Mr. Huggins' family down in about a week. The Monday following they will probably leave for Fort Snelling. Mr. Riggs will also go down to St. Peters at the same time & I shall be quite lonely I suppose, though not as much so as the time he first left home for any considerable time after we were married. I remember it well. Alfred was too little to comfort me much, particularly at meal time when I sat down alone at the table, & it seemed more difficult to swallow the food than it usually is for me to take medicine. I felt as perhaps did Kirke White when he wrote "It is not that my lot is less. . . . It is that I am all alone."

Traverse des Sioux, June 23, 1845
My dear Parents,

Having put our missionary cabin in order for the reception of Capts. Sumner & Allen, & Dr. Nichols of the army, I am reminded of home. I have not made half the preparations which you used to make to receive military company & I could not if I would, neither would I if I could. I do, however, sometimes wish it afforded me more pleasure to receive such guests when they occasionally pass through the country. We have so many uncivilized & so few civilized guests, & our circumstances are such that I almost shrink from trying to entertain company. I sometimes think that even mother, with all her hospitality, would become a little selfish if her kitchen, parlor & dining room were all one. I know ma'a has had the experience of four little ones, but I think not of the log cabin, still I feel conscious that I am not what her daughter should be. I have been reading Moffat's Southern Africa, & it encourages me very much to find that others have similar trials to our own, & in some respects even greater.

Our little Anna Jane cries & I must lay aside the pen. I hope you will like her name better than I do. If she is good it will grow pretty according to grandma'a's old adage. I well remember how she looked when she used to say to us "Handsome is that handsome does."

Mon. June 30

Since Miss Kephart left us I find very little time for writing, or rather no time. If I should wait to find leisure I should wait in vain. Sometimes I feel quite discouraged — the children have no school they can attend, & I must either neglect them or something else — domestic duties must receive attention &, setting aside sewing, my hands are full. Perhaps I might not complain thus lest it should grieve you, but I do it to relieve my own spirits by seeking a mother's sympathy. I doubt not but you have been tried in a similar way, at some period of life. We have had very little sickness in our family at any time & especially since we have been removed from a physician — surely for this we have great cause for thankfulness.

Our babe was baptized yesterday. Various reasons caused so long a delay—the principal one, my proposed visit to Oak Grove, the station that is occupied by the Messrs. Pond, which is about eight miles this side Fort Snelling. Anna was husband's mother's name & Jane that of a beloved sister. Our little ones would, I think, have preferred Henrietta for "baby's name," but, as we had no child named for husband's relatives, we did not decide by popular vote. Alfred [8 ½] takes some care of her & assists in various kinds of work. He is very fond of society, & apparently enjoyed the company very much that we have had for a few weeks past. Lieut. Masten, who brought up the supplies by water for the dragoons who are across the country from Fort Atkinson & Fort Winnebago, called quite frequently. . . & several times remained after Alfred's bed time, but he never grew sleepy, & went to rest reluctantly. When Lieut. Masten called on Sat. evening to take leave, he inquired of Alfred if he would like to return with him. He quickly replied that he would if he would wait till after the Sabbath. It apparently touched Masten's heart for he said in a softened tone, "I should like to wait, Alfred, till Monday."

Pa'a, I believe, mentioned that you thought of sending a box. In case you should I have a proposition to make, although I am almost afraid it may cause you more trouble than I ought to occasion you. Mr. Riggs will probably erect the fence around dear T's grave himself, & does not wish to retain the money which he would be obliged to use if he hired it done, & proposes sending it to you to use for benevolent objects. As I doubt not that you will choose to remember us in your benevolence, I will name some articles which I would like procured in case you can get them made, either in "the society" or by some of our friends. Good dark calico, not gay nor dear for myself, a dress made to fit Hetta, but not quite so long. Also one for Isabella, Martha, Mary Frances, & Anna Jane, made to fit little girls of the ages six, four, three, & one. I have put down their ages as they will be if they should all live till another year. Calico from 12 to 15 cents a yard by the piece would please me very well. Chocolate with very little white, but I leave it to you, or sister Lucretia's judgment.

I will mention some other things which would be acceptable & you can procure such of them as your circumstances may render most con-

venient. Colored cambric for a quilted skirt, if it could be quilted gratuitously. No cotton to be put in for a third of a yard from the top. A shirt
or two for Alfred, & two or three small chemises for some of our little
girls. Perhaps one a piece would be more than hands could be forced to
make. Some tape & thread to the amount of one dollar.

We send these two sheets together, to see if they will go for ten cents
under the new post office bars. Please write us about their weight. I
think three of them would not weigh more than half an ounce, but we
have no accurate way of ascertaining. Remember us most affectionately
to all our friends. I hope we shall hear from you all soon & frequently.

Or if, instead of these things you should choose to send Mr. Riggs a
pair of pants, I am sure I will not complain, for the making of pantaloons
is a more formidable task to me than dresses & chemise. I hope you will
be able to send me 1¼ or 1⅓ yds. green flannel for a cover to my bureau. 1⅓ yds. would be preferable but 1¼ will answer. The draft will
be $10, $9 of this will be of the sum we had consecrated to the grave of
dear T. As much of one dollar as is necessary you may use for framing
that engraving of T's if you think best. If you cannot without too much
trouble, please send it without a frame & instead get me a pair of gloves.

Traverse des Sioux, Aug 15, 1845
My dear Parents,

Your very precious letter commenced May 4th, reached us on the
9th inst. Rejoiced as I was to receive it, I was not satisfied it was so
short. But I hope if your letters are shortened in consequence of the
reduction in postage, the number will be increased, or we shall regret
the change. Your letter of February reached us safely & also the tablet
for dear T's grave. It now stands in our garden which is enclosed with a
rude picket, & I am very often reminded of the one who is gone as I
open the door of our bed room near which it stands. Our garden enclosure extends around the backside & both ends of our mission house,
which, in front, is a double log cabin with a porch between. Back of the
porch we have a very small bedroom which our children occupy, & back
of our cabin which was first erected, we have a larger bedroom, which
by way of distinction, we call the nursery. A door from this room opens

into the garden. The room does not extend half across "the double log cabin" so that Mr. H. has a room corresponding with our nursery, & then between the two wings we have two small windows, one in the children's bedroom & the other in our family room. Shading the latter, are Alfred's morning glories & a rose bush.

A shoot from this wild rose has often attracted my attention, as day after day it has continued its upward course. It is now seven feet high, the growth of a single season, & is still aspiring to be higher. Bound beneath it is a sister stalk laden with rose buds. Last year it was trampled upon & broken. . . but now our fence affords us some defense, & we flatter ourselves that our pumpkins & squashes would be unmolested. But we found to our surprise, one day that our garden had been stripped of the larger pumpkins the night previous, except a few vines belonging to Alfred which were nearer our door than those that were plundered. As it was quite early in the season, the little ones that were left us now promise a very good supply. . . . Our situation here. . . . exposes us to annoyances of this kind . . . . On our return here in 1843, we landed after sunset, pitched our tent & arranged our beds, baggage, including provision, baskets, etc. as expeditiously as possible. A large loaf of light bread, mixed on board the crowded barge & baked in a Dutch oven, or bake kettle, in the woods on the bank where we had taken supper, was an important article in one of the baskets. It was reserved for breakfast for our family which consisted then of twelve persons beside little Martha.

In the morning the meat & coffee were prepared, & as four of our number were at a distance, they were called. The bread basket was opened but our large loaf, our only loaf was gone. Our only alternative was to make & bake a substitute. All helped & none more readily than dear T. & as soon as possible the fire was surrounded with flat cakes in the various stages of baking from the newly placed dough in the frying pan to those that are propped up with a stick around the fire. In a short time we were at breakfast, rejoicing that the loss of our loaf was not irreparable, & thinking we would be more careful of our provision basket in future.

Tuesday, Aug 2

In the letter which we forwarded last was a draft for $10, 9 of which if I recollect rightly, was the value of various articles which we retained that belonged to brother T. I mentioned at that time that as we could not hire the fence erected around the grave, that Mr. Riggs hoped to be able to do it himself, & preferred that ma'a should have the control of the money rather than to retain it. And as I thought she, if able, would love to procure some articles of clothing for our children with a part of it at least, I mentioned several.

We are enjoying comfortable health at present, although some one of our mission has been rather ill during the warm weather. Our babe seems rather delicate & Mary Frances Hopkins quite so this summer. I fell partly down cellar a week since & sprained my knee, which is still weak & sore though I can now walk without limping.

Friday

Mr. Riggs has given a hasty glance at the far future [of statehood]. I cannot think that we shall soon be within the limits of a state. I should much prefer to have our own territory called Dakota, for I think it no more than justice to the Indians to transfer their name to the soil they inhabit.

Sept. 16, Monday morn before sunrise

Mr. Riggs left home for Lac qui Parle two weeks since tomorrow. Alfred was very near death a week since last Sat. night. I sent him out as I was removing the table cloth. As two horses passed him one kicked him in the face. He had his hand upon his face, which shielded it somewhat, though his nose & lip were considerably bruised.

Traverse des Sioux, Oct. 9, 1845
My dear Parents,

It is a long time since we have heard either from Alfred, Moses or Joseph. It seems to me that it is their duty to write to us, but I suppose they think differently. Surely I could find an abundance of reasons for not writing. Cooking, eating, & sweeping, & washing, ironing & mending, require no small portion of time. And then little Anna Jane must be nursed, & Martha dressed & Isabella's long fine straight hair, so much like her mother's, must be braided or it will be sadly tangled, & Alfred must have a coat & pants made before it is cold weather, & baby's calico suits must also be exchanged for flannel ones not yet made &c. &c. And who is to do all this & a great deal more? Alas, I fear I am in danger of becoming disheartened like the discontented pendulum, if I recount the pressing duties that throng around me. And so, like the silly ostrich that hides its head in the sand to screen itself from pursuers, I shut my mind's eye from the multitude of pressing demands upon my time & strength. I wish I understood how really & fully to cast all my cares upon the Lord. Remember husband & myself most affectionately to our kindred & friends who inquire about us.

I wish you would write to me the cost of such a sheet of (I think you called it zinc) as was under the airtight stove when I was at home. Would it be extravagant for us to have one? Is it purchased by surface or weight? And what is it called? We are in danger of burning our old puncheon floor quite through, & if we should ever make such an advance in civilization as to have a better floor, I should be sorry to burn it under the stove as badly as this is burnt by the "rousing fire" we have cold winter mornings.

Traverse des Sioux, Sat., April 4, 1846
My dear Parents,

Two weeks since I commenced this sheet & had proceeded thus far when a sudden & severe pain in my right side obliged me to lay it aside. Since that time I have been scarcely able to do my work, but with the assistance Mrs. Hopkins & Mr. Riggs have rendered, we have done all that was necessary. Today I feel somewhat like myself again & hope through the mercy of our God that I may renew my strength & not faint by the way.

For some weeks past our Indian neighbors have been scattered far & wide making sugar. Several of them have brought us a cake or two, but they will probably make much less than usual. For their own sakes I should rejoice were it otherwise, but I am very well contented to do with but little of it as few if any of these Indians either strain or clarify the syrup. A few days since a sick woman came in from the sugar camp, without bringing us any sugar. She apologized for this, & talked about her sufferings which the powows were unable to relieve. She has been a great conjurer & yet has so little faith in their skill, that for a long time she refused to have any one practice their "hellish charms" for her. She says her sickness is caused by some one of the fraternity who have "the medicine sack," who wishes to kill her. Poor creature, she knows very little about Him who holds our lives in his hand, & yet she doubtless knows more about His will than she is willing to obey. She has been a very wicked woman & has had fourteen husbands. The brother of one of them cut off her nose on account of her misconduct. Yet notwithstanding this she receives at times uncommon attention, such as being invited to a feast with men when no other female was invited! She has a daughter who is walking in her steps so rapidly that she is likely to outstrip her in crime, & still for ought that I know the Indians generally regard them almost as highly as others if they had lived more circumspectly.

I now expect to go to St. Peters with Mr. Riggs this spring, & perhaps may go farther. Mr. & Mrs. Denton of the Swiss mission near Lake Pepin on the Mississippi are very desirous that Mr. Riggs should spend a few weeks at their station & he purposes, God willing, to do so in May or June. We design taking Isabella and Anna Jane with us—Alfred & Martha are to remain with Mr. & Mrs. Hopkins. If their grandparents' house was near enough I should trouble them, perhaps, with one of the children, for it has been with considerable reluctance that I have concluded to leave both of them for Mrs. H. to take care of. We expect Alfred will go up to Lac qui Parle this Summer but perhaps not until our return. Miss Jane Williamson has kindly offered to teach him & he is very desirous to be associated with his former companions, John & Andrew Williamson.

I have written to you more than usual about our plans for the children perhaps because they have been upon my mind peculiarly of late. While I have felt admonished that "the house I live in" is at the best a frail abode, & may soon be demolished, the query has often arisen what would I wish for our children—to whom could we consign them?

Traverse des Sioux, Sept. 17, 1846
My dear Parents,

This is probably the last letter I shall write you from this spot so dear to us. Mr. Riggs has told you some of the reasons for leaving & also some of the causes for sadness on leaving. If I could see that it was duty to go, it would cheer me in the preparation for our departure. But I cannot feel that the interests of the mission required such a sacrifice as leaving this home is to me, & I know our children, if not my own health must suffer in consequence of the additional cares & labors which will devolve upon me. Husband & other friends would feign console me by saying that it will only be my duty to do that which I am able to perform, but my mind & body both are so constituted as to make too great exertions when I see a great deal that needs to be done. In addition to this, the excitement arising from a consciousness of a pressing of duties which at times seem to conflict, so affect my nervous system as to chase sleep from my eyes & slumber from my eyelids. Consequently, when oppressed with cares & labors more abundant, our children are & must be neglected. And if their own mother neglects them, who will instruct & watch over them? These are some of the thoughts that darken the prospect when I think of leaving the comforts & conveniences which we have only enjoyed one or two short summers, such as the enclosure for our children, our rude back porch which has served for a kitchen, the door into which, I helped Mr. Riggs saw with a cross cut saw because he could get no help. We located here in the midst of opposition & danger, yet God made our enemies to be at peace with us, & now we abandon it for Lac qui Parle.... Do pray that I may have faith that I faint not. Sad will be the hour when I take the last look of our low log cabins, our neat white chapel & dear Thomas' grave.

Lac qui Parle, Tuesday, Sept. 29

We reached here in safety on Saturday last, & are now occupying the same little old room we used to live in & where three of our children first saw the light. We met a horde of Indians a few miles from here. They greeted us in a friendly manner, but it reminded me notwithstanding, of that fearful encounter of the Ojibwas & Sioux the summer after our return from the States.

I hope you will write very soon, for my sad heart longs for a cheering letter from my mother, father, sister & brother. I have no time to write more as I must prepare dinner for both families.

Yours with affection,
Mary Ann

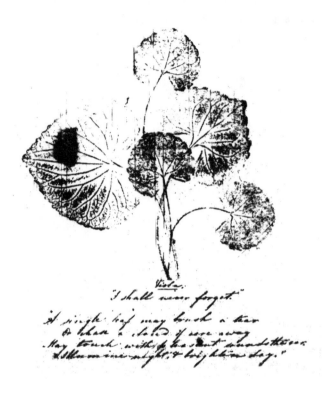

Viola
I shall never forget

A single leaf may brush a tear
Or chase a cloud of care away
May touch with pleasant sounds the ear
Illumine night and brighten day.

CHAPTER 5

Return to Lac qui Parle

1846 - 1854

Stephen & Mary Riggs, 1852.

Although Mary Ann did not want to leave a home that had so many memories, she followed Stephen because she felt that it was a wife's duty. In the new house, which they shared with the Adams family, Mary Ann had her first kitchen, a sitting room, and two bedrooms. Thomas was born there in 1847 and Henry in 1849.

Mary Ann's father died and concern for her Hawley family increased. With so many children to care for, and the frequent absence of her husband, she asked for help with her housework and teaching assignment. She tried to convince her sister, Henrietta, and her mother to come west, but Henrietta died before arrangements could be made. Her brother,

Alfred, also died during this time.

In 1852 Mary Ann, Stephen, Isabella, and Henry went east again, leaving Alfred at school in Illinois, Martha and Anna Jane in St. Paul, and Thomas with Dr. Williamson at Kaposia. During this trip Stephen's Dakota Dictionary was printed by the Smithsonian Institution and the ABCFM published Mary Ann's English and Dakota vocabulary, Bibliography of the Siouan Language.

Fire destroyed their home in 1854. The letters do not reveal that it was started by the candle that Thomas {9} and Henry {7} brought with them to get potatoes from the cellar. Boy-like they ignited some hay that was serving as insulation and after successfully putting the fire out, decided to try again, but the second attempt had disastrous results. There were fourteen people in the house at the time of the fire, three of whom were Dakota children living with the family. Mary Ann's health worsened with each tragic episode. Missionary boxes from Deerfield and Hawley arrived periodically supplying some of the family's needs, and Miss Cunningham joined the family to help with teaching.

Mary Ann and Stephen made plans for their older children's education. The family allowance at this time was $500 a year. In 1854, Alfred {17}, made plans to attend Knox College, Galesberg, Illinois.

Relations with the Indians continued to worsen. They were killing cattle, stealing horses, and complaining that the missionaries were trespassers in their country. Resentment toward the government, which was forcing them to live as farmers, continued to strengthen.

Lac qui Parle, Wed. eve, Dec. 16
My Dear Mother,

You will, I think, feel gratified to know that there are some things pleasant & encouraging here, notwithstanding the discouragements. The sound of the church going bell is heard—the bell which we pur-chased with the avails of moccasins donated by the church members here. True some of those contributors are dead & others have backslid-den or removed, still there are more hearers of the word here, than at Traverse des Sioux, although the large majority in both places turn a deaf ear to the calls & entreaties of the gospel. Quite a number of the women who attend the Sabbath services can read, but some of these are unable to find the hymns, & I enjoy very much finding the places for them.

The school is also larger here than at Traverse. I have not taught any yet excepting our own children & Mary Ann Huggins, & Nancy McLure, a half breed....

We have recently heard that the Indians have requested the Indian agent to make known their wish to Mr. Riggs to reside among them. We have received no official communication as yet & know not what may be our duty.

You know I love to travel, but moving to me is very painful. The sun-dering of old ties & breaking up of old associations are to me great trials to the flesh. Pray for us that we faint not. I feel very weak—almost afraid to encounter temptations & trials. We need, & I especially, need faith & strength from above....

Dec. 25

This morning a large number of the Indians encamped here started out to chase the buffalo, having heard that large droves were within 15 or 20 miles. Mr. McLeod, a trader here passed several herds on his re-turn from Big Stone Lake. He brought some fresh buffalo meat from the trading post there, a very fine piece of which he sent us. It is tender & excellent in all respects—the first fresh meat of the buffalo which we have ever eaten. Once or twice while we were living at Traverse, the buffalo were nearer this place than while we resided here. At one time a few passed not far from the mission premises. Although this arrival of buffalo has thinned our school, a hope that Indians will be enabled so to add to their supplies of food that starvation will not stare them in the face next spring as we have had reason to fear. The corn crop was smaller than usual in consequence of the drought last Summer.

Lac qui Parle, Feb. 26, 1847
My very dear Brother and Sister,

. . . . Perhaps you have been wondering why this sheet is dated at Lac qui Parle instead of Traverse des Sioux. A short explanation is this. Mr. Riggs thought it his duty to come here & I of course came too, although I have never been able to see the necessity of such a change. . . It was a sad, sad day when I last visited brother T's grave & left that spot which I had fondly thought might long be our home & around which clustered so many associations. Dr. Williamson who has resided here for the past eleven years received an invitation to locate upon the Mississippi at a Dakota village a few miles below Fort Snelling. As there had been much opposition manifested here during the last two or three years, Dr. W. felt as though someone else might be more useful here & Mr. S. W. Pond & Mr. Riggs were regarded by him & other missionaries as the ones best calculated to exert a good influence upon the Indians here. Mr. Pond declined but Mr. Riggs dared not, & consequently we came for a year. Whether we remain longer or not is uncertain—we have no certain dwelling place, & yet I find it difficult to realize that we are simply strangers & pilgrims on earth.

The love of home & the attachment to the place I call home, seems so inwrought into my nature that it costs me groans & tears to uproot it. Oh how I loved those low rude log cabins at Traverse & the picketed enclosure back of them where our children played secure from the Indians. How beautiful those scrub oak looked to me & how dear was the resting place of that loved one. I wish I could say I left all for Christ's sake but alas I have not this comfort—I left them because the wife must be in subjection, as Paul says. . . . I hope to learn a lesson from our removal & keep my affections from entwining around an earthly home in future.

The willingness you have both manifested to assist us in the care &
education of our children cheers me very much. My health has been
poor for the year past & I sometimes feel that soon our little ones may
be motherless. And although we wish to retain them with us for some
years to come, it is pleasant to feel that they have homes in prospect in
case they should need them. I, or rather we, have regarded Alfred as
provided with a home & paternal care, unless some change in your circumstances should render it impossible for you to receive him. On many
accounts it would be pleasant for one of his little sisters to be with him.
. . . You know we are at liberty to draw a certain sum for returned
children, if necessary, from our Board, which would in part at least defray expenses for education. . . . In indulging thoughts like these about
our children am I disobeying the injunction "take no thought for the
morrow." Usually I am enabled to feel that God will provide for them,
& to rest my cares in reference to their future lot upon Him who careth
for us.

Lac qui Parle, May 17, 1847
My dear Mother,
    It is past eight Monday evening. The children have gone to bed, Mr.
Riggs I suppose is at St. Peters & I am alone. When I have thought of
being left thus my mind has recoiled, but it seemed necessary & I have
tried to trust God for protection. I can say with some emphasis "Thus
far the Lord has led us on," & still I have not been without trials of
course. The Indians, young men particularly, seem to me to have no sense
of propriety, but come & sit by the hour & talk with each other about
my situation which in civilized lands would excuse me from their calls,
or if they chance to find our little daughters out of doors, treat them
with such rudeness that I could never again permit the libertines to cross
our threshold, if I were in a land where the rights of virtue were sustained. Besides such troubles & cares of our family, I am weary of being
begged. Since Mr. Riggs left home two weeks since today, I have had a
double share of wants to supply. I could almost wish he had locked up
the medicine case & taken the key with him, for I have not so much
confidence in my skill in dispensing it as to suppose the Indians would

have suffered if it had been out of my power to satisfy their wants. I purpose [proposed] giving only rhubarb & a few other samples, but I have been besieged until I have yielded & have now no relief to hope for until Mr. Riggs' return, which we hope will be the latter part of next week. In addition to the medicine there has been a great demand for garden seeds, to say nothing of the common wants of a little thread or soap, or patches for a ragged short gown, or a strip of white cloth for the head to enable them to kill ducks or buffalo as the case may be....

May 26

This morning a drunken Indian called while we were at breakfast to inquire when my husband would return. After being told that we were expecting him on Saturday, he said he would go when I gave him a little food. He did as he promised although it is quite often the case that supplying one request makes way for a second & third.

This afternoon 26 armed Indian men paraded before our door & discharged their fire arms. I was a little startled at first, but soon learned that they had been in search of Chippawas that were supposed to be concealed near & that they had returned unsuccessful & were merely indulging in a little military exercise without order of course.

Lac qui Parle, Jan. 10, 1848
My dear Mother,

.... I feel oppressed with care & labor & know not how or where to obtain the assistance I think I need. If I had more faith, I should not let such a seeming presence of duties discourage me, and even now I do endeavor not to be disheartened, but my faith is very weak. My mind as well as body suffer, & I expect ere long to be unable to do much more than sister Lucretia does in letter writing.

Tuesday, Jan. 11

The last Sabbath in December Mr. Riggs spent at an Indian encampment about 16 miles from this place. When he left home, Samuel Pettijohn, Mr. & Mrs. P's only child was ill, but we did not apprehend dangerously so, when he returned on Monday noon, little Samuel was dead....

Some few weeks ago an elderly woman with a young babe, begged me for clothing for the little one. I asked her if it was her child, she replied that it was her grandchild—that its mother died last summer & that she had nursed it ever since. At first she had no milk, but she continued nursing it, until milk flowed for the little orphan. This, thought I, is an evidence of a grandmother's love not often witnessed. I felt very compassionate for the babe & gave the grandmother some old clothing. After she left I noticed a knife was missing, which seemed rather like a gypsy's compensation for the kindness received. Perhaps she was not the thief, as our house was then thronged with visitors from morn-ing till night. We endeavor to keep such things as the Indians will be tempted to steal out of their reach, but a mother cannot watch three or four children & perform necessary household duties at the same time, without sometimes affording an opportunity for a cunning hand to slip away a pair of scissors or a knife unnoticed. But our losses from theft are not often very great. Potatoes & pumpkins, turnips & melons we ex-pect will be taken without liberty, particularly the two latter, & we are not greatly surprised when a chicken or even a sow is shot, but house breaking is a thing more uncommon.

Last fall however we found that we must prepare even for such events, or rather endeavor to secure ourselves against such depredations. While Mr. & Mrs. Pettijohn were absent last fall, their house was entered & various valuable articles taken. We suppose it must have been done in the day time, as several boxes & drawers were ransacked & things most valuable to an Indian selected. Suspicion rests strongly upon a young man, but we have no courts of justice—no sheriff—no jury, & no judges here.

Our Indians are luxuriating upon buffalo meat this winter, & we too are also enjoying a share of God's bounty. Our school & Sabbath assem-bly here is small as most of the Indians are encamped at some distance. Mr. Riggs has spent two Sabbaths at their camp. The devil is very busy at their camp as well as elsewhere—sending out war parties to scalp Chippewas—making sacred feasts—singing & dancing around the scalp they have taken.

Our children have enjoyed quite good health since the return of cold weather which served as an antidote to chills & fever. Thomas is the most fleshy babe we have ever had notwithstanding he was the least at his birth. I fear he will not aid in strengthening or straightening my back. He needs my care now, & I must lay aside the pen.

Lac qui Parle, May 25, 1848
My very dear Parents,

Hoping that you both still are spared us, I have taken the earliest opportunity of answering your letters, & expressing our sympathy with mother in her illness. It must have been a severe trial to pa'a to have been absent during your sickness & to Hetta also. When I read that sister Lucretia was with you in your solitude to watch by your sick bed, my heart gushed forth a thanksgiving to God for this mercy, that you had one child sufficiently near to succor you in distress. Yes, one of your twelve children to smooth your pillow & minister to your wants. But her account of your situation was so brief that many fond inquiries would arise concerning your welfare. Were you alone or did Mr. & Mrs. Eastman still occupy a part of the old mansion when you were taken ill? What prevented your spending the winter at South Deerfield with sister L.? How very quiet & green I think those lanes are—no noise save the whispering winds in those beautiful elms & maples, & those still rooms where rang the merry shout of children returned from school. I could almost fancy they would look as sober & sombre as those dark firs under which we played when we & they were small. They still are young & vigorous for ought I know, but we alas, are young no longer. Do the lilacs & roses & snowballs still blossom as brightly as ever? But the thought of those bright & beautiful scenes makes me sad, & I wish to write a cheering letter, so good bye to those visions of departed joys.

This summer we are building a plain, snug, one story house with a sitting room, kitchen & two bed rooms on the lower floor, & two rooms above, if ever they should be completed. We have been hoping to have a young lady to assist in teaching for an occupant of one of our bed chambers, but the prospect is rather discouraging. . . . There is some probability that a Mr. Adams from Ohio, a relative of Mr. Riggs may join us here next fall. If so, we shall have to dispense with the luxury of a kitchen, I suppose, for the needful comfort of our fellow laborers, or perhaps I should say the comfort of a kitchen for their necessity. I suppose in New England you would hardly class a kitchen among the luxuries of life, but here, where are dwellers in tents, some of which are not much better than a big umbrella, a Yankee kitchen would be a decided luxury.

Thursday, June 1

Alfred left home this morning with Mr. Pettijohn & his cousin from Illinois. . . . Their object is to procure buffalo calves & Alfred was very desirous to accompany them, as he had never seen a very large number of buffalo. It will be a fatiguing trip but it may make him more resolute & hardy. The buffalo are about 20 miles distant in large herds. I believe I wrote to you last winter of a ride of four or five miles which I took, to see these natives of the prairie. Before the herd perceived our approach they were quietly standing together, but on perceiving us, they waited a moment as if for consultation, & then commenced bounding away. Those who were prepared for the race entered their ranks & then the herd separated into three or four parts & scampered for life in as many different directions. Several were killed & dressed & we brought home the huge head for the children to see, beside the tongue & some meat which were given us as our share of the spoils.

Thomas is almost a year old but does not stand alone yet. He is too fleshy to walk as young as Alfred did. None of our children except Alfred have had any attacks of ague this season. His were slight & yielded to medicine. I should like very much to have you write a few lines to your grandchildren, it might stimulate them to improve in learning to write, to be able to answer your letter. Alfred & Isabella have both been neglected in penmanship as well as many other things. How can a mother do everything? I should love to have Henrietta with us a year or two, & yet I dare not cherish such a wish. She has written me but once & that before she commenced teaching. I presume she has written you definitely of her success, &c. Why not enclose it to us?

Lac qui Parle, Oct. 15, 1848
My dear parents,

It is a long time since I have received a letter from home, & longer still since I have written to its loved inmates. I should have written ere this. . . previous to the annual meeting of our mission at Kapojia, the station occupied by Dr. Williamson & family. I accompanied Mr. Riggs with three of our children. From Traverse des Sioux we went by land in ox cart through woods a considerable part of the way to Prairieville, as *Tintatonwa* signifies, where Mr. S. W. Pond is located. There we spent the Sabbath & reached Dr. Williamson's on the following Monday only eight days from Lac qui Parle, not a little fatigued though greatly prospered in our journey. . . . We passed nearly a week at Kapojia & then set our faces homeward, spending a night at Mr. G. H. Pond's at Oak Grove & one also at Mr. S. W. Pond's at *Tintatonwa*. Two nights we camped out & reached Traverse on Friday afternoon.

While there I often went to brother T.'s grave. The turf, which I assisted in planting is getting very green & the rose bushes flourishing. The cedar we planted withered, but a beautiful one placed by Mr. Hopkins near the grave is fresh & verdant. I enclose a sprig which Alfred plucked from it for you. While we were at Traverse Thomas L. Riggs was quite sick & I feared we should have to lay him to rest beside the uncle whose name he bears, but God mercifully restored him & brought us all together at home in safety. Isabella & Anna Jane were very much delighted on our return. Mrs. Pettijohn very kindly took pains in teaching Isabella to knit, so that with some pride she displayed a pair of socks she had assisted in knitting & a pair of mittens she had knit herself with some assistance, while during our absence of four weeks. I should have taught Isabella to knit before, but I have needed her assistance in sewing.

Thurs. eve, Oct. 18

Mr. & Mrs. Adams returned home with us & are to be located here. We have relinquished to them our kitchen & one bedroom for the winter, so that we have only two rooms & neither of them large, for our own family to occupy. Perhaps before it is very cold we shall get a chamber partitioned off with bedquilts, if not with boards for Alfred. If not, we shall still be more comfortable than our Indian neighbors. They seem astonished at ours, quite as much as I should be in Buckingham Palace, & occasionally one seems at a loss to know where to discharge his lungs or nostrils. Not long since a young man was about to disfigure the plaster on the wall when his eye caught mine—raising his foot a little he said, "I will wipe it on my moccasin & carry it out of doors." I felt much obliged for his politeness & smiling said, "you will do well"— indeed I think it was very gentlemanly for an Indian to use his moccasin instead of the wall for a pocket handkerchief.

Mon. eve, Oct. 23
We have just had supper of mush & milk. Isabella is washing the dishes, Martha wiping them, & Anna is seated at my left hand asking me "Are you going to write to my grandmother?" Alfred is preparing wood for tomorrow, his father is pursuing old White, whose young calf has escaped with its mother & robbed us of our milk. Last if not least, Thomas is asleep & I am thankful—for he is one of the most mischie' vous, steering [disturbing], noisy, boys that ever tired a mother, & if it were not that he can't quite dispense with sleep, he would be a speci' men of constant, if not of perpetual motion.

Please send me a few seeds of the mountain ash in a letter, say five or six seeds.

Lac qui Parle, Jan. 6, 1849
My dear Parents,
Another year has dawned upon us in this Indian land. . . . Some of the Indians have seemed in an inquiring state of mind. . . . The same foolish yet trying accusations are made, such as that we are to receive pay according to the number of scholars in the school here when their land is sold, that we are using up their grass & timber & land & making them no requital. As a proof of the falsity of such charges I will say that we have paid them as much for the timber used in our buildings as would have procured a greater amount of sawed timber at the lumber mill on the St. Croix. But the powder & lead are used up & the ox eaten up while our houses still remain, so that the past compensation is nothing

in their eyes, because forsooth, they want some fresh beef just now, &
the buffalo are not near. A few days since the old chief & his brother-in-
law, a chief soldier, came & rehearsed their supposed claims & said that
the Indians were tired of eating corn & wanted one of our few remaining cattle, hinting plainly that we should have to leave next spring,
unless we made to ourselves friends with flattering lips & bountiful.

Wed. Feb. 7

Last evening the letters from Hawley arrived apprising me that one
to whom this is addressed is where the letter cannot reach him, still, my
dear mother, it may afford you a sad pleasure to read what I had written
for you & my dear departed father.

Lac qui Parle, Feb. 7, 1849
My dear Mother & Sister,

The sad news of your & our bereavement reached us last night.... I
thank God for the comforting circumstances attending his last illness &
death, that some of your children were at home & kind friends near you
will sustain you in all your grief.

The members of our mission are enjoying comfortable health though
mine is not as good as usual, but I am able to supply the wants of the
family with such assistance as Mr. Riggs & the children can render. How
I should love to have you & Henrietta with us. Our children, if they did
not annoy you too much, would interest your feelings & occupy some
of your time. While I have been writing, Thomas has been standing by
me ransacking my escritoire — pulling out pencils, knife & India rubber,
& putting them in again times without number. I often wish his
grandma'a could see him, not that he is an uncommon child. Not any
evenings since, after sharing his bread with the cat, which lay on his lap
as he sat on the floor, to imitate the motion of his father's knee, he clasped
pussy's neck with both hands & putting her up & down said "Dot. Dot.
Dot." But the cat did not like such rude trotting & made her escape. He
seems to be a very affectionate little boy, but I fear his temper will occasion him trouble unless the Lord subdues it while he is young. For this I
pray & labor....

Lac qui Parle, Thursday eve, April 5, 1849
My dear brother Alfred & sister Julia,

.... In regard to the home property, I feel that we all have one mind that such a disposal should be made of it as will be most for our dear mother's comfort. I suppose that by will it was made hers to use at best during life if not under her entire control, but I do not know enough of such matters, to judge whether her children can do anything legally without applying or referring the case (what terms are correct I do not even know) to Probate. It would be pleasant to us all doubtless, and it would seem equally for mother's comfort to have our mountain home remain hers & ours still. But unless Joseph can take charge of the farm, would she not . . . be more comfortable with one of her children elsewhere? I presume that neither you nor Moses would think it your duty to make that your dwelling place, & as for my husband, his lot at present, is cast in this Indian land. We sometimes, however, fear that his labors in preaching may now terminate. Public speaking has been very fatiguing the past winter & often attended with hoarseness. We sometimes ask, is this the Bronchitis? But we have no physician near to answer the inquiry.

Friday eve

We feel solicitous about our children's spiritual interests. . . . The older they grow, the more reluctant their father is to send them from us. As for me if the trial should come I know not how I should bear it, still I feel less confident than Mr. Riggs that it is best for them, to keep them with us much longer. Isabella [9] & Martha [7] cannot write yet & Anna Jane [4] cannot read. Alfred was able to do both much younger than they are, for the simple reason that more time was spent in teaching him.

Lac qui Parle, Thurs. May 31, 1849
My dear Mother,

Hoping for a few moments of quiet as this last day of May is departing, I have taken my pen. The children are in bed excepting Alfred who is milking. Mr. Riggs is still from home having been absent more than three weeks. . . . During Mr. Riggs' absence our worship on the Sabbath both in Sioux & English has consisted in reading the scriptures, singing & prayer. I have been gratified that so many attended the Sioux service, about 30 each Sabbath. Anna Jane remarked the first Saturday after her father left home, "We can't have any Sabbath because two men & one woman are gone," referring to Mr. & Mrs. Adams & her papa. Still three Sabbaths have brought to us privileges even though the preached word & the great congregation have been wanting.

Friday, June 12

Mr. Riggs reached home two weeks since. He left for Big Stone Lake accompanied by Mr. Hopkins of Traverse des Sioux, last Monday. They have gone, hoping for opportunities to proclaim the word of God to the Sioux in that region. We expect their return here tomorrow.

The box from Hawley reached us safely. I should have been glad to have known their names, also what particular articles were designed for our family use & what for the station. I almost fancied that some old friend had dried the blackberries for me, but there was no name to designate for whom they were intended, so we divided them & the other things also, among the three families.

When Mr. & Mrs. Adams returned here a Miss Cunningham from Ohio accompanied them. She has been at Mr. S. W. Pond's during the past winter & is now with us. I cannot but hope her stay with us will be a blessing to us all. I believe she intends returning to Ohio in the fall. And then if Henrietta could be with us next fall or spring I should feel that our children would not be so much in danger of growing up like the heathen.

Lac qui Parle, June 30, 1849

My dear Sister, [Lucretia]

Doubtless you have looked for an acknowledgment of the box of donations from South Deerfield ere this. It did not reach us last fall as you hoped, but arrived safely only a few weeks since. We thank you all for this labor of love, though we cannot call each by name....

Not many days since a little girl stole one of Thomas' dresses which I had hung up to mend. She wanted to make herself a short gown. Before

I discovered the theft her father returned the dress to me, saying he had whipped his daughter to make her wise, intimating that I would compensate him. As they are suffering from want of food, I gave him a few potatoes, not wanting to reward him so freely as to cause it to be an inducement to steal and restore, as we have sometimes feared was the case.

The Indians are now almost half starving, and are about going out for buffalo meat, wild roots. A few have a little corn.

Our children were very much pleased with the presents sent them by their little cousins. They would be glad to see them here, and together gather prairie flowers by the apron full. Isabella & Martha have no idea of moderation in picking flowers in the big garden where bushels would hardly be missed. Very likely if they should pay you a visit, you would need to reprove them for taking liberties with your shrubbery, which your own children would not be tempted to.

I flatter myself that by having an early supper this warm Saturday afternoon, I should be able to finish this letter before sunset. But just as I had seated myself with pen in hand, an Indian came in with a catfish for sale. His story was this—the muskitos were eating up his child, and he wanted something for it, a shirt in exchange for the fish. This letter must be laid aside if the catfish was prepared for breakfast & thus the time has been occupied until the sun has just sunk behind Lac qui Parle. Its radiance still lingers on cloud & lake, forming a lovely scene which I wish you could enjoy with us. It is a more beautiful view at this hour than any we had at Traverse. . . .

Monday morn, July 2

A Miss Cunningham from Ohio is with us this summer. The children, consequently, enjoy what they have not done for a long time, a regular daily school. It is indeed a blessing to have her with us, but one we do not expect to enjoy but two months longer. We very earnestly desire Henrietta to take her place, if Ma'a can spare her. If she should reside with you, it will not, I suppose, be necessary for H. to remain with her, as I know you will be ready to do all in your power to render her comfortable. I long to hear how she is located.

The muskitoes are exceedingly annoying today. You can hardly imagine the like, and at night they are beyond endurance unless we are sheltered by a muskitoe bar or smothered in smoke. A few nights since, not being able to sleep, I listened for sometime to their dismal humming, wailing song. I could compare it to nothing but the howling of a pack of wolves, thirsting for blood.

My health is about as usual. We have a comfortable house which, though unfinished, is more convenient than the log houses we have hitherto occupied. How I should love to welcome you here.

Lac qui Parle, Sept. 18, 1849
My precious Mother,

I hope Sister Henrietta's health may be restored & her life be spared for many years.... We have written to her to join us here, & I still hope that her health will be such as to render such a course advisable. I should suppose that the atmosphere here would be more favorable to persons inclined to lung disease than New England. We would gladly do all we could for her comfort, yet she would doubtless lack many conveniences she would enjoy in New England. May the Lord direct you all in this decision.

You inquire what we are doing for the Indian females. The most that I am able to do is occasionally read the scriptures to, or converse with some of them. I sometimes feel as though I ought to try to do more, & last winter I had a small class on the Sabbath. Perhaps I shall be able again to teach those or some others. They were young married women & able to read the Bible with a little assistance. They came to our house at the time the Sabbath School assembled in the church.

I had not heard of Alfred's illness until I received your letter. How we are scattered & how little we know of each others afflictions.

Lac qui Parle, Minnesota Ter., Oct. 10, 1849
My dear Mother,

I do not like to have this sheet forwarded without my signature, & yet my head ache would almost excuse me from writing. But I am much better today than yesterday & have great cause to praise the Lord for his goodness in relieving the severe pain in my face & neck.

Previous to the birth of our babe I suffered more than usual both in body & mind. The promise "He will deliver thee in six troubles" sometimes comforted me not a little, still I felt unusually fearful about the result. And I think now that a skillful attendant could have saved me considerable suffering, but now it is past & I will remember "no more the anguish, for joy that a man is born into the world." When I recollect that you have been the mother of twelve children, & I of but six, I can only wonder that your life is yet spared after having suffered so much. I would rather not follow your example in this respect.

I feel very desirous to hear whether Henrietta purposes joining us next spring. (If it is best) how I should rejoice to see her. It would be a great comfort to me if she could be with me now while Mr. Riggs is absent. I have felt almost inclined to veto his leaving home now, but I am afraid I am losing all womanly heroism, & getting to be more & more timid & childlike not to say babyish.

Lac qui Parle, Minnesota, Nov. 10, 1849
My dear brother Alfred,

This Saturday eve my heart goes forth to thee. And thine perhaps is also now communing with mine on this our natal day. And can it be that Alfred is forty & I am thirty six? I have just been looking over the record which we have of our father's family, and it tells me that soon we shall have passed the noon of life. . . . I feel sometimes that both the spiritual & temporal suffer in consequence & that I am becoming slothful, stupid & melancholy. I have enough in my own family to keep alive my affections & my mental & bodily energies it would seem, but the poor body is so wearied with labor or worn with care or racked with pain, that the heart & the mind suffer with it.

I am thankful my husband retains more of youthful elasticity of spirit than I do. It is not pleasant to think of growing older unless we can grow wiser & better. The torpor of intellect, the decrepitude of age are not to be desired & still we choose & love life rather than death. Is it because the valley seems so dark & the river so deep?

You have probably learned of the addition to our family of another son. He is a healthy baby & cries about as much as babies usually do. The little girls take considerable care of him. Thomas wants to "diss him" (kiss him) very often & to pinch him about as often. I remarked today that I wished you could see Thomas. Isabella inquired if I thought you would like him because he was such a high tempered boy. I presume that would grieve you, but he is such an energetic merry boy, that mirth is constantly gushing forth, & that, I know would please you as it does us. For some two or three weeks past he has been learning to load & shoot a pop gun. His persevering efforts have been successful & the house has been made to ring, "Look papa! did shoot my popdun."

Dec. 6

This is your namesake's birthday. How vividly I can recall that eventful morning, when a mother's love first swelled my heart with its joyful throbbing. I was too happy to sleep. It was enough to know that my first born son slept quietly by my side. Now he is twelve years old — perhaps rather small for his age but active & industrious & if he learns to govern himself we hope he will become a useful man.

I must tell you that I am writing with an eagle's quill. My mind however does not catch inspiration from the proud bird that was doomed to die that its plumage might tell of Indian bravery (so called)! But is it bravery to murder unprotected women & children because they are enemies? This quill is from a Ruya's wing & is worn by warriors for women & children they have slain. For each victim one feather. If he is a man, a *Wanmdi* feather denotes the fact, fastened with a bunch of colored horse hair upon the head of the brave who killed him. Thus the warrior trumpets his own glory. We suppose the *Wanmdi* to be the Royal eagle, but are not enough of ornithologists to decide with certainty, from the feathers, & we have never seen the splendid bird. The Ruya, which the Indians regard as inferior to the *Wanmdi* we sometimes see on the wing.

Tues. eve, Jan. 1850

How strange this date looks after having written the forties for ten years. When this half century upon which we have now entered is past, the probability is that our children will have passed away with it.

We have thus far had very pleasant winter weather, not extremely cold. For ourselves we might wish it to continue but mild weather will not bring the buffalo from their northern haunts, and for the sake of the Indians, the approach of buffalo is to be desired. Their corn crop was small last fall, & besides other furs are scarce and some of them not very valuable; but the buffalo furnishes food, houses, furniture, clothing: no wonder the proximity of buffalo is to be desired by these northern Dakotas.

You are probably aware that we in these ends of the earth are now residents of an organized territory, Minnesota. Is it not a pretty name? The meaning is, water mighty turbid.

Our Indians are now returning from their fall hunt. A party came in last week bringing the corpse of one who had died a few days previous. She, with her husband & others, were on their way from Prairieville near Fort Snelling. After her giving birth to a son they rested one day! The next day they traveled too at night. She was sick—a day or two after they knew she must die & her husband left her to get new garments for her to wear in death and in the grave. When he returned to the camp she was already dead & had left another young child besides the babe. Mrs. Pettijohn, who has an infant son, but a few days old, nursed the little motherless one today....

Lac qui Parle, Minnesota Ter., Jan 10, 1850
My own dear Mother

I long very much to hear of your situation. Sometimes I wish that we were so situated as to offer you a home with us, & then again I think that even if we were, our children are so noisy, that you would soon be wearied with them. Indeed I am often tired by them, especially in the winter when they are so much confined to the house. And such a long imprisonment is to them equally wearisome if not more so than to me. Thomas in particular is exceedingly fond of outdoors & exercise, though not hardy enough to endure the cold. He has already frosted his ears & the fingers on one hand, & still has become no wiser by his painful experiences....

Some time ago I was reminded of a story which you told me years ago about a woman who wanted a floor painted. Old Thunderface, who considers himself a chief of "the five lodges," came one Sabbath for medicine. As he did not need it for immediate use, but for the future, Mr. Riggs told him that he would fill his vials & bottle in the morning, to which he apparently assented. They were accordingly placed in the medicine case. However, he shortly after demanded them, & as this wrath at the postponement waxed too hot to be repressed without some demonstration, he put them on the floor at his feet & furiously stamped them in pieces. Two of the bottles had contained oil, of which a sufficiency remained to mark for a long time the place where he sat & the print of his footsteps to the door as he angrily left the house. Thanks to soap & boiling lye, they are now effaced.

As I grow older I feel more & more the necessity of keeping very humble, when pride creeps into my heart I am sure to do something or say something which occasions me great sorrow. Doubtless pride is an inherent evil in the human heart, but it seems to me that it is greatly fostered in the education of children & youth.

How very difficult it is to do right, & to do so from right motives at all times, & still it is far more difficult to induce children to do so. May God have mercy upon our children.

Lac qui Parle, April 27, 1850
My dear Mother,

Sometimes I feel strong hopes that Mr. Riggs will meet you with Henrietta & Joseph at Mendote or Kaposia, ready to ascend the St. Peters. We will try & make you as comfortable as in our power. Today my husband said to me "If your mother & Henrietta come you will give them your bedroom," to which I assented, but I fear I shall not have the privilege. As my fears outweigh my hopes, I have concluded to commence this sheet. And yet how very superfluous writing would seem if you could come & spend six months, or a year or two with us. Our children feel very desirous to see their grandmother & doubtless will trouble you with their questions. But I believe grandmothers have considerable patience with their grandchildren.

Monday, May 8

.... A few days since I prepared for you & Henrietta some pillows of down, which shall be kept unused until I hear that you are not coming. If you think down will be too enervating I can furnish almost anything of the pillow kind which you may wish. But I am almost astonished at myself that I indulge any hope of your attempting to cross the prairie — to sleep in a tent, & upon a bed made on the ground. I should certainly send down a mattress if I knew you would dare make the effort necessary to visit us. But I will send pillows & bedding, & if, & if, & if — then husband will furnish a substitute for a bed. We often travel with buffalo robes for a bed but a mattress is more comfortable at night, though rather too bulky for convenience during the day.

Lac qui Parle, July 1, 1850
My dear sister Hetta,

You are now probably once more upon the hills of New England, & I cannot but hope with restored health.

Doubtless ere this you have received letters from us, showing how fondly & tenaciously we have clung to the hope that you might, although an invalid, be able to join us this summer. And now as this hope has faded, we are again hoping that by another spring, if not this autumn, you could join us. We so long to see you & to have the children enjoy your kindly influence that we think it would be right for us to bear your traveling expenses & furnish you with such clothing as you would need while here, if you will come & stay with us a year even though you are not able to teach a regular school. You can judge best whether you are able to assist me at all in the care of the children, sewing a little or anything of the kind. Whether you are or not, we should rejoice to see you, & we would take the best care of you & mother too that is in our power, but we have no funds of our own sufficient to defray the traveling expenses, & we ought not to use the funds of the Board unless the probability is that you would be able to render us some little assistance. ...

July 4

Where are my mother & sister now? And now I have a request to make of you to gather me some flower seeds during the summer. If you would send me a few occasionally in a letter it would not exceed 1/2 an ounce. Or in a newspaper—though perhaps that would be contrary to post office regulations & I do not wish you to transgress any laws. But if you cannot send them by mail, you can make me up a packet & send it to the Missionary Board before the middle of next winter. I desire particu-larly shrubs & perennials that are hardy & require but little care. Send me a few lilac seeds in a letter—or mountain ash berries.

Henry Martyn is creeping & of course getting into all kinds of mis-chief. This morning he tipped over the coffee pot—fortunately it was not scalding hot. Thomas is very active & noisy—fond of play & work. "Will chop for mama when I get bigger." We have not commenced teach-ing him to read yet. Anna Jane can read a little. She has not received as much attention as our other children did. They have studied a few lessons in Botany but I am not a very good teacher. So many other du-ties interfere, it is often hard to tell which is the most important.

Fort Snelling, Minnesota Territory, Lac qui Parle, July 1, 1850
My dear Sister [Lucretia],

I cannot thank you enough for your kind letters, & your equally kind efforts to aid me. Situated as we are, where hiring sewing &c. are out of the question, the relief they have afforded me, they can hardly realize who are able to obtain assistance when necessary. May the Lord bless you all for this labor of love . . . to aid me in clothing our little ones. But a few weeks ago I said to my husband, in reference to such supplies, "Last year so many of our friends remembered us, it is not probable that many of them will be able to again this year." God in his goodness has enabled our friends in South Deerfield to remember us again this year also.

You wish me to write how the dresses fit. I think very well & though I have not yet put them together, I thought I ought first to acknowledge them, as we have an opportunity of sending to the post office next week.

I was very glad to see the names of the donors attached to the articles. A name will sometimes call up forgotten scenes, but if it does not, it gives a reality to the present. It brings sister spirits into communion with my spirit. . . . dear sister, say to those other dear sisters, that although prairies & rivers, valleys & hills intervene, I accept with heartfelt gratitude the ready hands & willing hearts, which have been proffered me this service. . . .

You will be gratified to know that our children were very much delighted with the kind gifts sent. Each one of them seemed to rejoice as much (if not more) in the little wagon, & in Henry Martyn's shoes, as they would have done had they been exclusively for their own benefit.

Mr. Riggs was absent from home five weeks. We watched for him the last week of his absence day after day, as we used to watch for our dear father when on his return from Boston. Those recollections have been revived of late, indeed they always are when my husband is away from home. He reached here, to our great joy, June 22nd, Saturday evening just about dark. I have suffered sufficiently from poor health to sympathize with the sick in some degree. The album quilt will remind me of others whose names are written there.

July 4

Doubtless very patriotic demonstrations have been made all this morning in many parts of our land, but we are away from all the noise & parade connected with Independence day. Mr. Riggs & Alfred gathered a few strawberries this morning. How pleasant & yet how sad are the associations. Many a time we have gathered them together in our childhood. But strawberry time also revives the recollection of our dear departed brother Thomas. At this place strawberries have never been abundant since our residence here. At Traverse des Sioux they grew luxuriantly & plentifully. . . .

Lac qui Parle, Sept. 2, 1850
My dear Mother,

Last evening, which was Sabbath, hearing Thomas cry after he had gone to rest, I went to the chamber. Alfred was teaching him to say "Now I lay me," & the sentence "If I should die" distressed him very much. I soothed him by asking God to keep him through the night & make him a good boy. He has never seen a corpse, but a few weeks ago he saw Mrs. Antoine Renville buried & he has seen dead birds & chickens. He wanted to know "What is to die, mama," & evidently felt that it was something very incomprehensible & fearful. I felt a difficulty in explaining it & I wished also to soothe the animal excitement & not lessen the serious state of mind he manifested. . . .

God is blessing us with comfortable health.

Lac qui Parle, Oct. 28, 1850
My precious Mother,

Your kind letter containing the sad intelligence of H's departure reached us on the 25th. We are sorrowful, and we thank God that her last days on earth were so tranquil, & that the comforts of her own dear childhood's home were again granted her for a brief space — that kind friends ministered to her wants. I should love to mingle my tears with yours for those who have gone since last I left the home of my childhood, but it may not be now. Moses writes that Alfred's health is declining. . . .

The mission families here, received this week from Quincy Ill. a barrel of good apples! Mr. Adams who was associated with us last winter is now there on account of Mrs. A's health. Sometime since he wrote us that he had been endeavoring to procure us some apples in vain, because winter apples were not then in market & no one was willing to sell unless at a high price. The question passed through my mind, are these Christian brothers & sisters who are afraid they shall sacrifice a few cents on a barrel of apples, & are unwilling to do so for the sake of those who have never enjoyed such a treat at their mission homes? The tears started into my eyes, when I thought how regardless some of Christ's professed followers were, of those who are laboring for them in the dark corners of the earth. Then I recollected widow Taylor giving me, slipping into my hand, the wherewith to procure apples or something of the kind as she said, & the remembrance of that act affords me as much pleasure now & perhaps more than the enjoyment of the fruit did then. I had concluded that there were not many widow Taylors, but this barrel of apples proves that there are some of a like spirit.

Fri. eve, Nov. 27

We shall long for another letter from you soon, one of your precious long letters. Tell cousin Sophronia that I have just made Thomas a full suit out of the pieces of blue cloth she sent me some time ago. They were too small to use for Alfred when I received them. . . . The old fashioned sleeves were the right shape to cut into a sack coat, & almost every scrap found its place as though it had been designed for the purpose.

Martha is at Traverse des Sioux spending the winter at Mr. Hopkins!

Lac qui Parle, June 5, 1851
My dear Sister [Julia],

On the arrival of our last mail I looked for a letter from Chatham, but finding none, I instinctively opened the Oberlin Evangelist. It told me what I feared, of your & our bereavement [Alfred's death]. It is our privilege to weep, . . . and yet we should not abandon ourselves to selfish grief. We could not wish our love who is now free from sickness & pain & sin & sorrow, again to suffer, even though our own suffering would be lessened thereby. . . .

Mon. eve, June 9

I do, dear sister, sympathize with you most tenderly. I can realize something of the desolation you must feel, by the sadness I often feel when my husband is absent for a few weeks & the thought passed through my mind, if he should never return. You know too, what a deep & for a time what a dark sorrow to me was that of Thomas' death. Yet even then, I would thank God that he had spared my husband. . . .

My husband has been absent for three weeks, & we do not expect him for two or three more. Our oldest son—accompanied his father, & as Martha is still absent, our family is quite small for us, two of the children we had with us last winter having also left. We could easily make room for you & Charles, if you should think it best to join us. It would be very pleasant to us to have you with us & I think you might be useful.

Tues. June 24

My husband is still absent. We expected him last Saturday & again today but the rivers are so swollen by recent terrible rains that he has made very little homeward progress for nearly a week. He, with Alfred & Martha & a son & daughter of Mr. Huggins of the Traverse station, are encamped on the prairie two or three days journey from here waiting for the subsiding of the waters. I feel considerable solicitude on their account, & can only find relief by commending them to the ever watchful care of our omnipresent God & Father. Mr. Riggs sent me your letter which he received when at St. Peters. It is to me a precious letter....

We are now expecting to go East next fall... I wish either you or Moses would inform us of the mode of conveyance if any there is from Cleveland to Chatham or from some point on the canal from Portsmouth. What route we shall take is undecided. The fact that we must leave some of our children with our friends here until our return, detracts very much from the pleasant anticipations we might indulge. I hope the tour may be profitable to both body & spirit, though like all other joys & pleasures it must be mingled with sadness & sorrows. The funds for publishing the proposed Lexicon of the Dakota language are nearly raised.

Lac qui Parle, July 10, 1851
My dear Mother,

Why this long silence? Are you sick? If so, do ask someone to write a few lines for you. Under the new postal arrangement we have no excuse for being ignorant of the situation, & circumstances of our dear kindred & friends. I have but little time that I can take for writing, & yet I wish to prepare several short messages in readiness for our first regular mail. It will be due next Tuesday, & as Mr. Riggs is absent, I shall be obliged to act as postmaster's clerk. But I do not imagine the duties of the office will be very troublesome here.

Mr. Riggs reached home with Alfred & Martha a week ago last Saturday. They were nearly 13 days on the way home from Traverse on account of the swollen rivers which were impassable, or rather not fordable. I felt great anxiety about them but the Lord graciously preserved them. My husband has gone down to the Traverse to be present at a treaty now pending with the Indians of the Upper St. Peters. He had not intended leaving home quite so soon but the afflicting intelligence that we received of the death of Mr. Hopkins, determined him to leave yesterday morning.... We are informed that Mr. Hopkins went out to bath before breakfast on Friday last, & doubtless was drowned in the St. Peters. His clothes were found near the water, but his body had not been found when the messenger left on Sat. last. Poor precious sister Hopkins, how my heart aches for thee. I think she is not much past 25 & has four young children left fatherless....

Love to all. We are in comfortable health, though a painful sensation in my left side warns me that my time on earth may be short.

{Letter from Mary Ann to her brother Moses, who included it in his letter to Julia}

If you could look in upon us, you would doubtless think we were in an uncomfortable situation. But we are much more comfortably supplied than we supposed we could be two weeks ago. Before this reaches you, probably you will have received a copy of "The Pioneer," containing an account of the fire, on the third of March which suddenly consumed our dwelling & the greater part of what it contained. Even now it seems so dreamlike, that I occasionally forget that it is indeed a reality. All the momentos of friends, save a very few small ones that were in my escritoire are gone. But the remembrance of the givers abides with us still. Yesterday Mr. Riggs brought in a piece of glass from the ruins which from its shape, I recognized as a part of a small ivory box ornamented with Mother of pearl, an imitation of pearls, given me by Brother Alfred years ago.

At the time of the fire our family consisted of fourteen, three of these were half breed children. We had seven beds, three of which with the bedding were saved, tho' one of the comfortables & bed quilts was badly burned, one chair was also saved & an old pine stand. These were in the room occupied by Miss Spooner & the girls, & are all of that kind of furniture which is left us.

Not a table or a table cloth, nor anything to furnish a table was saved. A few cracked dishes were taken from the fire. No change of clothing for Mr. Riggs, myself, Alfred, Anna Jane, Thomas, Henry, or Joseph our half-breed boy of about 12, & not even patches or the cloth to mend our worn out garments. No flour, no butter, no sugar—no soap, no candles, nothing eatable, but two barrels of corn & a supply of potatoes were saved. The stoves were all melted, & the kettles all but melted or broken. The fire swept everything before it so rapidly that we were almost panic stricken. I cut my hand quite badly in breaking open a window to help secure an exit & everything I touched was marked with blood until an Indian woman picked up a scrap of calico & bound it up for me. We took refuge in the church & made a fire & warmed ourselves.

Before we had time to think how destitute we were, Mr. Frenier, a Dakota Gentleman, in charge of the McLeod's trading post came with a two horse team. He brought us a few plates, tea cups & saucers, knives & forks and a tea pot. Also a barrel of potatoes (ours were then beneath the burning ruins) part of a barrel of flour, some coffee, sugar, three pails & two small frying pans. This he doubtless did as Mr. McLeod's agent. Soon after, from his own wardrobe he sent or brought a coat, two shirts, a pair of socks, shoes & moccasins, & a black silk cravat. Another young man, three fourths Dakota, sent a shirt & brown cloth for Alfred's pants, some flour & a piece of beef, five plates & four knives & forks, & his little daughter gave our Anna calico for a dress.

A man who is full Dakota, gave Mr. Riggs a coat & a piece of beef, & his wife cooked some beans, our first meal after the fire.

A Dakota woman, who is a widow, gave me a candle stick & Henry a pair of boots. Another, who is also a widow, but whose husband was a white man, brought us, just as we were eating our first meat after the fire, a good loaf of white bread. I hardly know whether I cried or laughed when I saw it. Perhaps I did both for I was excited & nervous. She also brought me, the next day, a dress, a shawl & a pair of stockings, all of which were very acceptable in our destitution. Another Dakota woman, who is the wife of a Frenchman, sent me a shawl, which we also prize, as Isabella's & mine were now burned. Only a part of Isabella's was burned & the pieces were made the most of in our extremity. One piece was made into a cap for Henry, who, like his father & mother, ran out of the house bare headed. I have sometimes felt oppressed by these gifts from those who are not rich in this world's goods, but I hope some time, if the Lord wills, to return in part these favors. But if we never can repay them, the Lord can. It has been a great consolation to us to witness their generosity & sympathy....

On Saturday, the morning after the fire, we sent a Dakota man to Dr. Williamson to inform him of our situation. On Monday evening, he returned with Dr. W. bringing us a cooking stove, bed, bedding, clothing, some butter, sugar, dried fruit. Also three bibles, & several other things we were needing.

Thus, in the Providence of God, the many comforts which we possessed before the fire He has taken away from us, & supplied our necessities since in a wonderful manner.

Let us praise Him for His Goodness & Mercy. "He has not visited us according to our sins, nor rewarded us according to our iniquities."

The church which we occupy has two rooms. We have put up curtains at one end of them & purpose doing so in the other.

Nine of us sleep in one room & four in the other. One of our number was gone to her father at the time of the fire.

Miss Spooner is very nearly my size & she has generously given & lent me such clothing as the circumstances required. She has been a great comfort to us. May the Lord reward her.

Mission Chapel, Lac qui Parle, June 12, 1854
Dear sister Julia,

This second week in June I am thinking of you. I thought at first that I would not take time so soon to welcome you to your new home, but I have risen from my bed refreshed by a little rest, & have taken my pen. Both husband & myself thank you for your warm hearted letter. The kind expressions & deeds of Sympathy that have flowed in upon us since the fire has been truly wonderful, as wonderful as the Lord's kind care for you and Alfred during his sickness.

How I should love to see you, to talk over the Lord's goodness by the way to us both. I am not sorry for the change in your situation but I rejoice with you. Hope ere this you have written to mother about it. If no one objects, I shall love to have you retain the L. in your name even when Daniels is annexed. I think one who has been previously married would perhaps feel no objections. Of course if he does, you will regard his wish rather than mine.

My dear friend, Mrs. Hopkins, was married last April to Rev. G. H. Pond of this territory. My friends are coming nearer & the hope is almost forming, that I shall some day see them once more this side of Jordan. Yet hope cannot be my sanguine, while my health is so poor.

I long to hear from you from your new home. Please write how far it is from the Mississippi & what facilities for traveling to it—how large it is etc.

May God give you grace & patience for all your joys & trials in your new situation.

May the Lord bless dear Charles also. Tell him Aunt Mary hopes he will seek to make his new sisters happy even though he had to deny himself to do so.

With love,
Mary Ann Longley Riggs

CHAPTER 6

Hazelwood

1854 ~ 1862

Hazelwood Republic, Summer of 1862.

ollowing the fire of 1854, Stephen built a new home at Hazelwood, near the Santee Agency. Mary Ann was ill during much of this period of time. Riggs and Williamson, the only two remaining missionary families, consolidated their efforts and formed the Hazelwood Republic, an experiment to teach the Dakota, who were hunters and gatherers, how to become farmers. The experiment failed for a combination of reasons: the Indian land continued to be confiscated; Indians starved as food rotted in government storehouses; tensions grew between the *farmer Indians*, those willing to try to farming, and the *blanket Indians*, those who wanted to retain their own culture and way of life; the number of white settlers increased dramatically; and the federal government's attention was focused on its involvement in the approaching Civil War.

Changes in the immediate family, as well as the advent of the postal system impacted on Mary Ann's letter writing: her son, Alfred, was away at Knox College, Galesberg, Illinois and Chicago Theological Seminary; Isabella attended Western Female Seminary, Oxford, Ohio; in 1858 Mary Ann's mother, Martha, died and her daughter, Martha, went to Western Female Seminary; and Lucy Spooner, Mary Ann's confidante, returned east and became a correspondent.

Robert Baird was born nine months after the move to Hazelton, and Mary Ann's eighth child, Mary Cornelia Octavia was born in February, 1859.

In 1858 Minnesota was admitted as the thirty-second state of the United States.

Yellow Medicine, Sept. 22, 1854
Dear Lucy,

Though my heart went with you yesterday it was well my body remained behind to restrain & divert the children from their great grief. I hardly know what they would have done if I had gone too.

Mr. Hunter has a strong desire that you should leave for him *Old Folks at Home* & procure another for yourself in Cincinnati or else where. I have at his request written to Mr. Riggs to pay you if you are willing to spare it. If you are, mention it to him & send it up by Alfred.

I send Isabella a small package. The skirt she will give to Mrs. Huggins for one of her little girls with my love.

I wish her to send up the clothes for washing that she will not need. The sun has set Mr. [SIC] to you & Isabella.

My dear Lucy,

We left Lac qui Parle last Wednesday. It was a beautiful day & though we felt sad at leaving a place that had been so long home, everything in nature seemed bright & hope inspiring. Most of the Indians left us a few days previously. The war spirit had been very active notwithstanding the small pox had been making sad savages in some of the families at Lac qui Parle. *Wiyaha* had several of his children sick at one time. One died & he carried her in his arms to the grave & laid her in it himself. *Okiso* has buried two children & others also have died of the small pox whom you did not know. *Marpiya Sna's* "The whispers" daughter hung herself because her parents reproved her for something. She walked away to the cornfield as though she did not care what they said, & soon after was found with her neck broken hanging to the scaffold on which they watch their corn.

Monday morn, & such a beautiful morning! I wish you were here to enjoy it with us. Yesterday Dr. W. preached at the morning service in Dakota. It was quite well attended. In the afternoon Mr. Riggs preached in English to an audience of about 20 grown persons! Lorenzo was the only Dakota present. It was the largest congregation of white people that I have seen, this side of Traverse des Sioux.

Oh how much I long to know what your plans & expectations are for the future. Is there any room for me to hope that you will come back to us again? I hope your next letter will tell me all about it. If I hear soon, I will make no plans till then. . . . It seems as though we had been almost constantly receiving tokens of Christian sympathy since the fire. In many things our loss is not felt now, but only remembered among the trials of the past. When I was sick I could not but feel that God had been very kind in giving us so little sickness in our first days of poverty, when we had no change of sheets, & when I had to borrow clothing of you. I think I shall be able to sympathize more fully with the poor, & especially with those who have suddenly been reduced to poverty, than I could otherwise have done.

Hazelwood, Yellow Medicine, Min. Ter. Nov 24, '54
Dear Lucy,

I received a note from you a few weeks since, & was very glad, still I am hoping & wishing for a long letter. One that will seem like a talk in my bedroom last winter. I will not press you for such a chat, & yet my heart longs to know where Lucy's heart is, what her hopes & expectations are, her joys & sorrows.

As Isabella & Martha have both written, I can hardly expect to tell you any news. They have doubtless told you how the Indians are returning from the payment half starved & many of them are ready to steal anything they can find, such as cattle, corn & potatoes, table cloths, thermometers, iron heaters. When the *Sisitonwans* went down in September some one of them stole Mr. Riggs thermometer. . . .

Shall you be so situated this winter that you can either do a little sewing for me or get some one else to do it under your supervision? Of course I will pay whoever you think best to employ.

Will you make a trifling purchase for me & enclose it in a letter? 3 yds. narrow linen edging about the quality & width of that on the night cap you gave me which was burned up. I shall send for some other little things soon, & I will either send you the money or an order on Dr. Weed.

I do not know whether it is best to send to Cincinnati for a melodeon or not. We should love to have you select it, but we have lost so many things by the way this last summer, that Mr. Riggs thinks perhaps it would be safer to get one in St. Paul. I hope we shall be able to get one next summer. The girls have exerted themselves more than I expected. I think they will prize a melodeon very much now if they have one.

Hazelwood, Tues. Feb. 6, 1855
Dear Miss Spooner,
Knowing what you do by experience of missionary life, you will not suppose that we have been without trials since we came here, though you may perhaps be unable to imagine what they have been. One of the principal has been connected with the sawmill. It has used up the timber too fast while it was sawing. Mr. Riggs has given each man who is building a house enough boards to floor one room, but they expected the sawmill would supply them any amount of boards without expense for sawing! . . . .

It is very pleasant for us to have neighbors so near as Dr. Williamson's. We held a united communion there the last Sabbath in Jan. Ordinarily we have Sabbath services at both stations. . . . I have been over to Dr. W's four times this winter, the only times I have been out excepting when I have called in at Miss Pettijohn's. . . . We expect Angelique will live with us when we get a bedroom finished up stairs. . . .

If you can get a gingham sun bonnet made besides the gingham dress I shall be very glad. If you can get only one made, the dress is the most important. The bonnet is for myself or Isabella as circumstances require, suitable for occasional Sabbath wear. Please also procure me a hood if you can. Invisible green or some other dark color for the outside would suit me, still you will exercise your own judgment. I will abide by your selection.

The cloak that was your mother's is a great comfort to me this winter. Do thank her again & give her my kind regards.

Hazelwood, March 3, '55
Dear Lucy,
Doubtless you have remembered Lac qui Parle today and the scenes

that you witnessed there a year since, when we fled from the burning ruins of our house & took refuge in the church. Today we have lived over in memory that sad day with its sunny spots here & there gleaming through the clouds.

I have commissioned Mr. Stanley who is going to St. Paul to procure for me a daguerreotype of the new wire suspension bridge across the Mississippi at St. Anthony. . . .

In addition to all the troublesome commissions from me, will you make for me one or two more little purchases? 1 Linen collar. I wish it for a pattern for Mr. Riggs's collars. 4 yards sky blue basting riband about an inch wide. This riband I should like to have you send by mail. If capes are worn like the dresses please have one made like the gingham dress or send me a pattern if more convenient.

. . . . We had six days of inclement cold weather convening Feb. 21st & continuing til the 27th, the thermometer ranging from two to nineteen degrees below zero. . . .

Feb. 8, 1856
My dear Mrs. Drake,
. . . . The weather, that unfailing topic, has been so severely cold that we have had no day for nearly two months when the thermometer was up as high as 32 above zero, & most of the time it has ranged from 28 above to 30 below.

Friday, Feb. 9
Our baby, Robin had found a name before your letter reached us. He is a very pleasant child. . . . His smiles impart happiness to all around. Plain in features as he undoubtedly is, Anna Jane calls him "our beautiful boy."

Hazelwood Yellow Med., Feb. 16, 1856
My dear Mrs. Drake,
I wrote you last week & now send the list of articles I wish you to purchase for us. I have silk for Martha's apron & wish only for a girdle or strings. The under vests I mean, are like the unbleached cotton hose,

if they cost over 1.50 a piece do not get but one. If you can get better brass candlesticks of a square shape instead of round, get such as you think best. . . .

The French floss which we wish, I do not know how to specify the quantity, but I presume 12 1/2 or 15 cents worth is as much as we shall use. Isabella worked me a collar for a new year's present. Angelique & Anna Jane worked the edge for a pair of pantalets. It seems quite like old times when you were fitting & fixing work for the girls. But in some respects there is quite a difference. Music is sadly neglected & there is no one here to incite or excite by example.

Hazelwood, Feb. 20, 1857
My dear Mrs. Drake,
. . . . I am glad you still feel an interest in the Dakotas. . . . Lorenzo is now living with his wife & we hope will be kept from again discarding her. . . .

Angelique & Anna Jane often speak of you as though it was the great wish of their hearts to go & see you & Isabella also. There is a probability that Angelique may receive a share of certain half breed lands, if so she will have the means to obtain a better education than she can here.

Do you remember Henok? His wife (a little girl when he took her) has exchanged her cloth skirt for a dress made as nearly as she could like ours. Antoine Renville's wife also dresses in the costume of white women.

Hazelwood, April 18, 1857
My dear Mrs. Drake,
If you could take a bird's eye view of Minnesota at this time, I think you would compassionate our condition. During the present month instead of the warm southwest wind to melt our snow hills & dissolve our ice bridges, the cold north wind has given us a second winter in miniature. Some weeks since, a few pioneer ducks & geese came back to their old haunts, but poor things, those who escaped the Indians' gun have doubtless flown southward again. The Minnesota river is not open here yet, but the sun looks out upon us today genially & in a few more days we think its beams must melt even our ice & snow. . . .

Pajutazee, Hazelwood, Minnesota, Feb. 17, 1858
My dear Mrs. Drake,

....I thank God that Isabella has such a friend. I should love to visit you very much, & perhaps I may if life is spared, before all our daughters graduate at the Western Fem. Sem. We include on our lists for "the Great Western," our adopted daughters, but it is uncertain whether they graduate or not. I think Julia Laframbois intends to go through the course & I hope she may. . . . She seems teachable, conscientious, & studious.

Just now there seems to be a special effort made by traders & Dakotas against schools. It is probably owing to the education fund allowed by treaty, being left unexpended & permitted to accumulate till it excites the cupidity of those who care nothing for schools. Our boarding school consequently is very small, only four at the boarding house; two boys & two girls, & the three we have in our family.

Of late my attention has been called to the numerous patents for sewing machines. It seems as though some of them must be useful. Have you tried them or seen them tried? I feel very desirous to inform myself about them & this I must do through my friends. I should be glad to have Isabella with you when you see some machine in operation, either Grover & Baker's or Wheeler & Wilson's or both. I have no paper I can refer to their advertisements, but I presume they can be found without much difficulty. Mrs. Williamson & I are thinking some of procuring one. Grover & Baker have offered to deduct a third of the price to missionaries. We do not wish to be in haste & make a purchase we shall regret.

Remember Mr. Riggs & myself kindly to your husband & accept our united regards. We have been married 21 years yesterday. If we live, soon the "silver wedding" will be here. Time glides so rapidly away. It seems very probable that we may not both live till that time.

Fall of 1858
My dear Mrs. Drake,

Martha has every thing packed ready to leave in the morning for Oxford, Ohio. We have been so busy that we have hardly had time to think much about how sad we shall be. We have done the best we could for

her outfit. Her father wishing to attend the meeting of the A. B. C. F.
M. at Detroit, it seemed best to spare her my bonnet. It suited me well,
though I fancied it was a mite too small for me.

I suppose Martha may need another winter dress. On account of the
saving of expense I would suggest a dark half-wool delaine or plaid of
some kind of half wool material, but I confide in your judgment.

Hazlewood, Oct. 8, 1859
My dear Son, [at Knox College]

.... Robert was very much disappointed the morning that you left,
that he had not bid good-bye to you all. He was a mind to run after you
for that purpose, but I dissuaded him & promised to write his farewell.
He was quite sick a day or two after you left, something of a chill &
fever. We made a bed in the sitting room & I slept with him two nights.
I could have felt quite lonely & so could we all, but we repressed our
grief, lest indulgence should give it the mastery beyond control.

Andrew [Williamson] brought over our mail on Thursday, the day
of the opening of Synod. There was a letter from Martha. She was safe
back at Oxford, roomed with her cousin Maria Lizzin, daughter of your
uncle, Moses Riggs. The principal item of news or at least the last unexpected, was a deposit she had had made in her teeth by a dentist. Can
you guess the amount of the investment? What will your father say? I
can but think her satisfaction in being poor, is after all in a very easy
respectable kind of poverty. The kind of poverty which those with plenty
of clothing & good bread & butter suffer! in comparison with the
reputed rich. I think we may all still pray, "Give me neither poverty nor
riches."

Our tomatoes have done finely. We have had them on the table daily
since you left. Apprehending a frost we picked the few remaining ones
though green, & very seasonably too, for last night a withering white
frost robed every leaf & twig & flower. Everything looks drooping or
sear, except that tall mallow which still bids defiance to these frosts as
if it were determined to be perennial. But its fall must soon come. I
should also except the bitter sweet; it is still green & the leaves cling
to it lovingly.

Thomas & Henry have been digging potatoes the week past. They have hauled them in Thomas's little wagon. Twelve barrels in the cellar is the result of their labors.

Mon. Morn
Your father reached home Sat. afternoon a little before five in health & safety. While at Mankato he attended a meeting of the trustees of the University!, there being a vacancy he was elected a trustee. A vote was passed inviting Andrew W[illiamson], to visit the place & see whether classes could be obtained for languages & higher mathematics.

Hazlewood, Dec. 7, '59
My dear Son,
Our long looked for mail came today, but not a line for me. Your letter to Isabella was the only one in which I participated. We are glad to hear that you are prospering & trust the Lord's blessing will ever be your portion. I am half afraid you will find your purse empty sooner than you had expected, & although you may think it both logical & economical to choose between a Shakespeare & a coat, you will find a book will not conceal elbow holes or warm you this cold weather. It would be very pleasant to get a box from Chicago next summer, I could think of so many things to fill it, but we are making extra effort in the theory & practice of household economy this coming year. If however such a thing should happen don't forget to send your old pants & under shirts. The first to be remade for Robbie & the last re-modeled for under vests!

What is the price of those Sabbath School hymn books you named? The Traverse church introduced Longs for the Sabbath School & Vestry.

Has anyone written you that John W[illiamson] gives two lessons in singing weekly in a public school at Walnut Hills? Compensation a dollar an hour, I believe. Would it not be more profitable & more useful for you to impart rather than receive in this regard? I thought last winter you half repented having devoted so much time to music. Why should it not serve you in turn for the service you have paid it?

.... Oh! Such a woeful hard time as the boys have had reading your letters! I wish you would write with a little more uniformity, & avoid a few oddities which to me seem out of taste. For instance the use of a curved d in the middle of words. With me it is barely admissible at the end of words. Lastly, your small e, resembles the zigzag lightning more nearly than anything else I can think of. This "lecture on penmanship" is designed for your benefit not only, but for the boys accommodation also. The reading of your letter is a terrible task to them, & your papa & I are the taskmasters.

Write as often as you can to us all. I shall be glad of a good share of letters, but I don't mean to be selfish. Baby, [Cornelia] our pet & joy & pride, stands alone a minute in her basket!

Hazlewood, Jan. 11, 1860
My dear Son,
.... I am glad you find your clothing less expensive than you had feared. If you had told us the color of your coat we could think just how you look, but I fancy it is brown. ...

I sometimes think it unwise to have so much light reading as we do, still as we have commenced the "Troubles of Sandstone," we should like to have you send the Century until it is finished, & then send it to Martha. I fear Martha's health is really suffering from some cause. If she tells you "the secret," I shall trust you to tell it to me. If it is too hard study perhaps she should leave in the spring. Let us know what your plans are when you have formed them, in regard to the spring & summer. ...

The braid & silk came last mail. We will try the silk & let you know if we want more. If they had given the no. of yards on the spool, I could compare it with other silks.

Isabella is in school filling Mrs. Ackley's place. ... She has the older ones read in Dakota in the afternoon & some of the others.

Our darling Mary C. O. has outgrown her basket. She has just tipped it over & crawled out, & creeping to the table is now standing by my chair. She is as much petted & praised as ever & in a fair way to be the worst spoiled of any of our children.

Tues. night, Feb. 14, 1860
My dear Son,

We have had so much delightful weather this winter that it is likely to be a memorable winter on that account.

Our first Harper for 1860 came this month. Where the missing numbers are we know not. Is "The Woman in White" still continued in Harpers Weekly? Will you send them occasionally?

Isabella's plans for next year are just now seemingly frustrated. What school would you recommend? If it were not that we were very desirous that Anna Jane should go with her I think "Holyoke" would attract us most. Does the Female Department at Galesburg close in January? If so that would be an objection to Isabella. I should prefer to have her graduate at the Western Fem. Sem., but I do not think it would be wise to wait another year.

Oomahoo, Pajutazee, Min., March 15, 1860
My dear Son,

I was very glad to get your letter of Feb. 25 - 27th this morning. Thursday the 15th of March, & such a March, no poet ever sang. The weather is most delightful, & the roads about here, are as fine as the weather. I am sorry that you still catch such sorry colds, or let them catch you, but I can't complain of them if they bring me as the result so good a letter from you. . . .

Today's mail brought a letter from one of the proprietors at Ohio F[emale] College, Rev. F. Y. Vail, in which he says, "I trust you will commit this whole matter of your daughter's [Anna Jane] educational expenses, to your heavenly Father & to me, as I have for years been permitted to enjoy the privilege of doing as much of this delightful work as possible." We learn from his letter that he & Mr. Cary the other proprietor, wish to plan their institution on "a public & benevolent basis," & Mr. Vail is now, I suppose, soliciting funds for this purpose. He wishes your father to write him a letter which he can make use of in raising funds. It seems that their college property is estimated at $135,000 of this the proprietors will give $55,000 if the benevolent public will supply the $80,000, $30,000 of which is already pledged. It seems premature for your father to espouse this Institution when he knows so little about it.

I wrote Martha some days ago to take lessons either in music or drawing as she thought best, & I would defray the cost. Music lessons are most in demand here & your father preferred music to drawing, partly on that account. Isabella is now giving lessons to Mr. Huggins & Mr. McCullogh beside Martha Williamson & our girls.

Frolick had a side saddle on for the first time for Isabella to ride to meeting. She is very gentle & not very frolicksome, a wee bit of a pony.

Your father wrote you last week enclosing a draft for $40. I hope you will be successful in earning money in some pleasant & honorable way. The failure in getting help at the Boarding School has resulted in Isabella's teaching three months already. I think she succeeds pretty well in the teaching, though not uncommonly gifted in governing. Robert attends her school & has really waked up & is learning to read. He often gets his book after supper to read awhile before he goes to bed.

Friday

The south wind is bringing back ducks & geese to their summer homes. The first fowl for this season graced our dinner table yesterday. We spoke of you & Martha & wished you with us to assist, but managed to finish completely a large goose, without any aid excepting our family ten. Cornelia sat with one of the girls at table & was initiated into the art of eating wild fowl by a wing bone which she enjoyed as much as any of us. She has learned to walk very considerably of late. She can pass from room to room though she has to avail herself of the wall, partition & doors to aid her in her progress.

If your article on the Ojibwa mission is published, you will of course send us a copy?

Home, May 12, 1860
My dear Son,

.... I have just been out attending to our chickens. We have six very fine broods, & we keep them in the part of the yard north of the house & chicken house. The grass which is still short & but just green is fairly alive with chickens. The aspen grove looks beautifully.

Thomas has made us one flower bed, but the girls have not planted any seeds yet. As we have had no rain for a long time, it is very dry. The early flowers are dwarfed & vegetation is not as forward & abundant as it would have been if the clouds which have hovered over us day after day had distilled dew & rain. High winds have driven them away.

Hazlewood, Aug 1, 1860
My dear Son,

.... This morning I flattered myself that I should find a little time before cooking the dinner for writing, but I was occupied with Cornelia instead, & now our dinner which is to be chicken & beets is needing occasional care. Our chickens have done well this summer, notwithstanding we lost more than 20 one Sat. night. We have eggs quite abundantly during the summer, & some of the hens have been so very obliging as to lay their eggs in the back kitchen & pantry, & one had the presumption to intrude in my bedroom. They are about as unruly in the flower beds as usual, so that with their scratching & Cornelia's unconscious trespasses, Isabella has quite as much to try her patience as you had last summer. Beside these common predators, a visitor extraordinary has taking lodgings on one of her struts, but whether it is one of the Messrs. Gopher, Mole, or Squirrel is not fully determined.

.... Isabella is sewing on the machine this morning. She thinks that little grind stone a "nice little thing that will be a great deal of use." Martha has not made any progress yet in using the machine, she is so busy with other sewing. Perhaps she has told you that her lamp came in perfect safety, not a chimney broken. She packed her things very well indeed, with the exception of a can of peaches, sealed with cement. That of course got bruised & jammed off & the juice spoiled her Virgil & a calico dress.

Our yard & garden do not look as nice as they did last summer, & we all know the reason why. We are in tolerable health.

Home, Oct. 30, '60
My dear Son,

.... It is quite probable that you did not play enough in the open air in your childhood. If Thomas & Henry have better opportunities in this regard for physical development, I fear it is at the expense of their manners, if not of their morals. Living so near a Boarding School of Dakota boys is not to be desired.

I am very glad you were able to make Isabella's & Anna's time pass so pleasantly while at Chicago. I have no doubt their stay there will be a great benefit to them. . . . Cornelia is learning to talk very rapidly. She surprises us often with some new acquisition.

I wish you would take a little time to find me an attractive & easy book for Robert's Sabbath Reading. Cost not to exceed 75 cents. I will give you the titles & prices as taken from Carter's Catalogue of some that I would examine, if I could.

Mamma's Lessons about Jesus	75 cents
Sabbath Talks about Jesus	38 cents
First Footsteps in the Way of Knowledge	25 cents
Easy Lessons for Little Ones at Home	30 cents
Morning Star or Childhood of Jesus	30 cents

Hazelwood, Thurs. eve, Nov. 29, 1860
My dear Son,

Our Thanksgiving day is over & pleasantly over. Your father & I are alone in the sitting room. Dr. Williamson's family, with the exception of aunt Jane & "Smiley," a Dakota boy living with them, came over to meeting & took dinner with us. We spread the table for eighteen, & all sat down at once. Cornelia making nineteen.

Although we had no roast turkey we had beef, & chicken pie, & mince, & plum, & pumpkin pie, etc. etc. How glad we should have been to have had our scattered children home with us, but we are thankful that they are still spared us. We had hoped that the girls' daguerreotypes would have been here before this. . . . I wished to have theirs & yours taken in one group for our home circle, but I suppose they did not so understand me. I believe I often fail to express myself clearly & I fear this defect is rather increasing. A little extra care wearies & confuses me & fevers my brain. Perpetual youth & vigor would be more desirable than the decay & decrepitude of age, at least it would seem so to our imperfect sight. The idea of growing old is not pleasant to me, & if God wills it so, may I never outlive the capability of usefulness. . . .

Sat. eve, Dec. 1
Your father leaves for St. Paul next Tuesday. He hopes to get a law passed in favor of the Dakotas who have made certain attainments, becoming citizens. For my own part I do not feel at all sanguine that he will succeed, nor that success would secure very great blessings, but having confidence in your father's judgment, I endeavor not to damp his enthusiasm. . . .

Mon. Dec. 3
The thread & needles came last mail. Enclosed please find a dollar. Will you credit it to my account & let me know how much I am indebted to you & if convenient give me the items. How glad I should be to have you at home while your father is away.

Hazlewood, Jan. 11, 1861
My dear Son,
You probably know that we delegated to Isabella an especial charge of Anna Jane, with the particular injunction to go & see her before the close of her first term. Consequently she asked leave of absence for a week. Miss Peabody did not grant it, but intimated that if the request was for only two or three days it could have been granted. Isabella, having a short time before learned that her school bill would be $110 instead of $60, as she had expected, felt too poor to go to College Hill & return to Oxford so soon, consequently she relinquished our plan, & invited Anna Jane to the Little Western. The last two mails have brought us no tidings from Anna Jane. . . .

As yet we can hardly say we have any definite plans for the girls. We have wishes & thoughts. First among the wishes, is to have you all at home next summer. As yet we don't see how it can be brought about, but we hope it may....

Another of our wishes is to have Martha & Angelique go to school next year. A probable consequence is that either Isabella or Anna Jane will be needed at home. Circumstances will doubtless indicate which of the two it shall be. Another wish that has grown up quite recently is to have Thomas go from home to school in the course of a year {for} some five or six months, if the way is opened, where he can do some chores. An early friend of mine, Mrs. McKee is now living in St. Anthony. Her husband is the pastor of the Presbyterian church there. They have no children & would, I judge from her letter, be willing to board Thomas if the schools in St. Anthony were suitable.... I think it would be well for Thomas & Henry to be separated awhile. The habit of teasing might be weakened & if they would try to overcome it, it might be easier after a separation. I feel very solicitous about them.

The girls ambrotypes came safely. Sometime perhaps you can get yours taken for us. If it is convenient, I should like it either with Isabella or Martha or Anna Jane.

Have you tested the paraphene candles this winter? We like our lamp very well, but it would not be convenient for kitchen use. The question with us is, is there any economical substitute for tallow candles? Those we buy, are worse by far than those we make ourselves, & the former are often too unendurably troublesome I will say, for I can't describe them. Language that I would like to see in a letter is quite inadequate, too tame, & that which would be appropriate would be quite too revolting.

We are talking of buying buff linen window shades for our sitting room if they would not exceed $1.50 or at the most $1.75 for a window fixtures & all. Can you inform yourself & me about them?

Hazelwood, March 20, 1861
My dear Son,

.... Yesterday morning Thomas & Henry rode our horses down to the agency to get them shod as the roads are very icy. They reached home about 5 P.M. & brought a bag of mail. I emptied it out on to the carpet to hunt the letters, but found none to my surprise & disappointment. Just then the boys, who seemed rather to enjoy our disappointment, began to empty their pockets. Two letters from Anna Jane & one from Isabella & none from Alfred. . . .

We shall probably wish you to make a few purchases for us this spring. But the article that demands immediate attention is a portable desk for your father. I don't wish him to know about it until next February. I wish you to do as you think best about purchasing or getting one made to order. I should like the size to be nine & three eights 9 ³/₈ inches (9 ³/₈) wide, & fifteen & a half (15 ¹/₂) inches long. I should prefer to have solid mahogany, cherry, or black walnut, & not veneered. Black or green velvet is preferable to red for the writing tablet. Either on the outside or the inside, I wish to have a small silver plate marked S. R. Riggs, 1862 (provided such a plate will not exceed a dollar). I have written to my brother Joseph to send you ten dollars as soon as consistent. If he fails to do this, I will remit to you in some other way.

Your father & Thomas are very busy just now hauling logs to the saw mill. Robert is very much interested in learning to read, also in learning Bible verses to repeat at the breakfast table. How very thankful I am that your father is not an agency seeker.

Home, April 18, '61
My dear Son,

Your note of April 2nd to your father, reached us yesterday. He left home last Monday to attend Presbytery at Mankato. I suppose he will write you from there, suggesting that you engage to labor for two months or so. You can doubtless have an opportunity to preach occasionally here, & I think we can afford you as good wages as you mention for a month or two, if you will fill the office of "superintendent of gardening." I will pledge the spoons that I talked of getting towards defraying your expenses, & Thomas says if I can sell his potatoes I may have half of them for the same purpose. As for Henry's potato crop, it was a failure, the dry weather affecting the part of the field where he planted. Besides, he affects to be afraid of your authority when you are at home.

Sat. morn & oh so beautiful. A steamboat just arrived at Yellow Medicine. We heard the bell & saw the steam a few moments since.

Hazelwood, April 30, 1861
My dear Son,

The escritoire alias, "the box" you have purchased for me, I think will be very suitable. Please do it up securely with twine & strong paper & write my name on it before packing. . . . As many old pants, socks, etc. as you think are worth packing & can find room for, I shall be glad to get. Robbie has not yet outgrown pants made of old ones. I find them well worth remaking, when the original material was good & substantial.

I hope Thomas' coat will not exceed $1.25. If I could telegraph you now, while I'm in this seeming strait "betwixt" desires & means, I should say not purchase any coat, but keep the money to come home with. It was the fear about the cutting, that determined me upon the extravagance of purchasing a ready made coat for Thomas. In case you have not bought it when this reaches you let us know & we will try our skill.

Hazelwood Oct. 11, 1861
My dear Son,

. . . . We are waiting & watching with considerable interest the developments of this Republican administration among the Dakotas. Mr. Pierson, the new superintendent of schools, has disbanded the boarding school & dismissed the teachers, the why & wherefore is not yet apparent. He also intimates that he cares but little for either English or Dakota schools for reading, & that mechanical arts are more impor- tant. Mr. Pierson has returned to St. Paul, long may he remain there!

Hazelwood, Thurs. Nov. 14, 1861
My dear Son,

Anna Jane, & Cornelia are the only ones in the house with me. I have just sent Cornelia up stairs to stay with Anna, so that I may secure a quiet hour for writing. You know I haven't the power of abstraction your papa so preeminently possesses, & besides I write so seldom, that my escritoire is peculiarly attractive to little folks. . . .

Last Sabbath was my birthday, & I am 48. As I look back I feel that no regrets for the past can be of any avail, only as they induce greater diligence & watchfulness now & ever.

Wed. eve, Nov. 20

Your papa has Dakota meeting this evening in the church. We have our lamp with a double burner, which has been paid for by contribution. . . . We hoped to procure another one for the church. Rose gave a gold dollar last Saturday for this purpose, & *Winyan* brought a pillow on Monday.

No mail has come up from the Lower agency this week. We are consequently quite in the dark about the war, having heard however that Fremont is superseded. I feel a very strong sympathy for him, though I cannot but think his great wealth has led him into expenses inconsistent with republican simplicity & made him less regardful of "regulations" as well as outlays.

A week ago last Saturday Mr. Cunningham & Thomas went up to Lac qui Parle with potatoes for Mr. Huggins. Isabella went with them & she & Thomas spent the Sabbath. The house Mr. Huggins occupies is one of hewed logs, the ends above the logs, enclosed with green elm boards fastened up perpendicularly & without battens or weather boarding. Of course, the cracks are neither few nor far between. Mr. Huggins has had another attack of opthalmia. As yet it has not invaded our family, & I am sure we have special cause for thanksgiving in this regard. . . .

Isabella has one music scholar. . . . Not long since Isabella received two sheets of music, "Viva L'American" & "Our Banner of Glory." The girls are learning them.

Hazlewood, Jan. 1, 1862
My dear Son,

A happy greeting to all. Little Bell and big Baby have caroled this strain at various intervals all day long. We would extend the greeting to our loved ones away. How very glad we should be to see them face to face. . . .

Your father sends you a small draft with this. Seven of it is from Isabella, who of course will tell you how to use it. Two fifty (2.50) are from Thomas & Henry with which they wish you to get me a pair of spectacles, silver bows, & forward by mail. You know I have never worn glasses. I do not wish them to magnify but a little, also to diminish the distance of sight. I need to hold sewing rather farther from my eyes than is quite convenient. If there is a suitable place or places for M. L. R. 1862, I should like them marked. If not admitting the width of the letters, the figures alone could be used. I leave this with you to decide.

Has anyone written you that we have with us this winter Isabel Renville, a daughter of Madline R. Campbell? She is bright enough but very noisy.... So you see we are not quite solitary. Mr. Drew gave us one of the turkeys & Mr. Galbraith the other. He also gave Mr. Huggins one. Are we not civilized if we have tame turkey for dinner?

Home, Feb. 21, 1862
My dear Son,

I have put on my spectacles to try them while writing. They do not seem quite natural to me yet, although they answer a very good purpose in sewing. They are marked very neatly & arrived previous to the 10th. As the 10th was Sabbath we invited our friends on the Thursday preceding. It was a bitter cold day & the wind blowing furiously, but we succeeded in getting the turkey well cooked & had a very pleasant dinner in the library....

Your father is busier than ever, & our house is often crowded with Indians day after day, just as if it were "payment." I'm sure our house isn't "the house beautiful," perhaps it is the Interpreter's house. I'm afraid there is too much smoke even for that. The great men & the mighty men, the poor men & the weak men, the maimed, the deaf & dumb & blind old women & young women & children all come to present their claims & beg or command your papa's aid. He has already assisted in making them "kings in embryo" as Mr. Galbraith calls them.

Wed. Apr. 23

I am afraid I have not written a very intelligent letter. I am not in an intelligent mood. My health is poorer than usual. If I have not been able to impart my own intentions very clearly, remember I confide always very much in your judgment....

April 24

Your father intends leaving home the last of next week. He hopes to see or hear from you in Chicago or Cincinnati or both places.

If you haven't given your old pants to the contraband, send them home if it is convenient, that is if you have any to spare.

Hazelwood, May 5, 1862
My dear Husband, [at Lower Agency]

How very glad I am that you have such beautiful weather for your journey. May the Lord prosper you on the way, grant you a pleasant home & a profitable time during the sessions of the gen. Assembly & bring you home in safety.

Why does our sitting room stove make us so much trouble when you are away? This morning before any of the girls were down, it fell over backwards & the plates separated at the top. The iron rod behind kept it from tumbling in pieces & the burning wood falling upon the floor. As soon as the girls came to the rescue, we carried the fire out & set up the stove, but the last rod was broken & we had to gird it with a leather band. We needed a house band to straighten it up & bind it together. It wearied me a good deal & Isabella more. She didn't feel able to teach in the afternoon.

Dakota Mission, Pajutazee, Minn., May 15, 1862
My dear Husband,

Your notes from Lower agency & St. Peter were duly & gladly received.

We had a very refreshing rain last night, the first that has fallen since you left. Every thing looks charming this morning. I am greatly rejoiced that I had finished soap making & Thomas had carried the ashes to the field before the rain.

Mr. Gavins has not sent for the potatoes yet, & I shall not feel obliged to keep them much longer as I understood from you he was to send for them before the middle of this month. Isabella seems better while she is not teaching. She will make one more trial next week.

Henry is very desirous to get a "tip top" India rubber ball, not a solid one, but a thick firm strong one & he sends the commission to Alfred. If there is one of this description about two inches in diameter in the city, cost about 30 cents, Henry will be much obliged if Alfred will hunt it up for him.

Also 2 pieces Chamois Rubber for cleaning slates, advertised by G. L. Woodman & Co. 596 Broadway to be sent by mail for 15 cents apiece. Henry thinks papa forgot to put it down on his memorandum.

Hazelwood, June 5, 1862
My dear Husband,
I am very tired of the care of the garden, boys, etc. & am longing for your return very much. In addition to my other labors this week, I spent a day & night down at the mill! & it has used me up. A few nights since, after I had gone to bed, Cornelia asked, "Does papa pray before he goes to bed?" "I suppose so," I answered. She repeated the question & I repeated the reply, thinking she had not heard me, when she said in a quick decided tone, "Say, yes." Then she repeated the inquiry "Does papa pray before he goes to bed?" & I answered, "Yes," & she was satisfied.

I shall send this to Chicago. If while there you can conveniently procure & bring one or two ground glass chimney single burners we shall be glad as we have unfortunately broken both of ours. If you have no way to pack them safely, please get them at St. Peter.

. . . . Rumors that seem well founded, about the invasion of the *Yhanktonwans* for the coming payment are already rife. It is said the payment is to be earlier than usual.

Home, June 11, 1862
My dear Husband,
Your letters mailed May 28 & 29 came in Monday's mail. I wrote you last week at Chicago but very possibly you may not get it.

I sent down a jar when Bell went to Mrs. Huggins, requesting her either to get some one to fill it with good June butter or to send the jar to Mr. Ketchum's store to be filled there. I do not think that will be enough for us, if we don't have any more milk than one little heifer gives us. Thomas thinks we will have more after awhile perhaps. The butter sent up by boat was at most spoiled by heat, so that it doesn't last too well. Try & keep what you bring as cool as possible. Wrap it up well.

Mr. Shepherd's donation of bacon, lard & molasses has arrived. We have quite a supply for the summer. We shall need some sugar however.

The *Yhanktonwans* have not yet arrived. *Marpiya wicayta* came in last Sabbath morning, to tell me they would be here in ten days & that it was bad that you would not be home before they would come. I still hope if they come at all, they will not until after you return. We don't suffer from fear any yet.

Wed. afternoon

We tried some of Mr. L's sorghum molasses at dinner. Thomas said, "It tastes like licorice." "I wonder if people in Illinois like this," I inquired, "What can we do with it?" Anna Jane replied, "Maybe papa will take to it, as he does to squills," whereupon we all laughed & concluded to await your return before deciding what should be done with it. I wish I could sell it for berries.

Thurs. morn

The roses in our yard are exceedingly beautiful this morning. We wish you & the girls were here to enjoy them. May our covenant God soon bring you safely home.

Dakota Mission, Pujutazee P. O. Min. June 29, 1862
My dear Son,

I have been wishing for some days to write you, but I have been too nearly sick with a boil under my arm for more than a week, to be able to write much. For some days past it has been improving rapidly & I hope I shall soon be as well as usual. It is Saturday afternoon, almost six o'clock, & the loved ones we are looking for have not yet come home. I did not expect them until Friday & then was disappointed. And now today I have looked & looked in vain until I feel sad & fearful that some accident has befallen them. I was very sorry your father didn't take Rockford in his route when going on. He had time in abundance then & now we want him at home so much. He has been away so very long. And oh, if he should never come. May the Lord keep us from painful fears, & help us to endure & bear whatever He sees best for us.

July 1

The spoons please me well, the large ones perfectly. The small ones seem a little slight, & perhaps might have been improved by an additional dollar in weight, but I shall have saved a dollar for some benevolent purpose & I am satisfied & obliged to you for your trouble.

The clothing you sent will be quite valuable to us. I think Thomas can wear the pants without much alteration. As Thomas grows larger I feel more reluctance in cutting his clothing. I am doubting whether it will be better economy to get his clothing cut when practicable at St. Peter or to buy ready made clothing. What think you? And further, what think you we should do with Thomas this winter? He is a very necessary help in the garden & fields & besides the difficulty in sparing him —we don't know of any good plan to send him to school. If Isabella & Martha both remain at home, one of them can teach him next winter & perhaps that will be the best thing we can do, unless some more favorable opportunity is presented.

Yours with affection,
Mary Ann Longley Riggs

Refugee wagons after the uprising, 1862.

CHAPTER 7

After the Uprising

1862-1869

After the uprising. 1862.

In 1862, the pressure for survival among the Dakota reached a critical point leading to the great Sioux uprising in which many settlers were killed and homes and property destroyed. The Riggs-Williamson mission was not spared. Stephen and his family escaped with what little they could carry. They lived in a tent for a month until they found the house in St. Anthony.

Alfred was preaching in Hockport, Illinois Congregational Church when he heard of the massacre of the whites in the uprising. "Word was received that all white missionaries in Minnesota had been massacred by the Sioux. He insisted on preaching the next day, Sunday, [but]... in the concluding prayer... he broke down completely and left the church.

One of the members stated that he knew Rev. Riggs had no money with which to go to recover the bodies of his parents. . . so a collection was immediately taken for him . . . $250."

Mary Ann barely mentioned the uprising in her letters, but there are many bitter references about her loses. Her letters to Lucy Spooner Drake and son, Alfred, included many requests for replacement items. She told of her frugality and the complicated financial arrangements necessary to reconstruct three new homes during seven years of her life.

Stephen's absences from home became longer and more frequent, even during critical periods of his wife's illnesses. He served as chaplain with General Sibley after the uprising and also took many trips to Boston, New York, and Washington seeking publishers for his writings. Mary Ann's letters to him exposed the "frail vessel inhabited during these years," as her health deteriorated.

The children began to leave home and start their own lives. Alfred graduated from Chicago Theological Seminary, began to preach, and married Mary Hatch. Isabella graduated from Western Female Seminary, married Mark Williams, and they sailed to China to be missionaries. Martha attended Western Female seminary and married Wyllys Morris, Anna Jane graduated from Mr. Vail's Seminary in Ohio, Thomas and Henry attended Beloit Preparatory School, and Robert (14) and Mary Cornelia (10) were still at home when their mother died in 1869 of complications from a cold leading to pneumonia.

Tuesday, Sept. 2, 1862
My dear Husband,

. . . . Alfred now purposes leaving St. Paul on Friday morning but perhaps we may persuade him to wait till next week. Mr. Ketchum thinks we can rent a house cheaper in St. Peter than St. Anthony. He said he would make inquiries & write us. Would you have any preference for St. Anthony rather than St. Peter?

I should like to have you send me the bill of purchases at Ingersoll's, I think the bills will be of service in making an estimate of our losses. I wish you would send me an account of the girls' indebtedness to you as their guardian. I think I should keep their account as you have no books now.

This feeling is doubtless caused by the fear that you may never return, which fear may God grant may be never realized. I hope you will be careful of yourself & not unnecessarily expose your life to Indian treachery & cunning. I feel as though there is no wickedness of which they are incapable.

We are all as well as usual. Will you send a draft to Anna at Rockford for the first half of the school year?

St. Anthony, Minn., Friday morn
My dear Husband,

Yesterday we decided upon taking a house up town & today we are intending to move up there. It is convenient to school & perhaps we shall remain in it for the winter though I have the privilege of a few days to look around in. The cellar freezes they say, & the paper on the walls is soiled & torn & it is so far up town that it will give you a long walk when you come home! Alas that we have as yet no house, & will a rented place ever seem like home?

The sad catastrophe at Birch Cooley does not prove to my mind that an expedition could not be sent out with safety to rescue Mrs. Huggins & Julia. It merely shows a want of common prudence & wisdom in those who had the charge of the expedition. I think a company of equal size to that, with the addition of a piece or two of artillery could go to Lac qui Parle safely & successfully if they were wise. But if they forget they are in the enemy's country & that the enemy is with wily Indian, of course they will be hunted down & slaughtered. . . . Oh that the source of all wisdom would grant such a measure of it to our officers that they may out wisdom the Dakotas. I think they are gaining greatly by our delays as they will have time to gather & bury their corn that will enable them to subsist next winter while they prowl upon the white settle-ments.

Mon.

We commenced housekeeping last Saturday. Our present location is on 4th St. next door but one above the Congregational church on the right, the same side of the street. When will you come & see us? If you were here it might seem a little more homelike. I think I mentioned in a previous letter that Alfred drew $10.00 for Anna from Ingersoll's & I gave her some, I really don't remember how much. I am nearly out of money excepting what I have of my own which I shall use if necessary. Have you sent Anna a $30 draft?

Can you not write to the Bible Society asking for Bibles & saying that if we ever should get pay for those we have lost, we will refund the present loan. . . . good bye. May God keep you in the hollow of his hand.

St. Anthony, Sept. 18, '62
My dear Husband,

. . . . You write as though you supposed our houses were burned, though you only mentioned the burning of the church. . . . Mr. Van Eman, one of our neighbors sent in on Saturday, when we commenced housekeeping, a good wooden bucket filled with salt & several dozen eggs, a small box of beans, a paper of saleratus, ground coffee & pepper, a new tin pan full of nice cakes of butter, & a few candles. It was a bless-ing to receive it & I think it must have been a blessing to feast on it. . . .

I am astonished, it takes so much to begin housekeeping. I have bought neither bedsteads, chairs, nor tables nor stoves & yet I am almost out of money. The other ten of the twenty from brother Joseph came safely, & I thank God it did.

Isabella & Martha think we must have a sewing machine & I have given Isabella leave to draw on Mr. Ingersoll . . . .

I hope you will write to the boys. I don't think either of them try to endure as good soldiers. It is not strange that the sad & sudden change that has befallen us should seem hard to be borne, but I wish they could think less of themselves & more of the good they can do to others. . . .

We are all as well as usual. Isabella & Martha are great comforters & good helpers. I do not think Isabella gets as good compensation for her two hours a day as she deserves, & yet we thought it might be better to teach than not. If it had then occurred to us, we would have suggested that Thomas have two terms tuition & Henry one, instead of all three of the boys one term tuition. Robbie would then have read at home as we had previously intended, & Isabella would have been earning five dollars more than she now will.

How soon can you spare your plaid pants for Robbie? I have been patching his today with cloth of a different color & quality.

Mr. & Mrs. Wright, formerly missionaries of the A. M. A. among the Chippewas called. Mr. Wright says that he knows it to be a fact that Little Crow & Hole-in-the-day corresponded, & he thinks it was in reference to a general uprising. He does not think the Chippewas were generally prepared for a revolt, but that Hole-in-the-day & Little Crow were devising evil together under the guise of a "peace meeting!"

Fri. Sept. 19

Isabella returned last evening from St. Paul & brought with her several letters from you, one from your brother, Joseph, & a trunk from friends in Cin. & Walnut Hills filled with good clothing.

I am pained by the severe criticisms of the St. Paul Press upon Mr. Galbraith. We who know him know he would never have left his family in the Indian country if he had thought there was really any danger. Can you not write as much as that in his behalf? I am sure we have never had as good an agent since the upper Sioux have received annuities. Isabella did not get a sewing machine but made some other purchases.

St. Anthony Minn., Sept. 25, 1862
Dear Husband,

Your letters of Sept. 16th & 18th came yesterday, but they didn't satisfy the intense longing I feel for letters from you. . . .

The house we have rented at five dollars a month . . . is a very neat looking cottage on the outside, & although rather shabby within, is very comfortable at this season of the year. If you could be at home in season to fix us up for winter, I think we should find it as pleasant as we could expect to obtain in our circumstances. If the boys were cheerfully obedient, I shouldn't mind our other troubles much. . . . I wish you would write to them. I am afraid heavier afflictions will befall us, if we don't profit by the past.

I hope the drummer boy's coat didn't make you ridiculous. I think in your position a respectable appearance is necessary. I am sorry you haven't a blanket of your own, it is not well to depend too much on others.

Mr. Pettijohn sent us ten dollars of which I was very glad. The Indian department are owing us for eleven barrels of potatoes. Could not that be obtained now? We have used up all the money that was at Ingersoll's in getting articles of clothing etc. & now the boys need books & I expect I shall be obliged to get a cooking stove & some chairs & a table.

I wrote to Mrs. J. B. R. Renville to see if she wouldn't let the girls & me have the heifer of theirs that Dr. W. has. I thought if she would, I could transfer it to Smiley's father & Mr. Hunter would pay us what he has for the butter. She was owing me for 1 Hen $.50, Candles $1.00, Potatoes $2.00, Dress $3.00, Mosquito net $.30 total $6.80. Deduct $1 deep dish that I b'ot of her. $5.80 remains due me. Due Isabella for the lessons on Melodeon total $12. For making four child's dresses $1.50 to Martha for four lessons on Melodeon $2.00; total our due $21.30. There will be $6.30 due over the price of the calf & that I should be glad to have you include in what Mr. Renville owes you or average it all in the best way you can. We need the pay very much. What will the Board do for us?

St. Anthony, Oct. 3, 1862
My dear Husband,

I received your letter written from Wood Lake Sept. 22nd. I think you need not direct my letters to Mr. McKee's care, as I am sure the P.M. [postmaster] must have learned by this time that we are somebody, by the letters we get and write.

Before this you have passed by our old home, our desolate grounds, & seen the dear spot in ruins. If you think it possible that we ever return there I wish you could get some one to enclose the yard & protect what trees remain. Bring or send, a sprig of cedar if there is ought left. Please also take time to hunt for the smoothing irons & the old tongs that belonged to grandpa'a. They would both be in the back room not very far from the stove, if they were not stolen. I do not think they would steal the tongs & I should like them as a connecting link of the past, & the girls are very desirous to have one of the smoothing irons to commence housekeeping with! We had five & there would be enough for myself & each of the girls to have one, if you can find them all. What will be done about the goods taken by the *Wapetonwan* and *Sissiton* bands? Ours were not taken by the *Mdewakantonwans* of course. I hope you will inquire about our escritoire & my work box & spectacles. My pin was in my work box, & both escritoires & my work box & the senate clock & my best Britannia ware were in the closet in our room. Perhaps Simon or *Winyan* will know who broke upon the closet. The very thieves are ready for peace.

. . . . When are you coming down? Not till Mrs. Huggins is rescued I suppose. Is there a possibility of your staying there all winter? If so, do come down for a little while as bearer of dispatches, or on furlough, or with some other excuse. I have thought it possible that there might be more uncertainty about receiving your pay than if you had been chaplain of a regiment. What is a chaplains salary now? Mr. L. W. Pond told me it was reduced to the same as second lieutenant. I thought it was equal to that of first lieutenant, but anyhow do you know how much it is?

I have written a note to Mr. Treat inquiring if some Christian book seller or publisher, wouldn't cheerfully aid in supplying our lack of their abundance. I do hope the Messrs. Miriam will donate some copies of Webster's Dictionary. It seems as though we could hardly do without it this winter. Have you made any arrangement yet to supply us with bibles & hymn books? I wrote to you about it some weeks ago, or perhaps days only, but it seems weeks.

Isabella, Martha, Thomas, & Henry have gone to a singing this evening. Mr. McKee called in as he went to borrow my spectacles for the sing & I have written this with my own eyes. It seems strange to me that I can read & write without glasses better than sew. I hope you will send me a draft soon if you are not coming down. If you are coming soon, I would rather not buy a cooking stove until you come.

If the Whapetanwans & Sisitonwans are making peace I should like them to restore the stolen property, beside the articles I have named the horses & some of my good bedquilts, comfortables, & blankets, sheets, table linen, etc., etc., etc., etc. Is Mr. Freniere up there? I hope he will get his horse from Hanok. Who will settle up these accounts for stolen goods horses & cattle?

. . . . I wish you would speak about Taoyatiditas' (alias Little Crow) daguerreotype. I have written to Agnes about borrowing it. I think that some artist would perhaps give me a photograph for the opportunity of getting one. Good bye.

St. Anthony, Oct. 10, 1862
My dear Husband,

Thomas has just come from the office with your letter of the 2nd inst. I am very much disappointed that you are not coming, but if you are needed there, I am content. I thank God with you that Mrs. Huggins is rescued. Poor lone woman! How much greater her trials are than ours.

If the Indians are returning stolen goods I hope you will recover my work box with my breast pin & daguerreotypes. They didn't destroy them, I presume. I am almost willing to go up there to hunt up our things. I could identify them better than anyone else. A good part of my sheets & pillow cases & towels were marked with indelible ink & some of my table cloths. The newest white tablecloth was not marked. It was the snow drop pattern, a little figure in the weaving as big as a pea. I had three new bedquilts, one was dark furniture print (not patch work) the color was chiefly brown with red roses. I had a new comfortable of the same print. The two patch work quilts that were new, one was mostly pink & other miscellaneous colors pieces in a square, & the corresponding square was all of a kind, a buff or shade of orange. The other was an irregular star made up a good many pieces of various colors put together with squares of the same sort, a small figure in a drab ground. I had several other good bedquilts & comfortables & blankets. One blanket of very soft wool with red stripes at the ends & serged with worsted of the same color. I wish you could get it & another one equally good but of home manufacture & serged at the ends with blue yarn, both were new.

Will the troops pay you & Mr. Cunningham for wood & potatoes?

We are none of us sick. Mrs. Baird the mother of James Baird connected with the Expedition, called here yesterday & brought some tomatoes, squashes & beets to us. Martha is knitting some mittens for her son as she couldn't find any one who could. I think you would be glad of a pair that were in your drawer.

Where are *Wanmdiokiya's* sons? Were they not engaged in the war parties which attacked some of the towns near Hutchinson?

Who took our carpets? I wish they would give them back. Do you think they will? I have bought one & I would like one or two more. . . . Some of the Indians must have some of our pillows. If they give you two or three pair, it would save buying feathers. Inquire about them. All the daguerreotypes I had, but one of Alfred, Isabella, & Anna in a frame, were in cases in my work box.

Monday, St. Anthony, Oct. 13, 1862
My dear Husband,

What will be done with those Indians who are found guilty of murder? Is there no danger to the troops if the Indians are executed in the Dakota country? I should fear a second rebellion. You remember the story of the peace long ago between the Chippewas & Dakotas? If a peace is to be made ought not the Indians to give up everything they have taken from white people that isn't worn out! My breast pin &

spectacles can't be worn out & I am very desirous to recover them. I had daguerreotypes of Lucretia & husband & Mary & Ella—of Mr. & Mrs. Drake, & brother Alfred & his wife in my work box & my breast pin was with them. Also the daguerreotype of Alfred taken when he first left home for college & several others, any of which I should value. My spectacles were on the bureau in our bedroom & I think Paul or someone has likely got them. If he has got a good bedtick saved for us I hope he will send it down, under clothes too. Wearing apparel as well as bedding that is worth bringing down, we should be glad. If I had a dozen of tea knives & forks too small for Indian use I should like them.

. . . . I have trusted to others to engage wood till it has risen a dollar a cord since we came down; that is for hard wood $3.50 a cord. My head gets so pained & crowded attending to so many things, that I can't sleep. Besides, I have a boil under my arm, but its not yet as bad as the one I had last summer yet. You see how incoherent my note is, and if you don't think I am writing a la Anna Jane, you will think I am not very self possessed. . . .

I clip a snip out of yesterday's Pioneer about removing the Indians. I don't wonder people feel thus, but I think the Indians who have not participated in this rebellion should not suffer with the guilty & that they would be the best protection for our border. Mr. L. W. Pond thinks this late war would never have taken place if the *Mdewakantons* had been kept on their old grounds & not put so near other bands & the Winnebagoes. . . .

St. Anthony, Oct. 16, 1862
My dear Husband,

. . . . Have you any plans or expectations for labor of any kind the coming season? Do you wish for a chaplaincy? Can you have one if you wish it? The boys are doing rather better now than they were before I punished Henry. They have caused me care & grief & would better still if you were at home. . . .

Our means seem so inadequate to our wants that I find it difficult to pursue the wise & consistent medium in making purchases. I have done at all times what then seemed best, but I can see in some things I might have done better. We are not supplied with potatoes as yet, nor but partly with wood. We buy beef occasionally from the butcher & a pint of milk daily from a neighbor. Beside this, some of our friends give us milk occasionally.

. . . . The boil under my arm is quite troublesome but I hope the worst will soon be over. If you were only here to lance it, it would be a great relief to me. At times it is quite distracting.

I hope Gen. Sibley will not permit the Indians to out general him, but I fear treachery & surprise & slaughter. I feel very much afraid that the Indians sense of justice is too blind & dull to see the righteousness of their own people being executed. I wish those who are condemned could be sent to Fort Ridgely to suffer death. Miss Charles, who is staying in Minneapolis, hopes they will be sent to Fort Snelling for execution. But I do not think it would benefit white people to see them shot or hung & for one, I should not wish as she did to be "there to see." God spare me such a sight.

Does Gen. Sibley enjoin upon the Indians the return of spoils? I think they should all be required to give up all & everything that is left of what they took, & what is not worth bringing away they might be. returned them.

We are badly off without a "house band" or a time keeper.

St. Anthony, Fri. eve, Oct. 24, 1862
My dear Husband,

We have been expecting you home all this week, & today more than all the other days together. Of course we did not waste time in writing to you, when you were on the way down, but discussed the important questions whether you would find the house readily, & whether you would knock when you came. But the morning mail brought us two letters, & dashed all our speculations of your immediate coming. And, as you really can't come we were heartily glad to get such good long letters. . . .

The letter Mrs. Mattocks wrote in our behalf to Misses Wheeler & Wilson brought in return, an order to their agent in St. Paul to furnish a machine at the price for ministers. If your stay should be prolonged another three weeks could you send us another draft for $50? The one you sent us some days ago is converted into a stove & fuel. As for potatoes we have not yet laid in a supply. We have tried several kinds but don't find any equal to our Hazelwood potatoes.

I still feel as though the Indians should be made to return all the stolen goods that are of any worth. I wish the escritoire you found had been yours instead of mine. But tonight I care more for a small bird's eye maple box that brother Alfred made than for the escritoire. All my mementos of him are gone. I have wept tonight for the first time over our loss in that regard. It seems to me it would be perfectly right to search for stolen goods if they were not brought, in compliance with an order to that effect, & that means of forwarding such goods should be supplied by government. That is my opinion, but perhaps it is not Gen. Sibley's too. Of course only those that are worth transporting should be received. You didn't suppose that we wanted the smoothing irons & tongs, because we couldn't furnish ourselves here? We were thinking of them as substantial relics of the olden times. They were dug out from our fire eight years ago, & as people say are, "worth their weight in gold." Though I am afraid if that was their marketable value I should be too poor to keep them, even if I had them. Still there would be no danger of that, & they would belong to those valuables that are only valuable to the owners.

Today Martha sent you a copy of the Christian Herald, containing her letter about our escape. I think you will agree with me that it is a well written article. There are some parts very fine.

Today also we received a barrel & sack of clothing from College Hill, with the discretionary power of dispensing what we didn't need. We had previously received a trunk which we sent with a part of its contents to Mrs. Huggins.

We bought a barrel of apples this week for $3.00 hoping you would be home to eat some of the pies & dumplings! Be sure & come before they are eaten up.

If you think best, give my kind regards to Gen. Sibley. I am glad that he has been so successful & I am very thankful that the executions are not to be at Fort Snelling. Will Agnes & her mother come down? Is

Daniel among the suspected criminals?

We are as well as usual, with the exception of colds.

St. Anthony, Oct. 29, '62
My dear husband,

. . . . We are getting along pretty comfortably externally, but we all have troubles & cares, that seem doubtless to each one of us, quite as hard as we can bear. Isabella comforts me very much.

Thomas, age 15, has banked up the house very nicely, & is doing a job of wood splitting & piling for Mr. Van Eman. The boys like to work for pay.

Will it please you to know that we are not so poor that we have nothing to give away? We are rich in water privileges & some of our neighbors are not. At first, only one family asked a supply from our cistern, now I think several families depend upon it in part. When we are constantly receiving bountiful gifts, I don't like to refuse so small a favor as water, & so we "give to every one that asketh." I think, however, I will inquire where it is to be carried & wherefore the next time an ox team is sent for water, as was the case this morning. Besides, our family gave half of the collection in Sabbath school last Sabbath for supplying the soldiers with reading! Martha says, she doesn't know another family that give as liberally as we do. I said except Dr. Williamson. . . .

I am very sorry to learn that so many Indians are concerned in these massacres of the whites. Will those who kept themselves entirely aloof from the fighting, have to be herded up with the women & children in some island in Lake Superior or elsewhere?

Thurs.

Butter is very scarce here, I'm thinking of writing to Shakopee or Oak Grove to see if it can be had there. We are getting tired of doing without pillows, but it helps us to be contented to think that we fare as well & better than our soldiers. . . . I received letters from sisters Lucretia & Julia not long since. Charles Longley is in 24th Reg. Iowa Volunteers Co. E. & Edmund Cooley is in 65th Reg. Ill. F. It was thought probable these Regiments might be ordered northwest to defend the frontier.

The Ill. Reg. was paroled I believe at Harpers Ferry. If you hear of these Regiments in this state, I shall be glad to know it.

St. Anthony, Nov. 5, 1862
My Dear Husband,

Your last letter seems more discouraging than ever about your coming home soon. I think your coming is as much a necessity to us, as if we were sick. Indeed I am almost sick both mentally & physically. It seems as though I ought to feel very grateful for our wonderful deliverance, & I do when I think of what we escaped, but gratitude & joy do not so pervade my being but what I feel greatly the inconvenience of our losses. But I do not mean to allow myself to complain. And although the management of our pecuniary affairs, under such high pressure of economy is very perplexing & wearying, the management of the boys is more trying still. It has occurred to me that possibly Mr. L. W. Pond might, if you thought best to make the proposition, like to have one of his daughters board with us & go to school in exchange for Henry's board with them. I do not feel at all confident that the plan would work well, but I should be willing to try it.

Are you not delaying your efforts to influence the public mind too long? You will see by the Press that Gov. Ramsey in his letter to President Lincoln recommends their removal to some distant locality far beyond our borders. It seems to me that an article might be written inquiring how the faithful & loyal Dakotas can be rewarded, how we can repay the debt of gratitude we own those who assisted all the whites they could to escape, & by their influence saved the captives from a general massacre & aided in their rescue. Another thought I have in this connection is, that there will be a great many destitute children that will have to be fed & clothed by government, could not something be done in the way of a boarding school this winter, by our board either aided or unaided in the supply of food by the government? Would not Mr. & Mrs. Cunningham be willing to take a small number of children, if a building could be rented in some favorable locality?

Wednesday eve

Your letter of the last of October came today. May God help you to bear the burden of sorrow you must feel for *Chaske* & others. I hope your other duties, will not prevent your taking time to visit the poor condemned criminals . . . . Surely *Chaske* was not bound to criminate himself by confession. Were there no palliating circumstances? How came he to go to Birch Coolie? I am very sorry on his account & for Sarah also. . . .

St. Anthony, Nov. 8, '62
My dear Mrs. Drake,

It would have been pleasant to me to have visited our Ohio friends this winter, but it seemed best to go to housekeeping with such a family & three of them boys at just the age that they need watchful care. Mr. Riggs has just returned home, or I should say arrived. We rented a house & commenced keeping it, with about as little as we did eight years ago after our fire. But through the blessing of God & the kindness of friends in Ohio & here, we are supplied with many necessary & comfortable articles. This providing for a family is quite a new experience, buying flour, butter, beef, & laying in a supply of wood & potatoes for winter is very different from what I have been accustomed too. I should have felt very incompetent for such a task, if Isabella & Martha had not relieved me from a great part of the labor. But we are all very glad to lay down our "brief authority" & welcome home the "house-band."

Angelique will rejoice that Agnes is with us. She came here with Julia a little more than two weeks since. Julia went immediately to Rock-ford only spending one night with us. Agnes has had the measles since she came & we are expecting Robbie & Cornelia will soon have them.

Tues. Dec. 2

While Mr. Riggs was connected with the Sioux Expedition as Chap-lain, several of our Dakota friends returned articles belonging to us. The only dress we have received is an old debage, but I am thankful for that, this cold day. One good bed quilt & one old ragged quilt & three pair of sheets is the amount received of all my beds & bedding, but I am very thankful for these, for we need them more than personal clothing. In that regard, in consequence of the kindness of friends, we are comfortably provided for the winter. I shall love to hear from you at anytime.

St. Anthony, March 19, 1863
My dear Daughter, [Anna]

.... Your father left home on Wednesday last for Mankato, intending to spend two Sabbaths with the Indians there. . . . But I must not delay telling you my principle object in writing tonight, lest I forget it entirely. I wish to impress & enjoin upon you the propriety of abandoning some study for the present, rather than deferring music. Please say to your teachers that your parents wish to have you attend to both vocal & instrumental music. I can give you two reasons: 1st, we have no piano. 2nd, Isabella thinks if she should leave here next fall, & you should remain at home, that you could take her music scholars. Of course it is not certain that she will leave here, or you remain at home. I wish you would write me what expense will be necessary for dress until the term closes. You will need a bonnet, I suppose & something of the shawl or sacque kind for church wear, when your cloak is too warm. What will these cost you? We wish you to be comfortably & economically clothed, & if you & Julia think your duster will answer when your cloak is laid aside, very well.

You will be glad to learn that we have added to our home comforts by the purchase of a dark steel gray cow. We haven't decided upon her name yet. We call our horse Noble.

St. Anthony, April 22, 1863
My dear Son,

We were sorry to learn that it was "very doubtful" whether you would be able to visit us this summer with your bride. So we have discussed the matter, whether we could do anything to make it less doubtful. The conclusion is, that we will bear $25.00 of the expense, if that will enable you to come without incurring debt or infringing upon more important duties. I had intended to buy a carpet this summer preparatory to your coming, but we had rather see you than to have the carpet, &

you can see carpets elsewhere. We wish, of course, to see you & your wife & to feel that she is, indeed, one of our family. You need not hesitate to accept our offer of $25.00 for traveling expenses but regard it as the manifestation of our wish, that the trip you made in the time of our calamity, should not prevent your coming this summer.

If you decide to come will you procure for Martha one half dozen silver teaspoons & two tablespoons. The size & style of those you got for me would suit very well. The teaspoons might be a little heavier, if the cost would not exceed twelve or thirteen dollars. We should like to have them nicely marked with her initials, M.L.R. I think the initials in cipher, when skillfully done are prettier than otherwise. But custom & your own taste may decide that point.

My health is not good this spring, but I am hoping it will improve a little.

St. Anthony, June 8, 1863
My dear Husband,

Oh the boys do grieve me so, & especially Henry. This morning Thomas, having been invited to join a party to Mr. Baird's, went out with my consent to make some arrangements about it. Henry soon followed without permission & was absent at breakfast & worship & an hour afterward. He is certainly on the Broad Road to ruin. May the Lord have mercy on him & on us. . . .

The pay you get is a poor compensation for your absence. I wish to feel that you are filling a post no other one could fill as well & as faithfully as yourself.

St. Anthony, Minn., June 10, 1863
My dear Husband,

Your letter from Camp Pope came yesterday, & made us very glad. . . . Cornelia is not quite as well today & is lying on the bed, begging me to tell her a story. Alfred, Isabella & Martha are singing, & Mary is playing. They have just been singing "Watching for Pa'a."

I feel a deep sympathy for Gen. Sibley, just commencing this campaign, & one of his household group already gone. . . .

You will see by the Press, that there are or were Indians not far from the settlements in Wright & Stearns counties. The killing of Capt. Cody is a sad affair. It will only increase the anxiety between the Sioux & whites. Capt. C. is spoken of with a deep interest by his acquaintances here....

Tuesday morn

Alfred's Mary, is very companionable & as Anna J. says, "Isn't stuck up," & we are well pleased with her.

The garden is very much neglected, although T. has found time to finish his gun stock, & both of the boys wish to go when & where they please.

St. Anthony, June 27, 1863
My dear Husband,

.... Our hired house, is beginning to have the charm of home to me. When I go into the front bedroom there is the substitute for a wardrobe you put up the Saturday before you left. It was also Alfred & Mary's room when they were here. In the parlor are specimens of petrified moss which Alfred gathered & gave me. And in our bedroom the blinds you fitted are specially valuable in this scorching weather. I am afraid you & others on the Expedition will suffer. I fancy you can't have a hotter time than we have in the kitchen. We sympathize with you daily, but more especially on ironing & baking days. I am thankful that we have cooler rooms to rest & refresh ourselves in.

As you have no servant, do you pitch your own tent & take care of your own horse?

.... I am thinking of going to Mr. Pond's & Mr. Ellison's next Friday if I can, to inquire about a place for Henry. He was from home eleven hours on Saturday, including the singing school of a little more than an hour, being away from nine in the morning until eight in the evening. With prayers & wishes for you always.

St. Anthony, Minn., July 3, 1863
My dear Husband,

We had a delightful rain on Tuesday night, quiet & gentle. Fortunately we had cleaned out our cistern that very night. . . .

The Red River carts have been passing back for two or three days, they make me think of old times, but oh how changed the times, only the cart's the same. If their creaking wasn't so harried, I should feel a kind of attachment to the poor old things. They seem to me like the identical old set, always the same shaggy, creaking & tireless, but tiresome carts. I shouldn't fancy taking a trip in one of them from Traverse to Kaposia this fall. Was it fourteen years ago we took that trip? Ah me, how time flies!

. . . . How long a time is it expected the Expedition will be gone? I am in haste to calculate upon your return. God grant the Expedition success. There is a great deal of croaking about it by some, & disparaging comparisons made between it & Hatch's proposed Battalion. It seems to me that the utility of the one does not necessarily imply the utility of the other. Hatch's Battalion may fill a gap that Gen. Sibley's Expedition could not cover. Our war news is very discouraging.

. . . . This morning there was a sad accident on the St. Paul railroad. The cars coming up to St. Anthony ran upon a horse & wagon with two men in it. I have not learned whether they are still living. . . .

St. Anthony, July 6, 1863
My dear Husband,

This is Monday, another hot day, after a hot night. It is the first Monday of the boys' vacation. They wanted to go to St. Paul this morning. I told them I did not think it best to commence a vacation thus, especially as they had had Saturday for a holiday. I advised Thomas to go over to Mrs. Renville's & finish a job of wood cutting which he took some time ago, & told Henry I wanted him to pick some peas for dinner. Instead of obeying, they have both gone down town. Thomas said he would go to St. Paul & enlist in Hatch's battalion, but I do not really think he will. It seems to me now, that it would have been better if you had taken him with you, as you didn't find a place for him at Mr. Allison's. We should be far more comfortable without them, if they were with someone who would & could help them govern themselves. I would cheerfully spare them both, if I could find any suitable place for them.

Wed. July 8

Mr. Van Eman has furnished Thomas with work painting his barn. Thomas is very well pleased & works diligently. But Henry troubles me very much indeed. He has split but little of the wood we have, although he knows he gets ten cents a cord. This morning I told him that splitting wood would be his work, after considerable delay he went out & split a few sticks & the next time I looked out there was no Henry there. He was gone we could only guess where. This afternoon I sent him before one o'clock to buy two quarts of currants, as I had heard we could get them at half price if we picked them. It is now half past five & he has not come home yet. What shall I do with him? What can I do with him? My cry continually is, "Guide me O Thou great Jehovah, Pilgrim through this barren land, I am weak, but Thou art mighty, Hold me by thy powerful hand."

Tues. July 14

. . . . Thomas is at work for Mr. Van Eman still, & is very contented for him. Henry is doing rather better since Anna came home. She quite surprised us last Fri. morning. We heard footsteps while we were at breakfast on the porch & in the parlor, it was so very warm the doors were all open. I turned my head & there was Anna Jane just behind me. As the river was still falling, the teachers excused her immediately after her examinations were over, so that she could reach home before the Sabbath. She came by stage from Prescott, without her baggage, Thurs. night, & reached St. Paul just in time for the morning train for St. Anthony. . . .

Home, Wed. morn, July 15, '63
Dear Husband,

I have but just faith enough in this letter's ever finding you to put it in the mail. It seems like casting bread upon the water to send this out to you upon the prairie sea. . . .

Today's paper brings the news of a terrible riot in New York, several private dwellings rifled & burned, the Tribune office attacked, Morgan ten miles in the rear of Cincinnati, a skirmish at Camp Dennison, railroad trains intercepted, the track cut, etc. etc. Commotion everywhere.

St. Anthony, July 21, '63
My dear Husband,

Your package of home letters from the Cheyenne valley rejoined us this morning. It seems to bring you nearer home when we get a letter written only ten days ago. When we think of six weeks marching & camping, you seem a great ways off on a trackless waste, but getting a mail in ten days opens a road on the prairie, & makes communication between the Expedition & the homes from which it started very hopeful. . . .

Mr. Ketchum very generously offered me funds to send Anna to school. I told him I had not decided what to do, but he said he would leave me $50 until I had concluded, & would furnish more if necessary. I shall not like to take more. . . .

Thomas is doing pretty well under Mr. Van Eman's care. Henry perplexes & pains me very often. He does not wish to go to Oak Grove, & I am still undecided whether to take him there or not. He goes from home without asking permission, about as often as he asks leave to go & is unwilling to work when he is at home.

St. Anthony, Mn., Aug 4, 1863
My dear Husband,

We thank God you were well & that there is a prospect of your early return. I hope something will be accomplished by this Expedition even if Little Crow is not captured. You will see by the papers that there are a few Indians lurking around near the settlements stealing horses. Four or five have been killed, the two last on Tuesday a week ago, about 15 miles south of Kandiyohi Lakes. These two I presume were Dakotas, but those killed in Le Seur Co. I think were probably Winnebagoes.

I sympathize with Dr. W. & Alfred in their disappointment, but I hope good may come of it. The poor Dakotas are henceforth a despised race & an oppressed one also when the wicked have the power.

This morning's paper reports "three persons shot near Glencoe by Indians." Perhaps Little Crow is in that region.

.... If you are a mind to, you may give my compliments to Gen. Sibley & tell him that if he will name a lake, Lake Mary it will represent as many of the wives & mothers of the Expedition as any other name & perhaps more. Anna says of these women's names "They sound very tame besides Bear's Den & Devil's Lake."

St. Anthony, Aug 11, '63
My dear Husband,

.... Mr. Cunningham left on Friday last. They called here a few moments on Thursday. As they were leaving I handed him a note to this effect. "Dear Sir, I feel constrained to inquire, if you cannot fulfill your promise to Mr. Riggs in regard to the Board's claims before you leave Minn.? He will be pained & perplexed by this neglect. Will you pardon the thought, in case you & Mr. R. should not live until these claims are paid, could they ever be adjusted." I felt that I ought to intimate to him in a kindly way, that as I understood it, he had failed to keep his word. . . .

Mrs. Renville is publishing her book in Minneapolis. You see I have given you the skeleton of a letter. I really don't feel able to clothe it with sinews & flesh & I shall have to leave it to your imagination to make the dry bones live. . . .

Our family & friends are as well as usual.

St. Anthony, Aug 20, 1863
My dear Husband,

Perhaps it is quite superfluous for me to send a letter to Fort Abercrombie. Still if you do not return as soon as we wish, you may get another letter if we speed it on its way. I am exceedingly disappointed that Gen. Sibley did not open a communication with *Tatankanajin*. A single communication entrusted to one of the enemy for delivery was not sufficient effort for such an expedition I think. Who knows that the message was ever delivered? I am also chagrined that in the editorial heading of "the press" this unreliable messenger is called "a scout." The remark has been made to me, "One of the scouts proved treacherous." Of course I reply that I think they are mistaken, that the so-called scout, was one of the rebel scouts, that I am not informed that any of our scouts had proved faithless....

St. Anthony, July 15, 1864
My dear Son & Daughter,
.... Your father left home on Monday for a visit to the scouts' camp on the Coteau beyond Red Wood in company with Mr. Renville. Thomas went with them probably to St. Peter or vicinity hoping to visit a little & also to find work for a couple of weeks. Isabella reached home last week on Wednesday. She will probably remain at home if Martha leaves, but as yet nothing definite is determined about either. Your father expects to go to New York sometime in September & intends taking Thomas to Beloit. Thomas and Martha had a very providential escape last week on Thursday. Just after Martha got into the buggy, while Thomas with the reins in hand was upon the point of getting in, our horse scared at a new washing machine that had just been brought home and left at the gate. Thoughtlessly, Henry commenced working the machine at that moment, & the horse dashed off in a fright. He pulled the lines from Thomas by going so near the fence that Thomas couldn't run between it & the buggy. Martha sat very quietly till she thought the horse was about to run down the bluff, when she jumped out. The horse however turned on the bluff & came up homeward on the next street where Thomas intercepted him & brought him home. It seemed that no great injuries were received by persons, horse, or buggy. A few bruises, & jars & a general family fright, and the affair was over. Surely we have constant cause for thankfulness.

St. Anthony, Sept. 19, 1864
My dear Husband,
Your letter from Davenport & Lockport, to my great gratification reached us Saturday night. We hoped you were enjoying yourself at

South Deerfield. The first load of corn has been brought home to day. There will be three loads of ours at 2.50 a load. The whole cost, not including Henry's labor & toll, will be $21.50. Do you think it will be as valuable as two tons of hay? Mr. Renville paid H. some for his work, I think he should pay this toward the hauling of the corn. I bought a sack of flour this morning at $4.75, so that when I have paid for the hauling of the corn & some wood, I shall be nearly out of funds. There has been no wood brought yet, but the promise renewed.

St. Anthony, Sept. 28, 1864
Dear, dearer, dearest,

Why have you not written? Your last was from Lockport, reached us Sat. the 17th, & I hoped that we should get one the next Sat. from you in Mass. But the only message has been from brother M. announcing your arrival there. Henry took the horse to Mr. Pond's on Monday the 26th. It is quite a relief to me, to have him away, for I couldn't but know even if I tried to be "blind with one eye," that the horse was not well taken care of.

The money for Indian claims has at length arrived in St. Paul. I enclose a receipt for your signature. When it is received we can draw the money. . . . Mr. J. B. Renville had no difficulty in drawing the money for the half breeds for whom you & he had the power of attorney, but could not get the pay for the Indians! The one of *Makaahewin*'s which Martha presented was written across by Mr. Gilfillon thus "approved Sept. 23, 1864, Supt. of Indian affairs" but without his signature. Col. Thompson is not at home, but is expected daily. Will you write to him and tell him the circumstances of Ema's claim & death & of your sale of the buggy, to the widow & mother of the deceased? I fear we may never get the pay. . . .

I bought ten bushels of beautiful potatoes yesterday & paid $7.50 for them. I hope you will have a blessed meeting at Worcester.

St. Anthony, Minn., Oct. 7, 1864
My dear Husband,

Your first letter from New York came yesterday. Before this reached you, I hope you will be fairly at your work, & ready to make some calculation how long a time it will take to finish the printing & proof reading. . . .

Henry is cleaning the stable for the first time since you left. The corn has kept him out of school about two weeks already. He will go to school again, when he finishes husking what has never been set-up, which is about two thirds of it.

I have not been very well but am better today. God bless you & keep us all, always.

St. Anthony, Oct. 19, 1864
My dear Son,

I do not remember that I have ever written you how pleasant is the remembrance to me of my visit at Lockport last summer. I can think of you & Mary so much better than before. I can see you at home & at church, & also at your social visits. These, I think, require as much or more wisdom & grace for a pastor & his wife, than any other duty they have to fulfill. Of course in your social intercourse with your people, there should be relaxation & enjoyment, & at the same time I think there should be improvement, intellectual & moral. . . . I feel especially encouraged & thankful just now, by the letters I received from both Anna & Thomas. Anna says, "I have taken a stand in school very different from what it has been, that of a hoping Christian." Thomas seems to feel penitent for the past, & resolved for the future to try & do the best he can. I wish I could say the same of Henry, but he is yet a great grief to me. Although he united with the church last winter, I fear he is yet a rebel against God & a stranger to grace. . . .

We have at length received the pay for our claims, over two thousand dollars. They were cut down several hundred, I don't know on what principle or for what reason. We are glad to receive what has been awarded us, & think some of buying a house somewhere, sometime.

. . . . I suppose you hear from your father so that I need not tell you he is attending meetings, eating pears, grapes, peaches, & apples, while we can only imagine how nice they are. Apples are from nine to twelve dollars a barrel here & dry maple wood, ten dollars a cord. Wood we must have, apples we can do without. I have not yet quite decided that we must.

St. Anthony, Oct. 25, 1864
My Dear Friend: [[Mrs. Drake]]

I was very glad to get your note, & learn that you were enjoying so many blessings. . . . A letter came from my husband yesterday. He is at length fairly at his work reading the proofs of the Dakota New Testament, but not sufficiently advanced in it to make any calculations in regard to his return home. He visited my brother & sister in Mass. & attended the meeting of the Board at Worcester. On his calculations returning to New York after the meeting of the Board, he found the electratypes still uncast, & improved the time which would intervene before the printing could proceed, to visit Mr. Moore & wife who were boarding with us at the time of the outbreak & who reside in New Jersey. . . . Mr. M. came with him to Philadelphia on his return & at parting handed him a present for me. I do not suppose it will buy me a silk dress, but if you are well enough & not too busy to send me a sample or so of silk & also of Irish poplin or something else that you think suitable for me I shall be obliged. I do not yet know whether we shall remain here, or where we shall go if we leave, so that I cannot tell what I shall need, but I should like to be informed as to what I may need, with prices. . . .

The Quakeress with the white shawl, stands on the mantel piece still.

St. Anthony, Sat. Nov. 5, '64
My dear Husband,

You will thank God with me that I am again able to sit up & write a little. It is eight days since I have been into the Kitchen & most of that time I have been obliged to keep my bed. I have made vain attempts to sit up several days in my haste to get well, but they have only increased the fever & protracted the disease. I hardly dared allow myself to think of you much, lest I should too longingly wish you at home, so I only just wished for a kiss & a prayer. My head has troubled me a good deal so that I couldn't comfortably think, nor stop thinking. Such a confused mixture of wood, butter, beef & 7-30s, Mrs. Cunningham, Mrs. Renville,

& Miss Wheeler, interluded with snatches of hymns & bible verses. I tried vainly to put worldly affairs all out of mind, but they would come back again, so to be relieved, with Martha's help, I gave them the attention they seemed to demand, & they afterward staid dismissed, not a ghost of them came back to haunt me. . . .

Looking from a sick bed upon our training of our two boys, I feel that we have sadly failed. I think a firmer & more watchful government would have probably saved them from such grievous rebellion against their parents & their God. I have strong hope that Thomas has passed the crises, & that he will recover from the effects of reluctant & murmuring obedience. But Henry is more defiant & determined. He seems bent on doing just as he pleases & making every one in the family do the same. He teases the children & worries everybody. I have seen this spirit growing more & more intolerable for a long time, but have felt unable to root it out. Since he received your letter there has been a little improvement in work, & since I have been sick a little in behavior to me, but there is a sad deficiency still. He will do just as he chooses, & he generally chooses his own ease & gratification. I see little that I can do but repent past sins & neglects. . . . I see that I ought to have governed him in days past more indepently [sic] of you. I think I unwittingly slid into that defect, from several causes. One that you sometimes objected to my plans before the boys, another, that you gave them reason to suppose you thought me too particular by saying "Don't fret yourself, I'll attend to the boys." I do not see that I can remedy the evil now. But there are evils which you can in part remedy. You can, in some way punish him for delinquencies in work never on any ordinary occasion relieve him from the entire fulfillment of his own duties. This is one reason why the burden I have to bear when you first leave home is actually heavier than afterward. Accustomed as Henry has been to your supplying his deficiency in wood, he is irritated because he had to chop wood to make the morning fire & we have to bear both the bad temper & the lack of wood. I mention this not chiefly on my own account, for I feel that as I have sown I must reap, but it seems very desirable for the sake of the children, now my health & life are so uncertain, that in your arrangements for the future, you should be at home as much as possible. And that in case you cannot be at home, Henry should not be left any length of time with the family, unless there is great improvement.

It will at least dwarf Robbie & Cornelia soul & body, & perhaps worse. It makes the one who has the care of them prematurely old. Burn this! I have written this, sorry to pain you yet desiring to help you to see that we have failed in training up our boys. If we can produce a better let us try. Now, I lay my hand on my mouth in the dust.

Monday Nov. 7, 1864
My dear husband,

.... Mr. & Mrs. Renville called here this morning with Paul. Mrs. R. tells me that Noble has been sick ever since Mrs. Theresa has had him. Paul is going back to Ft. Wadsworth. If there should be a deputation of Dakotas to Washington in January, I think Paul should be one. Have any of the scouts but *Naupexin* been over to Ft. Thompson? Aunt Jane was very hopeful that the Indians on the Missouri might yet be located somewhere on the Coteau, & if this "Indian's aid Society" that is to be organized according to Miss Wheeler, can do anything to help them I hope it will be done. Do you consider yourself as fitted to take a secre-taryship in such a society? Miss Wheeler thinks the Devil's lake country a poor country. Do you know anything definitely about it? She will write to you or call upon you at the Bible House or both when she goes east. If I understand her position she is one of the committee for organizing such a society, & is also acting as one agent in gathering facts in refer-ence to Indian wrongs.

Mon. Nov. 14, '64
Dear Husband,

I am getting better very slowly, I seem to have lost the elasticity I usually have after sickness. I have not eaten with the family yet, neither have I had tea or coffee for more than two weeks. Last week on Thurs-day I was fifty one. Martha bought a peck of apples on that day & paid $1.10 for them. She has had a very good opportunity to teach in Wis-consin, but how could I spare her? She is our entire dependence. I wish Henry felt willing to exert himself to help her. He professes to make the kitchen fire, but it is not uncommon for her to make both fires. I went to the kitchen door & called him until I was taken sick, since then I ring the bell at six o'clock, & stay in bed until the room is warm. Robbie & Cornelia are generally pretty good children, & if it were not for a thorn that goes deeper than the flesh, we should be very comfortable.

It snowed last night & all the forenoon & the ground is covered. I should think it three or four inches deep.

Saint Anthony, Nov. 18, '64
My dear Husband,

I see he [Henry] has written about getting into the river on Friday, but he hasn't told the half of the story. M. had been sewing all the time she could get on a jacket for him for a week. He had been told early in the week that we should need water hauled for washing on Friday, & that we should depend on him to get it done. Friday morning he was reminded of it, & told that M. wanted to prepare for a two weeks washing on Sat. He chopped some & played some till noon, & then was ready for skating. I told him he could skate after he had found some one to haul the water, but he must arrange about the water before he went skating. . . . He demurred but went as I hoped to get the water. He stopped at the Negro neighbor of ours & found he was from home, & then went to the river & skated but a short time, before he broke in. He came home dripping wet about two in the afternoon. I feel that he ought to be punished, but I see no way in which I can punish him effectively. Some days he behaves very well, & I feel as though it was in answer to prayer. He pretends to think that both his mother & teacher should request & not command.

St. Anthony, Nov. 19, 1864
Dear Husband,

. . . . Yesterday morning we expected Isabella & Julia on the cars. I told H. that he must see to their trunk & get it brought up without expense if he could. I mentioned several ways & said he could choose the way he pleased. I trusted in him, & as the day passed & it began to grow dark, I sympathized with him in not being able to get Mr. Renville's horse & wagon till it would be so dark that I feared the depot would be closed. After we were seated at supper he came at last. I said "Did you succeed in getting the trunk?" He replied, " I haven't seen any trunk, I have been skating!" Yes, the boy that I had trusted with a special commission, had skated two whole hours after school was over, not getting home in time to cut any wood before dark. In the morning we hadn't wood to get breakfast with, but I forbear. The inquiry is, what shall we do? Isabella proposes that he go to Lakeland & stay at least during the vacation there which will be in about three weeks. I feel doubtful about it. I fear he would be drowned in the lake. I think it doubtful whether my health will improve under present circumstances, & yet I can't wish you to come home before your work is done, unless you could finish it nearly as well here.

Prompted by a consciousness of my critical health, & Martha's urgent request & Mrs. McKee's advice, I sent for Miss Fairchild. She came today & examined my case. She gave me a less favorable opinion than I had expected, though she spoke hopefully of restoration under favorable conditions. She would prefer to have me under her care at "the home," but if that was not practicable would prescribe home treatment. She said the disease was a very common cause of insanity, & I think gives me much credit for power of endurance & self control. I told her that the expense would be an objection to "the home" with me & especially while you were away. We shall try "home treatment" awhile & I am to commence dieting & bathing immediately. It will give Martha additional labor.

Monday morn
.... Much as I should like to have you go to Washington, I am not sure but we need you more at home than the Indians need you at Washington. I think it would be difficult to get up a good deputation this winter. Please let us know when you expect to finish the printing. I know you will be as industrious as possible.

Saint Anthony, Nov. 24, '64 Thanksgiving day
My dear Husband,

Perhaps I led you to think that I was getting well. I did not mean that. There is internal inflammation somewhere, until that is subdued, I may feel better one day than another, but I can't regard myself as getting well. But I do not wish you to come home, glad as I should be to have you here until I feel that there is not a reasonable hope of recovery. Till then work at the Dakota Testament as God may give you strength, praying as you labor, & may He enable you to finish it & the other parts of the Dakota scriptures also. Providence permitting, I go to the Hygiene House tomorrow, by the wish of the girls & advice of friends. It is a great trial to me to go, but it may be blessed to my recovery, or it may help to wean me from my earthly home as a preparation for the heavenly home.

I do not think H. is burdened with the ordinary work at home. He finds a great deal of time to read & play & tease. I think the present is a very critical time with him. The Devil has great power over him, & yet I think the Holy Spirit sometimes strives still. If any one of our children have had especial reason to suppose they had a mother's love it has been Henry. . . .

Tues. Morn. Jan. 24

Martha is washing this cold morning, & I have been trying to do a little mending. Since I came home I have spent almost all the strength I had in mending & darning. Martha has done admirably this winter, but she has needed double diligence & energy to perform all her varied & responsible duties. The sleigh bells are ringing right merrily this morning. We have had no sleighing this winter until now, & it is not very good yet. God bless you always.

St. Anthony, Minn., June 5, 1865
My dear Daughter, [Anna]

I am lying propped up by pillows in bed in the parlor, while I answer your letter which came on Sat. I sat up a few minutes yesterday & day before, after having been kept prostrate three months. I have tried to be patient, but it has seemed a long time to be helpless & useless.

We can't spare you to teach more than three months or so, if at all next year. . . .

St. Anthony, July 4, 1865
My dear Husband,

I am glad you made the purchase of a house without referring it to us. With the data you gave us, we shouldn't have been able to make an intelligent choice. Isabella is loyally gratified, Henry pleased, & I judging from what you wrote & the natural inferences from what you didn't write, have our private opinion that the Miller property is really the cheapest & would be much preferable if we could afford a horse & buggy. But as we can't, I am satisfied with "the home" you have selected. . . .

I shall shiver in prospect of that cold parlor with three outside thin walls, four windows down to the floor & one door opening onto a porch & not into a hall. I can't divest myself of the feeling that the shady house & sickly body sustain the relation of cause & effect. But it may not be so, & even if financially & esthetically, the house with larger grounds might be desirable, the proximity of our home to church, is certainly a strong reason in its favor. . . . All our other homes have their memories, four of them as the birth places of our children, but in God's great mercy, no sad memory of the death of child or parent. My Brother, Thomas, so suddenly taken from our Traverse home, is the only one yet summoned from our family group. Perhaps I shall next be called.

I have written this sitting up in bed without resting. But I must lie down. I went into the kitchen & boys' bedroom one day last week, & have been obliged to keep [to] my bed most of the time since. May God watch over us all & bring our family all together in our new home.

Beloit, Oct. 24, 1865
Dear Husband,

I am glad to say the pain & swelling in my face came to a crisis on Sabbath morning. The night after I slept delightfully. I think those who have never known the painful unrest of wakeful nights, can hardly appreciate the blessing of a quiet sleep. . . .

The certificate of shares in the Amity Oil Co. came on Saturday. Henry chopped wood in the forenoon, & thus secured the whole afternoon for play. I should like to make such a division of the odd jobs that he wouldn't slip out & leave those not to be paid for, for Thomas. Will you not write to them about their work? If Thomas would make a bin for the potatoes, Henry could remove those you bought, if you would so direct, the first Wednesday or Saturday afternoon, after your letter came. The potatoes would be much less exposed to the light & air, under the stairs, than under the window. I shall be glad to hear you have found a less expensive boarding place, if one with as good accommodations can be had at a cheaper rate. If not, I hope you will not make any change. We can try & economize some other way.

Thomas & Isabella have brought the Sewing Machine into the parlor. Isa. has put it in order & used it this afternoon.

Beloit, Wis. Dec. 12, 1865
My dear Husband,

Our Thanksgiving passed very pleasantly. Although we should have been very glad & thankful, if you could have helped eat the nice turkey you bought, we had a great many other things to thank & praise God for. Since Thanksgiving the weather has been very mild & our beef was thawing, but the cold west wind of today is freezing it again. The beef is very good, better than most of what we have had this fall.

Wed. morn
We had a cold windy night, the thermometer at zero at seven in the evening. This morning the ink on the parlor table was frozen, & isn't quite thawed now at ten A.M., though I am sitting by the stove writing. The little coal stove draws very well, but we have had so few calls lately, that the boys study chiefly in the parlor. They will find it very nice at the Christmas vacation.

Anna has tried skating once, with quite as good success as is usual for beginners. Cornelia went over to Mrs. Hasences last Saturday & brought home a little grey kitten. It is lying on the carpet between the wood box & stove. Cornelia commenced sewing up a pillowcase yesterday for China.

Beloit, Wis. Jan. 24, 1866
My dear husband,

Your letter to Henry & myself came today. He has recited one lesson in the Greek Reader to Thomas, & has, I believe a spelling lesson on Saturdays. Isabella received a draft from Mr. Treat last week & went to Chicago yesterday. The ladies have just become interested in helping furnish & prepare her outfit.

Mr. Williams proposed their being married a week earlier than had been contemplated, but Isabella does not think it will be practicable. I am sorry on Mr. W's account that he can have no longer time for his friends in Ohio. "Rev. Doolittle," [Secretary Treat] as Mr. W. calls him, is hoping for a ship by the first of April, so that between his wishes & Isabella's, Mr. W. is not likely to make a very long stay at his father's.

The boys have been to attend their Societies this evening & Henry has just come hooting & screaming home! The wood contract is filled, though not quite as fully as Thomas thought it should have been. Still he preferred to pay him according to agreement. The beef was duly delivered & is as good as that you bought in the fall. It was so nicely cut up that I am afraid I shall be more particular than ever about the shape of roasts & steaks.

Beloit, Wis., March 5, '66
My dear Husband,

Alfred is still with us. He preached & attended Monthly concert over the river yesterday. He is making a Photograph Album for Anna today with her assistance.

It is a sore trial to leave home & country, especially so to woman, but there are sorer trials still. And were it not for troubles here, we should be too much attached to earth, & earthly friends. I don't feel like writing. It requires so much effort for me & I have nothing pleasant to write about. My sense of justice compels me to try, though it is such a laborious task to write. But I want to hear from you just as often as if I could write longer & oftener. Is that selfish? If so, it is a loving selfishness. Good bye.

Beloit, Fri. June 1, 7 p.m. 1866
My dear Husband,

I have felt very sad all the afternoon without knowing any special reason why. Perhaps our pecuniary expenses for the last two years is one cause. It doesn't seem right to me to be spending our own funds simply to eke out our family supply of food & fuel at the poverty rate we have lived, while the Presidential Com. doubtless supposes we have been comfortably provided for at their expense. Where is our clothing to come from?

I had thought about it while Mr. Treat was here, I should like to have asked him his opinion. At least I would have told him that our pictures & melodeon were chiefly gifts, & that so far as food & clothing were concerned we practiced as close economy as most home missionaries. Perhaps I have thought about this just now because you had to sell 7-30 to subsist us during the month of June. Those that were sold during the winter for fuel, I flattered myself would somehow be canceled when summer came, but to be still falling back on our private funds, is something I don't understand.

I hope you will be successful in getting Lorenza's & Makachewin's claims for them, & I am sure they will be glad to compensate you liberally for your trouble. I almost have a share in your labors for Makachewin.

Sat. afternoon

I am alone in the house. Martha is playing croquet, Thomas has gone down town, Robbie is away & Cornelia has a picnic party in the backyard. Martha made her a cake, Robbie popped some corn, & Cornelia made a couple of small pies, that being the extent of her capability. . . . Robbie has worn out the sole of his shoe. He worked very well at hoeing corn this morning, & was brave enough last evening to buy us some beef. I hope he will "get a man" after awhile, if we give him time enough. . . .

Martha wishes to know if you wrote to Dr. Wood to inquire about ship letters sent to China by New York?

Beloit, June 5, 1866
My dear Son,

We were very glad to hear that Mary & the baby went with you to Ottawa. I know by experience that mothers don't have a very easy time when they take babies with them from home & have neither sister or nurse to relieve them in the care. Of course on public occasions, their husbands can't take the babies with them, nor stay away to take care of them. . . .

Mr. Treat came on Tuesday last & spent the night with us. Your father left with him on Wednesday noon by way of Dubuque where Mr. Treat designed attending Association. We hadn't reduced the chaos of building & repairing into order when he came, but we were in far more comfortable circumstances than when he visited us at Lac qui Parle just twelve years before.

Enclosed you will find a dollar. Please get for us one bunch of thin envelopes, & as much paper as you can get with the remainder.

Beloit, Fri. June 22, 1866
My dear Husband,

. . . . We have sent a letter to Fort Wadsworth. Martha copied in hers, a note to you from Bishop Whipple, in which he says, "Will you give me as briefly as you can a statement of bros. Paul & Simon & any others who rendered positive aid?" The Com. Ind. Af. "Wishes to know only of such who preferred extraordinary acts of bravery & not those of merely a friendly disposition." I see no objection to mentioning the cases of those you named, though they do not all exactly come under the class of "extraordinary acts of bravery." Simon & Paul & Elctukiya are entitled to a place on the wall of honor, & perhaps Henok, Antoine & Rera. But Enos I think was a truer friend than Henok. As he is dead, if Henok received anything, why should not Enos' relatives? Bishop Whipple has the statement of Other Day & Lorenzo. . . .

Beloit, Wis. July 19, 1866
Dear Husband,

For some days past, I have wanted to write you & yet felt very reluctant to commence until I had something pleasant to write. I feel greatly at a loss what to write & what to refrain from writing. I used to think if I wrote frankly & freely you would know better how to pray for us, but I have found this longing for human sympathy worse than useless. So, instead of saying this child did so & so & that one thus & thus, I will ask a few questions. Did you tell Thomas that, in your absence, he was to accompany his sisters to such places as it was needful for them to have an escort, whenever it was practicable for him to do so? Or was he to consult merely his own preference? In case Henry doesn't get work when the next term commences, do you wish him to go to college? Mr. Payne has advertised for a trusty lad from 14 to 16 in the printing office. Henry made some inquiries about the terms but was not very definitely answered, was told to call again some weeks hence. Do you think printing would be active & engrossing work enough to enable him to persevere?

Beloit, Wis. Aug 2, 1866
My Dear Husband,

Your last three letters mailed at Fort Wadsworth, Fort Thompson, & Fort Randall are all safe. The one last mailed being the first received. I have copied from each of your home notes something for Isabella, & shall forward a letter China-ward soon.

I have been hoping to tell you that both Thomas & Henry were at work in the harvest field, but Henry is at home today. . . . Our funds for the month were used up before the month was out, but today Martha got the $75.00 draft cashed & we bought some wall paper for the bedroom. I went down town with her in Mr. Bushnell's carriage. I do not think we ought to try to live on $750 & your traveling expenses next year. It will oblige us to use our 7-30s & they will not last long if we make up what is lacking out of them. You & I need clothes, & a hundred dollars wouldn't more than comfortably supply us.

Our garden, I hope, will be some help to us. Thomas worked in it pretty well, but he cut off instead of hoeing out the weeds, & the heavy & frequent rains of late, have made the weeds come to life & spring up most abundantly. Henry don't incline to work in the garden very much. Robert & I have been weeding the strawberries. I hope we shall get the upper hand of the weeds after a while, but their name is legion.

Beloit, Wis. Aug 14, 1866
My dear Husband,

My head doesn't seem to improve with my physical strength. I am very much stronger bodily than last summer, but my head troubles me still.

Thomas & Henry both worked in the harvest fields last week & the one before. Henry is still harvesting this week. Thomas weeded the turnips yesterday & today is papering our bedroom. I concluded, after careful & economical calculation & deliberation to have the front door painted with "private funds." The painter put on the first coat yesterday. Our dining room is not painted yet, but will probably be painted soon, if Thomas doesn't find more remunerative work away from home. . . .

Alfred is expecting to make a trip east as far as Boston with a part of the gift for that purpose from his brother-in-law [Mr. Hatch]. Mary thinks it better for her to stay at home on account of Freddy. I hope she will go sometime. I don't think it wise or just for women to be "keepers at home" always.

Last week the cord to our "Landing of the Pilgrims" broke & the picture fell upon the melodeon, & didn't break the glass! A little piece was cracked off the frame, & a bigger piece from the melodeon. It seemed very wonderful to me.

Beloit, Jan. 11, 1867
My dear Son,

The excitement connected with Martha's marriage didn't make me sick, though it exhausted my nervous system considerably. I hope to feel as well as before soon. I am glad you found such a comforting present for Mary for New Year's & that your friends in New York remembered you. Isabella's gift to help educate Thomas came during the first week of the New Year. Truly we have great cause to thank God & to trust him. With much love to all always.

Beloit, Wis. Jan. 12, 1867

My dear Mrs. Drake,

We were all glad to hear of your safe arrival home. Your visit here, did us so much good. I am really obliged to him [Mr. Drake] for being willing to spare you occasionally.

Mr. Morris & Martha had a long trip—stayed over a day at Owotanna as the two stages were filled by lunatics being transferred from Iowa to the Minnesota state asylum at St. Peter. They commenced housekeeping on New Years, & I presume Martha will ere long report to you of her success. Neither her vases nor pictures were broken nor her husband nor self frozen.

Beloit, Wis. Jan. 28, 1867

My dear Son,

If you are "fully persuaded in your own mind," that your father should have a larger salary, & that you ought to try to have it increased, I wish you success if God wills... I should think any effort of that kind should be made through Mr. Treat.... Probably I have felt the care & contriving required by the close economy we have practiced since the Dakota outbreak, more than your father, & perhaps too, my faith for the future is weaker. I don't know as you have been told that, notwithstanding our careful economy, we have used during these years in addition to our salary, two or three hundred dollars yearly of private funds, which are now exhausted.

My poor health has of course been one cause of our increased expenses, but not the chief one, for all this time, we have tried to curtail them in various ways, by dispensing with the daily use of tea & coffee, by purchasing very few books & but a scanty supply of clothing, hoping that the high prices would soon be lessened. When the appropriations for 1867 were being made, I hoped your father would at least ask for $850 instead of the $750 which we had been receiving. But he shrank from asking for more than an additional fifty, for two reasons, one that we are living away from the Dakotas, the other, that we are already receiving a larger salary than any other family in our mission. We have not been informed whether $800 has been granted us for the present year, but we think it probable. How a family of seven can live comfortably on $800, I don't now see, but I can try & trust. I have written you these particulars, that you might understand the circumstances, & judge wisely. We wish to live in such a way that we can render a good account of our stewardship. . . .

Your father doesn't want a hand in this matter, not even impliedly. He has trained himself from early life, to "endure hardness as a good soldier of Jesus Christ." And shall a soldier complain of hard tack & thin blankets? Let the officers see to those things.

Sat. eve, March 9, 1867
My dear Husband,

I asked Henry to write to you tonight. He sat down & scribbled a few minutes, & then said he must make a call. Thomas has not been very well for a few days past, & Henry made both fires two mornings very cheerfully. I think you should have a fire in your room even if it costs $2.00 a week, though that seems high for this season of the year.

. . . . How long a time will you probably stay in Washington? Henry carries your letter to him in his pocket & has read most of your "home notes." When reading the last one, he said "Father ought to have a fire in his room Sundays at least."

If you go to Mt. Vernon please bring me a sprig of Holly. It is a large, smooth leaved evergreen. I should like a sprig of Cypress too if [you] should go to "the Soldiers Home." This, in war time, was a few miles from Washington on the Maryland side. You will recollect that President Lincoln had a country house there, & on a certain time gathered specimens there of "spruce, pine, cedar & an illegitimate cypress." You may perhaps get a specimen of cypress if you should go there.

Beloit, Wis., Sat. March 9, 1867
My dear Son,

I am anxious to know what you are going to do the coming summer. If you are going far away, will you not come to see us & stay two or three weeks before you go? Cornelia {8} would write to Freddie {4} & tell him that she will try & be less selfish, next time he comes, but she feels too old to print letters & she can't write them yet.

If you are expecting to go up to Chicago soon, we should be glad to have you do a few errands for us, if convenient. Anna would like a few sheets of music & we are wanting some pocket hdkfs. Beside these I have a desire to know the price of moss mattresses. Now the war is over, they ought to be in the market again, & they are much better than shucks. The smell of mold in the bedroom you slept in was from the mattress. I didn't perceive that it was injured in that way until it was brought home.

Beloit, Wis. July 17, 1867
My dear Son,

Commencement week passed very pleasantly, though we were quite disappointed that you didn't come. We hoped to the last. Mr. Kent... was impressed with the idea that Thomas should study for the ministry & has since written him a fatherly letter.

I am glad that Mary & Freddy are having a pleasant summer. The summer we spent in Mass. when you were four years old, seemed to benefit you greatly.

Our house with only four at home is large & lonely.... We had a very good supply of strawberries. We could easily have used them all ourselves, but we chose to give some away. Currants are now taking the place of strawberries, with occasionally a dish of raspberries.

Beloit, Wis. Feb. 28, 1868
My dear husband,

I wrote you a few lines some days ago, & Thomas & Anna have written since your letters to them reached us. Henry read the whole of your letter to Anna, but I couldn't say as much of the one directed to him. Still he does manifest more interest in family matters than he did a year ago, especially in regard to Isabella. If he stays at Brittens' another year, he says he will send her some forks. If he could only be induced to spend his evenings at home instead of playing cards, I should feel more hopeful.

.... The box for China was sent yesterday by express to New York. A letter followed in today's mail....

I flatter myself that you put on your cravat & collar before breakfast, even though the ladies there don't care half as much as your wife would when you neglected it. Perhaps too, you use your fork as others do.

My fears in regard to Martha's situation, were too true. Poor child, without a home & poor teaching school during the week, playing the melodeon on Sabbath & then trying to help write a book! In answer to my inquiry she says,

"I want you not to feel distressed about me in any way. We shall get along somehow. I thought if I taught through into April we could get along quite comfortably with economy, of course. But I do not expect I shall try to finish out the term. If it had not been that we needed the money so, there would have been less mortification if I had stopped last vacation. Aside from this, I doubt if the purse would hold out for me to come home, things cost so, & Wyllys can't get any work that pays, sad to say. "

It is some consolation that we tried to do right about her marriage, but I wish we could do something to help them now. I should like to send the sheets & some other articles by express, even if I do without a bureau a while longer. I'm weary of poverty, but I want to be patient & thankful for the blessings we have. I suppose Mrs. Reynolds, our wash woman, thinks we are rich compared with herself. She is sick & we had no help this week.

Dr. Strong vaccinated Robbie, notwithstanding he told him you didn't think it necessary. His arm has been rather lame, but it is well now. Cornelia was not vaccinated.

Is there a possibility that the Smithsonian Institution would make any appropriation for expenses in comparing Indian languages?

I should very much like a photograph of Sen. Ramsey if he would only give me one.

Beloit, Wis. March 6, 1868
My dear Husband,

The beautiful ink you use in your letters, makes this mauve, more distasteful than ever. I hope you will remember the name of the maker of that deep glassy black ink. I wish I had some. . . .

March 7, Sat. eve

Our three days rain, ended this forenoon, & to our great delight the sun, moon, & stars have appeared again, as usual. Your very interesting letter mailed March 3rd, Henry brought when he came home to dinner. I read it at table. Henry seemed considerably interested. I am pleased with the change in your commencement from home notes to Dear Home. Perhaps it is better than to address individual members, & yet I am not sure but you would get more answers if the letters were to someone in particular. I must confess I love to read Dear wife at the beginning, but I intend to write as often as I can conveniently, without regard to the address. I have tried to sew a little more than usual since you left, but it quite unfits me for writing. Close attention to anything, wearies me wonderfully, especially if it is long protracted. The consciousness of the decay of our physical powers is very depressing, unless we can comfort ourselves with the renewing of the inward more day by day. If the spirit is not benumbed & beclouded, by bodily weakness, I don't think life's decline would seem so sad. If it is God's will, I hope to be spared a long lingering decay. . . .

Perhaps had you been here this afternoon, you would have thought us not very wise. Just before tea, a man with a basket of shells called at the door. I asked him in & called Anna & Cornelia. We looked over his shells, of which he had some very beautiful ones, & each of us bought one of the less expensive shells. I should be delighted with a cabinet of shells & a knowledge of the science. I love beautiful things just as in-tensely as when I was young. There are some things I haven't yet grown too old to enjoy. This love of beauty will, I think, be satisfied in that world where [there] will be no physical or moral deformity or ugliness. Good night.

Beloit, Wis. March 16, 1868
My dear Husband,

We were very glad to get your letters written just before & after your pilgrimage to Mount Vernon. I thank you for the small Holly branch. I can't think it vandalism to gather a few leaves from the home & tomb of Washington.

Last week Alfred, & Mary, & Freddy came on Monday & stayed till Thursday. Mr. Warner came Tuesday & left on Saturday. So you see we didn't suffer from loneliness last week, except an hour or two on Friday & Saturday evening when Anna was at prayer & choir meetings. Robbie has finished Physical Geography & commenced Natural Philosophy! He likes to study better than to chop wood or practice on the melodeon.

Two full letters from Isabella came last week, containing letters from Mr. Williams for Paddy's Run. They have generously remembered Thomas again....

Beloit, Wis. July 16, '68
My dear Husband,

The intense & long continued hot weather has slightly abated today. The Champion peas, that were so young & tender a week ago, are almost too old for use....

Thomas & Henry are quite disturbed by the loss of their boat. They took Miss Jennie up the river in it Friday evening. The following Monday Thomas & Ed Salmon prepared to take a short trip & camp out, but found the staple broken & the boat missing. Thomas has spent considerable part of two days searching for it in the rain. As yet no clue is discovered & he has offered a reward for it being found & returned.

.... It is half past eight & I must prepare string beans for dinner. I should like to send you a dish, or rather have you here at noon.

Beloit, Wis. Aug 6, 1868
My dear Husband,

Your letter containing items of the treaty came a day or two since & was sent to Alfred this morning. The one describing your reception at Santee Agency by the Dakotas, I took over to the Ladies Missionary prayer meeting the last Wednesday in July. I didn't feel quite able to go it was so warm, but I was so impressed that this was their special time for prayer for the Dakotas that I went....

Last Sabbath I had the satisfaction of sitting in church with the four younger children. I think Cornelia is trying to do right. Of course there is a good deal of wrong still, but I do thank God if He will teach her what is right, & help her to do it. . . .

We have had new potatoes, corn, beans & beets. The potatoes are about the size of robin's eggs, with occasionally one as large as a hen's egg. Notwithstanding they are so small, they are sprouting, & the bugs are eating the tops. The tomatoes are not ripening well. The leaves are shriveled & the fruit rather small. I think they would keep the ground moister, without a trellis. . . . We are not likely to be troubled with apples this fall, as the hot, dry, weather thinned the trees suprisingly. I should have thought there were so few apples, that they wouldn't have burdened the trees.

We received a short letter from Isabella last week written in April, just before their proposed trip to Peking. A long letter from Mr. Williams was sent us a few days later, as characteristic as usual. I can't recall much of their letters to tell you. Isabella was still troubled with that old trouble & in fasting & taking turpentine according to prescription had fainted & had a slight spasm. She was having her Chinese boys learn to sew. To make labor honorable to the one who some day may be a mandarin, she told them that her oldest brother sewed with an "Iron tailor" a sewing machine.

We have finally commenced our rag carpet. This beginning makes the magnitude of the job more real & appalling. Still there is a kind of fascination about the work, that would make it quite attractive, if I could forget the mending that is meanwhile neglected. Cornelia sews her twenty pieces regularly, & usually without fretting. I'm really hopeful in her case, & I don't despair about Henry, but the burden is very heavy—not on my own account, so much as for his own sake & that of Robbie & Cornelia. . . . He studied considerable for him as the weather was so unfavorable to close application. The study is really a very warm room at this season of the year. The heat from the kitchen stove these hot days, has made us all wish for a wood shed, or summer kitchen. . . .

Fri. Aug 7

We had a refreshing rain last night, for which every thing seems to rejoice. It was so hot & dry, that not more than a dozen turnips came up from the seed you sowed just before you left.

Thomas hurt his left thumb yesterday, which was an unfortunate beginning at lathing. He is at work at it today notwithstanding.

Beloit, Wis. Aug 25, '68
My dear Son,

As the boys were from home, I didn't send to the P.O. on Friday, & so didn't hear of the birth of your daughter until Sat. morning. I rejoice with you, & hope Mary may continue comfortable, until she is quite restored. I don't think I can spare Anna longer than three or four days....

Beloit, Feb. 11, 1869
Dear Mrs. Drake,

I have felt so much for you in your sickness, that I have wanted to write to you & hear from you. And now that I learn from Mrs. McKee that you are getting better, I wish to tell you some of my experience in sickness.

I thank God that through all my disquietude & pain, he kept me from losing my trust in Him. ...

And next to trust in God, I wanted to feel such trust in my physician, husband, Mrs. McKee & Isabella, that I could leave them to decide things, about which I differed, as I often did, from anyone of them. I often felt very much disturbed by what I then thought their wrong notions, especially of Isabella's, but usually I could see that it was best to yield to their opinions.

Now I am pained to think I made Isabella's last year at home such a trying one, but am comforted in her present happiness & usefulness in China. In one of her late letters, she writes "For several months I have been feeling such a degree of gratitude for life ... that I cannot but tell of it. It seems to me that next to God this gratitude is due to one's parents. I think of it so often, & feel very grateful & happy. There is cause of grief that this realization has come to me, when the time has past when I could have truly shown that I realized it. Now the only way is [that] I try & do something for the Lord."

I'm afraid I shall tire you, if I write more now. Accept for you & yours our tenderest love.

Yours truly,

Mary Ann Longley Riggs

Mary Ann Longley Riggs died on March 22, 1869 from pneumonia.

Index